P9-BJR-765

ARIZONA
IN YOUR FUTURE

The complete relocation guide for job-seekers, retirees and Snowbirds

By Don W. Martin & Betty Woo Martin

Pine Cone Press, Inc. • Henderson, Nevada

BOOKS BY DON AND BETTY MARTIN

Adventure Cruising • 1996
Arizona Discovery Guide • 1990, 1993, 1994, 1996
Arizona in Your Future • 1991, 1993, 1997
The Best of the Gold Country • 1987, 1990, 1992
The Best of San Francisco • 1986, 1990, 1994, 1997
The Best of the Wine Country • 1991, 1994, 1995
Inside San Francisco • 1991
Las Vegas: The Best of Glitter City • 1998
Nevada Discovery Guide • 1992, 1997
New Mexico Discovery Guide • 1998
Northern California Discovery Guide • 1993
Oregon Discovery Guide • 1993, 1995, 1996, 1998
San Francisco's Ultimate Dining Guide • 1988
The Toll-free Traveler • 1997
The Ultimate Wine Book • 1993, 1998
Utah Discovery Guide • 1995
Washington Discovery Guide • 1994, 1997

Copyright © 1998 by Don W. Martin & Betty Woo Martin

All rights reserved. No written material, maps or illustrations from this book may be reproduced in any form, including electronic media, other than brief passages in book reviews, without written permission from the publisher. Printed in the United States of America

Library of Congress Cataloging-in-Publication Data
Martin, Don and Betty —
Arizona In Your Future
Includes index.
1. Arizona—Description and travel
2. Arizona—Relocating, job-seeking, retiring

ISBN: 0-942053-23-0
Library of Congress catalog card number: 97-66327

COVER DESIGN • **Dave Bonnot,** Columbine Type & Design
  Sonora, California
PHOTOGRAPHY • **Betty** or **Don Martin,** unless otherwise
  credited
CHARTS AND GRAPHS • **Jil Weil,** Oakland, California

CONTENTS
PART ONE: THE STATE

ARIZONA: A STATE FOR EVERYONE

Most relocation guides focus on a particular group—usually job hunters, moving families or retirees. Why not, we wondered, produce a guide for everyone? Whatever your reason for contemplating a move to Arizona, you all share common interests and curiosities. You'll want to know the nature, character, physical appearance and amenities of your future home town. You'll be concerned about climate, cultural lures and nearby attractions.

To create a complete relocation guide, we've ridden off in three directions. Part I has special chapters for job-seekers, permanent retirees and those long-term winter visitors called Snowbirds. We then offer detailed descriptions of Arizona's major communities in Part II, followed by lists of regional attractions in Part III.

If Arizona is in your future, for whatever reason, this is your book. It's not only full of information; it's straightforward and honest. Our reviews of communities are based on facts and impressions gathered during our visits, not on chamber of commerce puffery. If a city is economically depressed, if an area is scalding hot in summer, if a town is hound dog homely, we say so.

Like all of our guides, *Arizona in Your Future* contains no paid listings or advertising, so it's free of outside bias. No agency, organization or community listed herein has asked to be included. All of the information—and opinions—have come from our own research and observations.

Of course, most of what we have to say about Arizona is positive, because it's a stimulating, growing, vibrant and attractive state.

During the past years, we've spent months prowling about the state to research this relocation guide, and our popular travel book, the *Arizona Discovery Guide.* We learned why Arizona has been, and will continue to be, one of America's fastest growing states. It's amazingly diverse, with pine forests as well as cactus deserts. It offers two major metropolitan centers with their cultural variety, fine dining and—yes—commute-hour traffic. Or, one can settle in a tiny hamlet where nothing changes but the stoplight—if there is one.

Phoenix is America's seventh largest city, with a population topping a million, and Tucson has nearly half a million. Yet overall, the state ranks very low in population density, with about 40 folks per square mile.

Many people think of Arizona primarily as a Sunbelt state. Indeed, eighty-five percent of its population resides in warmer climes. Yet, you can live under the pines of Flagstaff and ski the slopes of the next-door San Francisco Peaks. You can play cowboy, or be a real one, on the high prairies of the state's southeastern corner.

You can run rivers, hike the high country, fish in crystalline streams and explore prehistoric ruins left by the very first Arizonans. On the flip side of the activity coin, you can attend opening night at the Tucson Opera or Phoenix Symphony, dine in style in a skyroom restaurant, prowl through excellent museums, putter around fine golf courses and—obviously—laze at poolside. Arizona is one of the few places on the planet where you can soak up both culture and toasty sunshine in January. (In Tucson, you can do these things and even go skiing—at nearby Mount Lemmon.) Other than the absence of an ocean, the state offers a bit of everything, and most of it is bathed in warm sunshine.

Is Arizona in your future? Come and check it out!

A BIT ABOUT THE AUTHORS

The Martins have written more than a dozen guidebooks, mostly under their Pine Cone Press banner. When not tending to their publishing company, they explore America and the world beyond, seeking new places and new experiences for their readers. Both are members of the Society of American Travel Writers.

Don, who provides most of the adjectives, has been a journalist since he was 16, when classmates elected him editor of his high school newspaper. (No one else wanted the job.) After school, he left his small family farm in Idaho, wandered about the country a bit, and then joined the Marine Corps. He was assigned as a military correspondent in the Orient and at bases in California. Back in civvies, he worked as a reporter, sports writer and editor for several West Coast newspapers, then he became associate editor of the California State Automobile Association's travel magazine. He now devotes his time to writing, photography, sipping fine Zinfandel and—for some odd reason—collecting squirrel and chipmunk artifacts.

Betty, a Chinese-American who's varied credentials have included a doctorate in pharmacy and a real estate broker's license, does much of the research, editing and photography for their books. She also has sold articles and photos to an assortment of newspapers and magazines. When she isn't helping Don run Pine Cone Press, Inc., she wanders the globe—with or without him. Her travels have taken her from Cuba to Antarctica.

CORPORATIONS: IS ARIZONA IN YOUR FUTURE?

If you're planning a move to Arizona, opening a branch office or transferring employees there, *Arizona In Your Future* is a great reference source. We offer special discount prices for bulk orders and we can customize the cover and some inside pages on larger orders. Contact Pine Cone Press at the address below.

CLOSING INTRODUCTORY THOUGHTS
Keeping up with the changes

Nobody's perfect, but we try. This relocation guide contains thousands of facts and a few are probably wrong, or have become outdated. If you catch an error, let us know. Also drop us a note if you find that a phone number, office location or other bit of information has changed in this ever-changing state.

All who provide information that's particularly useful for future editions of this guidebook will earn a free copy of a Pine Cone Press publication. (See listing in the back of this book.)

Address your comments to:

Pine Cone Press, Inc.
631 N. Stephanie St., #138
Henderson, NV 89014

PART ONE
THE STATE

Like a sunny magnate, Arizona lures millions of people across its borders each year. About 18 million tourists annually sample the state's seductive climate and its rich variety of scenic attractions, historic and cultural offerings.

While some come to play, many come to stay. Hundreds of thousands of families, soured by January blizzards and stagnating economies back home, snip their roots and head for Arizona. Additional legions of retirees choose to spend their golden years under the state's smiling sun. Another million or more long-term seasonal visitors, called Snowbirds, fly south to winter here.

In this section, you'll meet the state itself. You'll learn all about its history, its alluring desert climate (and how to handle it) and its various departments and services. Later chapters discuss schooling, job prospects and the best places in the state for retirees and winter visitors.

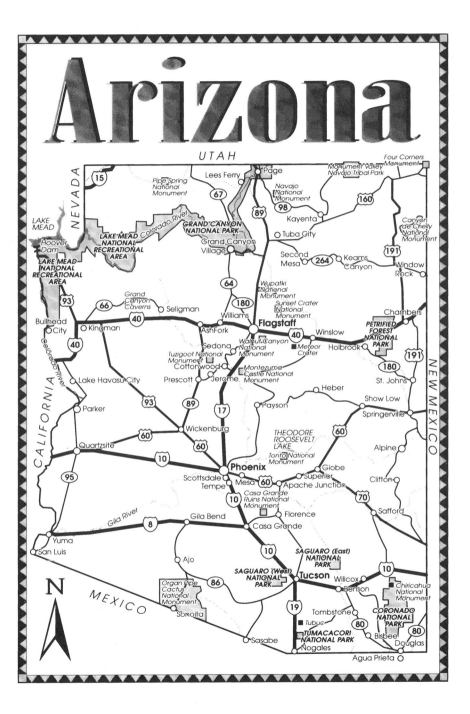

Chapter one

WHY ARIZONA?

MAKING THE DECISION

During the past two decades, more than a million people have come to Arizona—to stay. They made a profound decision—to pack their families, their worldly goods and possibly their pets. They chose to relinquish the comfort of familiar terrain, friends and relatives.

Uprooting and relocating a family is not a task taken lightly. What has prompted so many to undertake such a move? Why Arizona?

We'll sum it up in two sentences, and then spend the rest of this book on elaboration.

1. Arizona offers that rare combination of pleasant climate, natural attractions, cultural and recreational facilities and essential services.

2. It's all wrapped up in an alluring package of affordability.

If you and your family are planning to join this statistical surge to Arizona—or if you are retirees leaving your family behind—this is your book. It's packed with information for job-seekers, retirees and winter Snowbirds. On the pages that follow, we'll tell you everything you need to know about the Grand Canyon State—how to find a job, which communities offer the best climate, cultural opportunities, schools, retirement and medical facilities and housing prices.

Arizona has been the third fastest growing state in the nation during the past two decades, after Nevada and Alaska. According to census figures, its population leaped by more than 30 percent—from 2,716,546 to 4,228,900—between 1980 and 1995. It has become western America's third most populous state, after California and Washington. A survey taken a few years ago revealed that nearly 70 percent of the residents of metropolitan Phoenix have been in the state less than 20 years.

Growth slowed a bit toward the end of the 1980s as the economy flattened, and then it surged forward again in the middle 1990s. Average unemployment figures were cut by fifty percent between 1990 and 1995. It was only 5.1 percent statewide in 1995, compared with 7.3 percent in 1985. The U.S. Census Bureau predicts that Arizona will be America's fastest growing state in population numbers as we reach for the millennium. Nevada may out-perform it percentage-wise, but with a larger population base, Arizona will gain more people. At century's end, its population will nudge five million, say the experts. Early in the next century—or even before—it could pass Washington to become the West's second most populous state.

The hot spots

Arizona's growth is focused in several areas, while other regions show very little gain. Percentage-wise, the fastest growing county between 1985 and 1995 was Mohave along the upper Colorado River corridor, with a 68.7 percent increase. The greater Phoenix area in Maricopa County gained the most people, soaring from 1,812,700 to 2,454,525; that's an increase of 35.4 percent and 641,825 folks. Pima County (Tucson) went from 582,600 to 758,050 for 30.1 percent and 175,450 new people, trailing Maricopa by just over four percentage points. It was second to Maricopa in total people gain and it remains the state's second most populous county.

Other hot spots were Yavapai County (the Verde Valley and Prescott), from 85,500 to 129,500 for a gain of 51.5 percent; Yuma in the southwest corner, from 85,100 to 121,875 for 43.2 percent; Santa Cruz (Nogales, south of Tucson), from 23,800 to 33,875 for 42.3 percent; and Pinal (the I-10 corridor between Phoenix and Tucson), from 98,100 to 139,050 for 41.7 percent.

The slowest growth area was the northeast corner, where Apache County gained 9.4 percent, Navajo gained 8.5 and little Greenlee lost 12 percent. Apache and Navajo counties cover much of the large Navajo, Hopi and White Mountain Apache reservations. Greenly, on Arizona's eastern edge below the Navajo Reservation, is the state's least populated county and it appears doomed to stay that way, slipping from 9,600 to 8,450 from 1985 to 1995.

Much of Arizona's growth is rooted in tourism, which generates $7.2 billion a year. Folks come to play, and then decide to stay. This is no accident, since the state operates one of America's most aggressive tourist promotion campaigns. Officials realize that visitors and conventioneers require few services and leave behind lots of money.

The state-sponsored *Arizona Highways* magazine has wooed visitors for decades. Its pages brim with color pictures of pristine canyons, handsome Native Americans and cactus wrens looking quite at home in giant saguaros. The slick magazine has projected Arizona's vast sweeps of sunny terrain into millions of American households.

Many individual communities work to lure and accommodate newcomers as well—both visitors and residents. Phoenix, for instance, is unabashedly pro-growth. Its promoters have placed ads in *Fortune* magazine, the *Wall Street Journal* and other publications, touting this area as a sunny place for business.

The Phoenix metropolitan area, which local promoters like to call the "Valley of the Sun," cradles more than 60 percent of the state's population. Phoenix proper has more than a million residents, and 2,500,000 live in the greater metropolitan area.

Valley of the Sun bedroom communities of Mesa, Scottsdale, Gilbert, Glendale, Chandler and Tempe are among the swiftest growing cities in America. Between 1985 and 1995, Gilbert was the growth champion, increasing by an amazing 354 percent. Mesa gained 37 percent, Scottsdale 51 percent, Glendale 47 percent, Chandler 18 and Tempe 17.

Tucson, while not quite as growth obsessed as Phoenix, isn't exactly locking its gates to newcomers. Percentage-wise, it actually outgained Phoenix in population growth, 26 percent versus 22 percent between 1985 and 1995. Its people count rose from 354,533 to 447,075.

Both population hubs have broadened their employment bases by attracting high-tech industries and promoting white collar and service jobs. Several major corporations have moved their headquarters to the state. Service industries, including tourism, account for 25 percent of Arizona's payroll. Another 20 percent comes from retail trades and 11 percent stems from manufacturing.

Other factors that motivate migration to the Grand Canyon State are moderate home prices and a rather conservative state government that tries to keep the lid on taxes. Although both housing prices and taxes are rising, they're still far below those of some other Sunbelt states, notably neighboring California. For instance, home prices in the San Francisco Bay Area and Los Angeles basin are nearly double those in Phoenix and Tucson. At mid-decade, the median price for a new home was $127,600 in Phoenix and $127,156 in Tucson. Used homes are a better buy; prices average $90,500 in Phoenix and $90,116 in Tucson, compared with a national average of $112,900.

If you're renting, the average cost is about $500 a month in Phoenix and $477 in Tucson.

Arizona's Department of Commerce and Department of Economic Security collect and eagerly disseminate statistics that track, and thus promote, Arizona economic boom. The commerce department issues in-depth community profiles of more than a hundred cities and 23 Native American communities. They cover employment, population, climate, history, transportation, communication, utilities, educational facilities, churches, recreational and cultural lures, nearby attractions

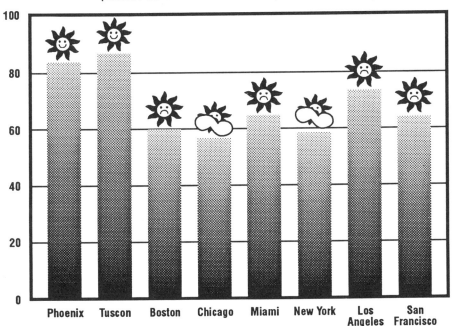

PERCENTAGE OF SUNNY DAYS
(Source : National Oceanic and Atmospheric Administration)

and lodging—all crowded onto a single two-sided sheet. A complete set of these profiles are available for $18 with a binder and $15 without, or 15 cents for profiles of individual communities.

Call for current prices:

Economic Research Division
Arizona Department of Commerce
3800 N. Central Ave., Suite 1400
Phoenix, AZ 85012
(602) 280-1321

You also can receive a list of the department's other publications by calling the number above.

WEATHER OR NOT

Many families or retirees contemplating a move to Arizona may be concerned about summer temperatures. Certainly, it's a great place for a winter retreat, but can one handle the August heat? Bear in mind that Phoenix set an all-time record of 124 degrees during the summer of 1990.

Sizzling summers don't seem to bother most of the state's residents. Eighty-five percent of them live in desert climes, well below the cooler heights of northern Arizona. With air conditioning and a little common sense, they do just fine.

Heat is not a problem if you keep a cool head. For one thing, Arizona's desert heat is dry. Humidity, not heat alone, causes the greatest discomfort. It slows surface evaporation from your skin, which is nature's cooling device. For instance, at zero humidity, 115 degrees has a "discomfort rating" of only 103. (Only?) The discomfort rating, incidentally, is like a wind chill factor in reverse. If the mercury hits 115 and the humidity is 40 percent, the discomfort factor spirals to 151, which would make survival impossible. Fortunately, that combination never occurs in the Arizona desert.

We often travel about the Southwest in summer and we function quite comfortably. On the other hand, during trips to the soggy tropics, we've wilted at 85 degrees because of the humidity.

Beating the heat

Follow these steps to keep your cool when the weather's not:

✹ Don't be a mad dog or an Englishman. Plan active outdoor activities in the early morning and evening.

✹ Avoid dehydration by drinking plenty of water. And we mean plenty. A gallon a day will keep heatstroke away. If you're hiking—and you'll want to do a lot of that in the Grand Canyon—take all the water you can carry. If there are water sources along a hiking trail, carry a ceramic water filter to replenish your supply. Never drink untreated stream or spring water, even if it does look like Evian.

✹ In desert areas, the ground absorbs and then radiates the sun's rays, so temperatures may remain high until sundown and even beyond. It's best to do your summer hiking in the morning. In the Grand Canyon, we mean *early* in the morning. Trails begin on the rim and descend, meaning that the end of your hike is always uphill. While it may be cool on the rim, the inner canyon has a desert climate. People have died of heatstroke down there.

✹ Avoid sweet drinks or alcohol, which speed up dehydration. Besides, you chubby little rascal, a typical twelve-ounce soft drink contains about 12 teaspoons of sugar!

✹ Don't take salt tablets, despite what they told you in boot camp. Salt causes you to retain water, and you want to perspire. That's what keeps you cool. You should keep plenty of fluid circulating through your system.

✹ Don't exert yourself on a hot day. Your body will lose more fluid than it can replace.

✹ Wear light colored, reflective clothing—preferably cotton or linen. Avoid nylon and polyester, since these fabrics don't "breathe" and this traps body heat against your skin.

✹ If you must work outdoors in the heat, dip your shirt or blouse in water frequently. The garment's evaporation, along with that from your body, will help keep you cool.

Shielding the sun

Southwestern states such as Arizona have high skin cancer rates. Because of the southern latitude, clear air and relatively high altitude, more of the sun's damaging ultraviolet rays reach the earth. With the ongoing depletion of our ozone layer, scientists tell us that the skin cancer rate is increasing dangerously. It can develop late in life, even years after you've stopped getting your annual tan. One form—melanoma—can be fatal. Even if you don't get skin cancer, which is nearly 100 percent preventable, constant sun exposure will lead to premature wrinkling.

Some drugs increase the skin's sensitivity to the sun, so check with your pharmacist. Among the suspect items are hormone based drugs including birth control pills, some tranquilizers, diuretics, sulfa drugs and antibiotics such as vibramycin and tetracycline. Even some artificial sweeteners and perfumes are suspect.

Take these precautions to keep your hide from being fried:

✻ Use sunscreen with a high PABA content; it ranges from five to 33 percent (which is a virtual sunblock). Even if you're working on a tan, use sunblock on sensitive areas, such as your lips, nose and—yes—the tops of your ears. If you have a bald pate, remember to protect that—preferably by wearing a hat instead of a sun visor. In case you're curious, PABA stands for para-aminobenzoic acid. (No wonder people use the acronym!) A few individuals are allergic to PABA; if a rash appears, try something else.

✻ Bear in mind that suntan lotion will rinse off when you swim or perspire, so re-lather yourself after swimming or exercising.

✻ Always wear a broad brimmed hat or visor outdoors. It'll shade your eyes and protect them from sun glare and shield your face from sunburn. There's some evidence that sun glare may be a cause of cataracts. The vaqueros knew what they were doing when they created the sombrero.

✻ If you spend a lot of time outdoors, some specialists recommend getting a careful, light tan. Moderately tanned skin will resist sunburn—up to a point. You can still get singed from prolonged exposure. Get your tan very slowly, limiting your initial exposure to a few minutes a day. Do your tanning in the morning or late afternoon when the sun's rays are less direct. Take Rudyard Kipling's advice; avoid the noonday sun.

We prefer to keep moving when we work on tans—hiking, swimming, bike riding and such. If you baste yourself in the sun, you may doze off and get too much exposure. Besides, it's boring. Incidentally, clouds don't block all ultraviolet rays. Also, reflections from sand, pool decks or water can intensify burning. Wet T-shirts may look rather fetching on the right bodies, but they offer little sun protection, despite their cooling effect.

If you do get burned, ease the pain with a dip in the pool or a cool shower, then use one of those over-the-counter anesthetic sprays. Antihistamine will relieve the itch. That's right; the same stuff that you take for the sniffles. Keep your skin out of the sun until it's fully healed.

Avoiding "heat sickness"

Heat exhaustion and its lethal cousin heatstroke are real dangers on hot summer days. Both are brought on by a combination of dehydration and sun.

Signs of heat exhaustion are weariness, muscle cramps and clammy skin. The pulse may slow and you may become unusually irritable. If left untreated, heat exhaustion can lead to deadly heatstroke. The skin becomes dry and hot, the pulse may quicken and you'll experience nausea and possibly a headache. Convulsions, unconsciousness, even death can follow.

At the first sign of heat sickness, get out of the sun and into the shade. Stay quiet and drink water—plenty of water. If you're near a pool, faucet or stream, douse your face and body with water, and soak your clothes to lower your body temperature quickly.

Driving and surviving the desert

Arizona's deserts occupy thousands of square miles of open spaces; population is thinly scattered. These can be intimidating places if you're stranded. If you're tempted—as we often are—to explore this remote and beautiful world, save the urge for fall or spring, when it's not so darned hot. Winters can be biting cold in higher desert elevations such as southeastern Arizona, creating hypothermia risks if you become stranded.

When you venture into the wilds, let someone know where you're going, and when you intend to return. Keep these pointers in mind if you wander off well-traveled asphalt:

✸ First, foremost and always, take plenty of water. Water to drink, to soak your clothes, to top off a leaky radiator. It's cheap, it's easily portable and it can save your life.

✸ Give your car, four-wheel-drive or RV a physical before going into the boonies, to ensure that it'll get you back. Take extra engine oil, coolant and an emergency radiator sealant. Include spare parts such as fan belts, a water pump, radiator hoses—and tools to install these things. Toss an extra spare tire into the trunk, along with a tire pump, patching and sealant.

✸ Take food with you—stuff that won't spoil. If your vehicle breaks down, you may be out there for a while. Also pack matches, a small shovel, aluminum foil (for signaling), a can opener, a powerful flashlight and a space blanket so you can snooze in the shade of your car. The shiny side of a space blanket also is a good signaling device.

✻ A cellular phone or CB radio can be a lifesaver. Remember that channel 9 is the emergency CB band, monitored by rescue agencies.

✻ Never drive off-road, particularly in an on-road vehicle. Loose, sandy desert soil can trap your car in an instant, even if the ground looks solid. We don't leave established roadways as a matter of principle, because tires are hell on the fragile desert environment.

✻ Even if you keep to the roads, you might get stuck in an area of blowing sand or a soft shoulder. It could happen when you leave the road to set up camp. Carry a tow chain and tire supports such as strips of carpeting for soft sand. An inexpensive device called a "come-along"—sort of a hand winch—can get you out of a hole, if you can find something for an anchor.

✻ If you become stranded in the desert, stay in the shade of your car—not in the vehicle itself. If you're far from civilization and not sure of your bearings, don't try to walk out, particularly during the heat of the day. Besides, a vehicle is easier to spot than a lone hiker. Use a mirror, foil or space blanket as a signal device if you see a plane approaching, and build a signal fire. A spare tire will burn, and a douse of oil will make the fire nice and smoky. Start your blaze in a cleared area away from your vehicle. You don't want to launch a wildfire that might compound your predicament.

✻ If you're on a road and you know that you can reach civilization on foot, do your walking at night. Take plenty of water, a flashlight with extra batteries and some food for nibbling.

Heat isn't your only problem in the desert. Flash floods can roar down dry washes and across roadway dips, particularly during spring and summer rain squalls. If you're driving or hiking in the desert and a sudden rainstorm hits, keep to the high ground until it passes. Storms can be unpredictable, so avoid camping in dry washes.

Chapter two
GETTING TO KNOW YOU
THE WAY IT IS

Asking someone to describe Arizona is like asking one to describe an elephant in the dark. It depends on which part you're feeling.

The state fits its well known desert stereotype. Indeed, two thirds of it is arid. It's the only state in the Union with a national park and national monument named for varieties of cactus—Saguaro and Organ Pipe.

At the same time, it defies this stereotype. Humphreys Peak north of Flagstaff is one of America's highest mountains, at 12,633 feet. A fourth of the state is covered by forest, and it shelters the largest stand of virgin ponderosa pines in the country. And of course it contains the deepest gorge—the Grand Canyon, which is Arizona's grandest stereotype of all.

The state's physical appearance is summed up rather well by Reg Manning, Pulitzer Prize winning cartoonist for Phoenix's *Arizona Republic.* In his whimsical book, *What is Arizona Really Like?*, he says the topography can be taken in three bites, starting from the Four Corners area in the northeast.

The first bite is a remote, often hauntingly beautiful semiarid plateau containing the large Navajo and Hopi reservations, Monument Valley and the Painted Desert. The second semicircle, curving from northwest through east central Arizona, is a green belt of ponderosa pines, including the forest-rimmed Grand Canyon. The Mogollon Rim, a great fault extending in a 200-mile arc, marks the edge of this high country.

The final bite—consuming nearly two thirds of the state—is a great sweep of desert and high prairie, reaching from the western edge to the southeast corner. This is the Sunbelt. That term originated in Arizona and now is used to describe just about any place south of a Pennsylvania blizzard.

Although most of Arizona is desert, it isn't necessarily hot. Much of this land, particularly in the central and northeastern areas, is high desert that's often quite cold in winter. Southeastern Arizona is more of a prairie than a desert. Naturally, the northwestern mountain regions get regular snowfall. Even in the southern Sunbelt, evenings can be quite cool, so don't put *all* of your winter clothing into the Salvation Army collection box.

Nearly 85 percent of Arizona's population is focused in this warm belt—mostly in and around Phoenix and Tucson. These two metropolitan centers offer every imaginable service and convenience, and an abundance of cultural and recreational lures.

However, Arizona's greatest charms lie in its open spaces and scenic wonders; in its small towns with their affable wanna-be-cowboy attitudes. We found our Arizona in the high, silent reaches of the San Francisco Peaks and in the hidden depths of the Grand Canyon. We discovered it in the dignity of the Indian nations and the scruffy charm of Mexican border towns; in the solitude of a wilderness cactus garden reached only by a dusty road.

THE WAY IT WAS

Arizona is one of the youngest states in the union, admitted as the last of the lower 48 in 1912. Yet, river-runners and hikers in the Grand Canyon will see two-billion-year-old Precambrian schist, some of the oldest exposed rock on this third rock from the sun. Native Americans have occupied Arizona's deserts and high plateaus for about 20,000 years.

Its first residents were nomadic hunters who drifted down from the Great Plains. When droughts drove the mammoths and antelope away, they swapped their spears for plowshares and became—about 11 centuries ago—North America's first farmers. Freed from the constant search for food, they developed complex societies and built large pueblos whose ruins survive today. The state is a treasure-trove of archaeological sites.

Anthropologists call these early people Hohokam, Anasazi, Sinagua and Mogollon. We don't know what they called themselves, for they left no written language. Like most ancient tribes, they probably just referred to their kind as "The People." Through the centuries, they evolved into highly-developed societies, occupying great pueblos of adobe or stone atop mesas or tucked into hidden canyons and precipitous cliffs. They dug irrigation canals and became excellent farmers.

— PHOTO COURTESY ARIZONA DEPARTMENT OF ARCHIVES

Spain was the first outside nation to explore Arizona. Francisco Vasquez de Coronado came looking for golden cities in 1540 and found mostly trouble.

Their pottery, weaving and other crafts were among the most advanced of their time.

About eight centuries ago, this highly developed society began coming apart at the seams. The great pueblos were abandoned and left to weather away in the wind and hot sun. Scientists speculate that a persistent drought may have driven them from their corn and bean fields. Some experts blame their downfall on disease, soil depletion or the arrival of more aggressive tribes.

People identify Navajos and Apaches with Arizona, yet these were latter-day arrivals, coming from the cold north. They were Athabaskans who drifted down from Canada, starting about six hundred years ago. Warlike hunters, they may have driven off many of the native tribes. Ironically, they adopted some of the original residents' farming and weaving techniques, particularly those who would become Navajos. Scientists have been unable to pinpoint the ultimate fate of the Hohokam, Sinagua or Mogollon. Similarities in culture and crafts suggest that today's Hopi may be Anasazi descendants.

Historians have fun feuding over the origin of Arizona's name. There are four Indian versions: Arizuma, an Aztec word for "silver bearing"; *Ali shonak* or *Ari-son,* meaning "small spring" or "young spring," which were names of Pima settlements; and a Tohono O'odham term, *Aleh-zone,* also meaning young spring. Basque settlers insist that Arizona comes from *Aritz ona,* their term for "good oak." This name was given to a silver strike site in 1736. Some unimaginative scholars suggest that "Arizona" is merely a derivation of "arid zone." The name "Arizona" first appeared in print in a 1750s document by one Padre Ortega, a Spanish missionary.

Spaniards were the area's first outside visitors, and they got here by accident. In 1528, a group led by Alvar Núñez Cabeza de Vaca set out to explore Florida's west coast. Part of the group became lost after an Indian attack and spent more than eight years wandering through what is now Texas, New Mexico, Arizona and northern Mexico. Some accounts say they were befriended and protected by the locals, after De Vaca convinced them that he was a powerful medicine man. When four surviving members of the group finally stumbled across some of their countrymen in western Mexico, they reported Indian legends of fabulously wealthy cities which lay to the north.

Antonio de Mendoza, viceroy of New Spain, knew of an eighth century Moorish legend about seven golden cities, hidden somewhere in the unexplored world. Could these be the same? In 1539, with golden greed glittering in his eyes, he dispatched a party of explorers from Mexico City to find these treasure-laden towns. It was led by Franciscan Father Marcos de Niza. Accompanying the group—probably reluctantly—was a Moorish slave named Estévan, one of the survivors of the De Vaca trek.

The legend of Cibola

As the Spaniards entered present-day Arizona, local Indians said the area through which they traveled was called "Cibola." Thus, the legend of the Seven Cities of Cibola was born. Learning that a Zuni pueblo lay ahead, Father de Niza sent an advance party to investigate, led by Estévan. The Zunis weren't very nice hosts; they killed the visitors.

An intimidated Father de Niza kept his distance. But he drew near enough to see that the pueblos glittered in the sun. He returned home and advised the Viceroy of Mexico that he may have found one of the golden cities. However, the good padre most likely had been fooled by the glitter of mica, embedded in the adobe.

A year later, that great and brutal explorer, 30-year-old Francisco Vásquez de Coronado headed north to continue the search. He found no gold, pillaged a few pueblos and explored as far north as Kansas. After two years, he returned to Mexico City empty-handed. More than a century passed before the curious Spanish again began pestering natives of the Southwest. In the late 1600s, Father Eusebio Francisco Kino and other padres came to establish missions throughout the Southwest. They succeeded in converting thousands of Indians to Christianity—an act most likely encouraged by accompanying soldiers, who set up military presidios to protect the missions.

However, many of the Indians did not yield their land or their free spirits easily. Angered by abusive treatment from the Spanish intruders, they staged several violent revolts. The Hopi emptied their pueblos of Spaniards in a savage rebellion in 1680. Spanish occupation—punctuated by Indian uprisings—continued into the early 1800s. When Mexico won its independence from Spain in the 1820s, most of the soldiers were withdrawn from this northern outpost. In the absence of the military, Indians—primarily Apaches—again went on the warpath, driving frightened settlers to the safety of the walled cities of Tucson and Tubac.

Much of what is now Arizona and New Mexico was ceded to the United States in the 1848 Treaty of Guadalupe Hidalgo, at the end of the Mexican War. Sandwiched between California and Texas, they were lumped together as the New Mexico Territory. However, as far as the original residents were concerned, this was still their land and warfare with the intruders continued. In the late 1800s, more than a dozen U.S. Army forts were built to protect American settlers. Not until Geronimo surrendered in 1886 was the area considered safe for settlement.

A major force

Today, Native Americans are a major force in the state, culturally and politically. Vast tracts of land were set aside as reservations, which have become self-governing entities. The Navajo and Hopi nations occupy a huge chunk of northeastern Arizona. Combined with other reservations, they comprise a fourth of the state's land area.

The California gold discovery in 1848 spurred the greatest human migration since the Crusades. Many gold-seekers traveled south through the New Mexico Territory to avoid the precipitous Sierra Nevada range that formed a barrier on California's eastern edge. Part of this southern route dipped into Mexico, so the government decided to make it all-American by negotiating the Gadsden Purchase. In 1854, cash-poor Mexico sold 30,000 square miles of its northern desert for $10 million. This would become a large chunk of southern Arizona.

Four years later, the government awarded the Butterfield Overland Stage Company a contract to forge a mail a route through this area, from St. Louis to San Francisco. It was needed to link fast-growing California with the rest of the U.S., which then ended at the Missouri border.

The New Mexico Territory, settled primarily by Southerners, sided with the South during the Civil War. A Texas militia seized Mesilla, New Mexico, in 1861. The Texans claimed all of the land from the Rio Grande to the Pacific as Confederate territory. But a column of Union-sympathizing Californians soon put an end to that. In 1862, the Confederates were routed in the Battle of Picacho Pass, south of Phoenix. Little more than a skirmish with only eight casualties, it was the Civil War's westernmost engagement. The following year, President Lincoln moved to ensure the area's Union support by signing a bill creating separate Arizona and New Mexico territories.

For the next two decades, the Arizona Territory epitomized the Wild West. Cattle barons battled over water and grazing rights and knocked down sod-busters' pesky fences. Tombstone and its O.K. Corral shoot-out and Yuma's infamous Territorial Prison became the stuff of which legends—and certainly movies—were made. Then in the 1880s, several minor gold strikes, major copper discoveries and Mormon migrations from Utah brought a more settled brand of citizens to the territory. The railroad arrived late in the century to complete the taming of this last outpost of the Wild West. Then on St. Valentine's Day in 1912, portly President William Howard Taft signed the proclamation making Arizona the last of the 48 contiguous states.

Hampered by lack of water, the new state grew slowly in the first half of this century. Several military air bases were built in its wide open spaces during World War II, and many GIs who trained here returned at war's end. In the Fifties, Arizona's numbers began to swell, aided by air conditioning, the creation of the Snowbird cult, and a court ruling granting it a larger share of Colorado River water.

And suddenly, Arizona was on a roll. It grew by a whopping 53 percent during the 1970s, second only to Nevada in percentage increase; in the next decade it added another 35 percent, outgained only by Nevada and Alaska. In numbers of people, it is considerably larger than both, with an estimated population of 4,228,900 in 1995. Among Western states, only California and Washington have more people. Phoenix has blossomed into a major city. Its suburbs of Mesa, Glendale and Chandler doubled their populations between 1970 and 1980, and Gilbert nearly quadrupled its people count. As the millennium approached, Phoenix and several other Arizona communities again were numbered among the fastest growing cities in the nation.

THINGS ARIZONAN

Several things—cultural, historic or climatic—are distinctly Arizonan, or at least distinctly Southwestern.

Bola tie • This curious form of neckware, with a braided cord drawn through some kind of Western ornament, was born in Arizona and hopefully will die there.

Cowboys • The American cowboy's roots are mostly Mexican, and the cowboy himself originated in Arizona, New Mexico and west Texas. His standard gear—wide-brimmed hat, lariat, saddle with a horn (used for snubbing the lariat) and chaps—are all of Mexican *vaquero* origin. The rodeo originated in Mexico and the guitar that cowboys like to strum is Spanish. Levi's were contributed by Californian Levi Strauss, although the originals were grey tent canvas; blue denims didn't come along until the late 1800s. We have no idea why all those Southern country singers dress like cowboys and play guitars. Round 'em up and head 'em out to—Nashville?

Howling coyotes • That coyote, wearing a neckerchief and howling at the moon, is a typical object on Arizona jewelry and ceramics. No one seems to know where he came from.

Native American casinos • A phenomenon of recent years, Indian casinos are cropping up all over Arizona. They range from a small slot machine parlor above Pipe Springs National Monument on the Arizona Strip to the large, handsome Mazatzal Casino just outside Payson. Since reservations are sovereign territories, Native Americans are free to establish casinos and there is of course an abundance of native land in Arizona. Most gaming parlors are small by Las Vegas standards, offering primarily slot machines, video poker and keno. Some, however, are quite elaborate. The largest, which rivals some of the big Nevada resorts, is the Avi Hotel and Casino operated by the Fort Mohave Tribe. Although the tribe has land in Arizona and Nevada, the casino itself is in Nevada, challenging the gaming resorts of Laughlin, just to the north.

Indian fry bread and Navajo tacos ● Common among most Arizona tribes, Indian fry bread is something like pizza crust without the pizza. It's used like bread, or it can be turned into a pastry by sprinkling it with cinnamon and sugar. A dish popular with Navajos and many other Arizona tribes and a few hearty whites is the infamous Navajo taco, also called the Indian taco. Neither Navajo nor taco, it's more like a Mexican tostada, with pinto beans, chili, ground beef, grated cheese, chopped onions and shredded lettuce layered over a disk of fry bread. Served in many Arizona restaurants, they're usually quite huge. After a Navajo taco meal, you won't want to eat again for hours—possibly for days.

Silver and turquoise ● The Navajo and Hopi of Arizona and Zuni of New Mexico are noted for their beautiful silver and turquoise jewelry. The Hopi work primarily with silver while the Navajo jewelry often combines silver with turquoise, particularly in the famous "squash blossom" necklace. However, it is not native to their culture, despite their love of adornment. The turquoise-silver concept was introduced to them by none other than Fred Harvey, who had gotten his start by developing Southwest tourism in the late 1800s. It was crafted then as it is now—primarily to sell to tourists.

Southwest cuisine ● The *nouveau* cuisine movement started about 20 years ago in California, featuring fresh ingredients simply prepared, interestingly spiced and lightly cooked. Chefs in Arizona and New Mexico, where fresh year-around vegetables are abundant, started adding chili peppers and *polenta* to these recipes and *voile!* Southwest cuisine.

Southwestern architecture ● The look is earthy, squarish and adobe, with salmon and turquoise as the preferred colors. Probably more of New Mexican origin than Arizonan, it was inspired by a combination of Hopi and Zuni dwellings and Frank Lloyd Wright's earthy, geometric architecture. Wright spent his final years at Taliesen West, near Scottsdale.

Saguaro cactus ● Pronounced *sa-WHA-ro,* this large and thick-limbed plant is often portrayed as a "typical" cactus in illustrations, cartoons and Western souvenirs. Yet its habitat is strictly limited; it grows only in the Sonoran Desert of southern Arizona and northern Mexico. It's also found frequently on bola ties.

JUST THE FACTS

Size • 113,909 square miles; sixth largest state; about 340 miles wide by just under 400 miles deep.

Population • About 4,228,900; largest city is Phoenix with just over a million residents. Tucson is the second largest city with just under half a million. Arizona's population density is 37.1 per square mile.

Elevations • Highest point, Humphreys Peak north of Flagstaff, 12,633 feet; lowest point, Colorado River as it enters Mexico below Yuma, 70 feet.

Admitted to the Union • February 14, 1912, as the 48th state; capital—Phoenix.

Time zone • Mountain; one hour later than the West Coast, two hours earlier than the East. Except for the Navajo Reservation, Arizona doesn't switch to summer Daylight Saving Time; apparently those warm desert evenings are long enough!

Area codes • (520) for all of Arizona except the Phoenix metropolitan area, which is (602).

Official stuff • STATE MOTTO—*Didat Deus* (God enriches); STATE SEAL depicts the five "Cs" of copper, cotton, climate, citrus and cattle; STATE BIRD—cactus wren (medium brown with speckled breast, likes to hang around saguaro cactus); STATE FLOWER—saguaro cactus blossom (white with yellow center); STATE TREE—paloverde (desert tree identified by green limbs, which is what *palo verde* means in Spanish); STATE GEM—turquoise.

State nicknames • The Grand Canyon State; the Copper State (appropriate, since it produces more than half of America's copper supply).

Alcohol • None may be imported from another state (although there are no border checks). It's sold by the bottle in any licensed store; minimum drinking age 21, Legal bar hours 7 a.m. to 1 a.m.

Motorists' laws • Safety belts required for drivers and front seat passengers. Children under five or weighing less than 40 pounds must be secured by child restraints in vehicles. Helmets required for motorcyclists under 18. Speed limit is 65 to 70 mph (as posted) on rural freeways and 55 mph on most urban freeways and other highways. Highway patrolmen use radar, and to even the score, radar detectors are permitted.

Road conditions • Call (602) 279-2000 and punch R-O-A-D to learn about driving conditions.

Hunting and Fishing • Out-of-state hunting and fishing licenses are available at most sporting goods stores. Anyone over 14 may get one; fees vary. State licenses aren't required on Indian reservations, but each has its own laws and permit fees; check before you go.

To learn more about Arizona, contact:

Arizona Department of Commerce, Economic Research Division, 3800 N. Central Ave., Suite 1400, Phoenix, AZ 85012; (602) 280- 1321.

Arizona Office of Tourism, 1100 W. Washington St., Phoenix, AZ 85007; (800) 842-8257 or (602) 542-TOUR.

Arizona Game & Fish Department, 2222 W. Greenway Rd., Phoenix, AZ 85023; (602) 942-3000.

Arizona Wine Commission, 1688 W. Adams, Phoenix, AZ 85007; (602) 542-0968. (For a brochure listing the eight wineries in the state.)

Arizona State Parks, 1300 W. Washington St., Phoenix, AZ 85007; (602) 542-4174.

Arizona Travel Parks Association, P.O. Box 11090-275, Phoenix, AZ 85061-1090; (602) 230-1126.

Native American Tourism Center, 4130 N. Goldwater Blvd., Suite 114, Scottsdale, AZ 85281; (602) 945-0771.

U.S. Bureau of Land Management, 3707 N. Seventh St., Phoenix, AZ 85014; (602) 650-0504.

Chapter three

ESSENTIAL ARIZONA

ALMOST EVERYTHING YOU NEED TO KNOW

As you contemplate Arizona in your future, it's a good guess that one of your first concerns will be taxes. By law and impulse, Arizonans try to keep them down. Property tax has a cap of one percent of full value, similar to California's Proposition 13. With their basic pro-growth attitude, officials try to rein in business taxes as well. If you have any taxing questions, contact the **Arizona Department of Revenue,** 1600 W. Monroe St., Phoenix, AZ 85007; (602) 542-3572.

Individual income tax

Income received while you reside in Arizona is subject to state income tax, whether or not you're a permanent resident. Tax credits are available for seniors, renters (including mobile home occupants) and low income people. Renters must occupy property in the state for more than six months to qualify for this credit. Other credits are given for installing solar energy equipment or groundwater measuring devices.

State income taxes have been reduced in recent years. The rates are as follows, based on the adjusted gross income on your federal return (assuming all of it was earned while you resided in Arizona):

Single or married taxpayers filing separate returns

Up to $10,000—3 percent of taxable income
$10,001 to $25,000—$300 plus 3.5% of excess over $10,000
$25,001 to $50,000—$825 plus 4.2% of excess over $25,000

$50,001 to $150,000—$1,875 plus 5.2% of excess over $50,000
$150,001 and over—$7,075 plus 5.6% of excess over $150,000

Married taxpayers filing joint returns
and unmarried heads of household

Up to $20,000—3 percent of taxable income
$20,001 to $50,000—$600 plus 3.5% of excess over $20,000
$50,001 to $100,000—$1,650 plus 4.2% of excess over $50,000
$100,001 to $300,000—$3,750 plus 5.2% of excess over $100,000
$300,001 and over—$14,150 plus 5.6% of excess over $300,000

Estate (inheritance) tax

Arizona is rather generous with estate taxes, allowing a $600,000 exemption. For estates valued higher, a return must be filed with the Department of Revenue, Estate Tax Division, within nine months of the person's demise.

Property taxes

Real Estate taxes in Arizona are well below the national urban average. In fact, according to *Money Magazine,* Phoenix is ninth lowest among all major American cities, with an average annual residential property tax of $1,501 for a 2,600-square-foot home.

To help keep taxes down, counties, cities and schools can increase their levies by only two percent a year. Reevaluation of property for taxing purposes is limited to ten percent a year, even if the appraised value is higher. Owner-occupied property is assessed at ten percent of its real value, with a tax rate cap of one percent of the full cash value. Other rates are ten percent for rental property, 16 percent for farm land and vacant property and 25 percent for commercial property.

The state property tax bite is 47 cents per $100 assessed valuation. Above that, tax rates vary widely from one community to the next. They're listed in our community profiles in Part Two.

Like most states, Arizona offers property tax breaks for certain people, including surviving spouses and the disabled.

Sales tax

Arizona collects a five percent sales tax on most items purchased, except for food and pharmaceuticals. In addition, most cities levy another one or two percent, and they have the option of taxing food and drugs. The state also levies tax from three-eights of a percent to five percent on business sales.

THINGS AUTOMOTIVE

Since you will likely be driving to Arizona, you'll need to know about vehicle taxes, insurance requirements, registration and such. For details, check with the nearest office of the **Motor Vehicle Division** or the main office at 1801 W. Jefferson (P.O. Box 2100), Phoenix, AZ 85001.

MOTOR VEHICLE AND FUEL TAXES • Motorists pay an $8.25 per vehicle registration fee each year (and an extra $4 for new first-time registrations), plus a Vehicle License Tax (VLT) in lieu of personal property tax. It's based on $4 per $100 of assessed value. New cars are assessed at 60 percent of the manufacturer's base retail price, and the assessment drops 15 percent a year as the vehicle ages. Vehicle taxes are paid annually, in the month that the vehicle was first registered. And yes, you can get personalized license plates in Arizona for a one-time fee of $25.

State gasoline and diesel tax is 17 cents per gallon, plus whatever federal fuel levy currently is in vogue.

AUTO INSURANCE • Arizona drivers are required to carry liability insurance in the amounts of $15,000 medical per person or $30,000 per accident, plus $10,000 property damage. As an alternative to insurance, one can deposit a $40,000 surety bond or certificate of deposit with the state treasurer. Evidence of insurance or other financial responsibility must be carried in the vehicle. This can be the policy itself or an insurance company's ID card.

If you can't prove financial responsibility, you face penalties of $250 for the first offense and possible suspension of your driving license and vehicle registration for 90 days. Penalties go up to $750 and a year's suspension for three violations within three years. Also, you must notify the Motor Vehicle Division within ten days of any change in liability coverage, such as switching vehicles or changing insurance companies.

AUTO REGISTRATION • See "Vehicle registration" below.

AUTO REPAIR • The Arizona Automobile Association (AAA) provides a list of approved auto repair establishments. Call (602) 274-1116 in Phoenix, (602) 949-7993 in Scottsdale, (602) 979-3700 in Peoria (for the west side of the Valley of the Sun), (602) 834-8296 in Mesa (east side), (520) 296-7461 in Tucson and (520) 783-3339 in Yuma.

AUTOMOTIVE LEMON LAW • The state has a "lemon law" that protects new car buyers. It requires the dealer to offer a full refund or replacement vehicle if a defect can't be fixed after four tries within a year; or if the vehicle is in the shop for more than 30 days during that year.

DRIVER'S LICENSE • If you become a resident, you must immediately obtain an Arizona driver's license. Seasonal visitors are not considered permanent residents and may use their back-home licenses. Arizona defines a resident as anyone who remains in the state for seven or more consecutive months in one year. Also, you become a resident if you enroll a child in school, set up a business or accept employment other than seasonal agricultural work.

For teen drivers, a restricted learner's permit can be obtained at age 15 years and seven months, and a regular license at age 16.

Fees are $2 for a learner's permit and $7 for a new or renewed passenger vehicle or motorcycle license. State ID cards are $5. You can get a copy of your motor vehicle record for a $3 fee (or $5 for a certified five-year record).

When applying for a license, you must surrender your license from the previous state, and show evidence that you have a clear driving record in that state. For details on fees and requirements, contact the nearest Driver's License Examining Station.

DRUNK DRIVING LAWS • Arizona is tough on drunk drivers. You are presumed to be under the influence if you have a blood alcohol level of .10 percent or higher. A law enforcement officer can require that you submit to a blood, breath or urine test if he or she has "reasonable grounds" to believe you were driving under the influence of alcohol or drugs. You can lose your license for a year if you refuse to submit to a test, even if you are cleared of the drunk driving charge.

A DWI conviction results in a mandatory jail sentence of at least 24 hours, a fine of $250 or more and a 90-day license suspension. A second offense within five years results in a year's license suspension, a heavy fine and mandatory jail term.

DRUNK DRIVING REPORTS • If you see someone driving erratically, call the police hot line at (800) 535-5555.

HANDICAPPED LICENSE PLATES • People with physical disabilities can obtain special vehicle license plates that permit parking in blue spaces designated for the handicapped. They must first obtain a statement from a physician confirming their disability. To qualify, they must meet two of these requirements:

- Be physically unable to use public transit.
- Be extremely deformed or disfigured.
- Have a severe loss of dexterity and/or coordination.
- Be physically unable to perform manual activity for more than six hours.
- Be unable to climb a flight of stairs without a pause.
- Be unable to walk 50 yards without stopping to rest.

Plates may be obtained at any office of the Motor Vehicle Division. You also can get a temporary permit while recuperating from an illness or injury that has impaired your mobility. Again, a statement from a physician is required.

Able-bodied people who use a handicapped parking space face a stiff fine.

MOTORCYCLE HELMET LAW • Anyone under age 18 must wear a safety helmet when riding a motorcycle. Also, all motorcyclists must wear protective eyewear if their cycle is not equipped with a windshield.

SAFETY BELTS • Safety restraints are required for front seat passengers in all vehicles. All children weighing up to 40 pounds, or age four and under, must be secured in an approved child restraint.

SMOG CHECKS • If you register a vehicle in Maricopa or Pima counties (Phoenix or Tucson areas), it must be checked to ensure that it meets federally required emission standards and that emission equipment hasn't been tampered with, removed or bypassed. To learn the location of the nearest vehicle testing station, call (800) 2-VIP-SITE. Electric and diesel powered vehicles and those with engines under 90 cubic centimeters are exempted.

SPEED LIMITS • The limit is 65 to 70 mph on rural freeways (as posted) and 55 mph on urban freeways and most surface streets (or as posted). Highway patrolmen use radar and, to even the score, radar detectors are permitted.

VEHICLE REGISTRATION • If you become a resident, you must immediately register your car at a state Title and Registration office. Anyone who remains in Arizona for seven consecutive months in a year, enrolls a child in school, starts a business or accepts employment other than seasonal agricultural work is considered a resident. (See "Driver's license" above.) A vehicle must be checked at a smog testing station before it can be registered. To learn the location of the nearest testing station, call (800) 2-VIP-SITE.

Fees are $4 for a new title plus $8.50 annual registration and a $1.50 Air Quality Fee. In addition, you must pay an annual Vehicle License Tax (VLT); see "Motor vehicle and fuel taxes" above.

Once your vehicle is registered, if you move or change your name, you must notify the Motor Vehicle Division with ten days.

EVERYTHING ELSE YOU NEED TO KNOW
and now you know where to ask

ACCOUNTANTS • To find an accountant, contact the Arizona Society of CPAs at 426 N. 44th St., Phoenix, AZ 85008; (602) 273-0100.

ALCOHOL • Alcoholic beverage sale hours are 7 a.m. to 1 a.m. Monday through Saturday and noon to 1 a.m. Sunday. Legal age for buying or consuming alcohol is 21. It may not be drunk in a vehicle or in public areas in its original container. Wine, beer and distilled spirits are available in liquor stores, supermarkets and other outlets.

ARCHITECTS • For a list of AIA members, contact the American Institute of Architects at 802 N. Fifth Ave., Phoenix, AZ 85003; (602) 257-1924.

ATTORNEYS • To find a lawyer, contact the Maricopa County Bar Association Lawyers Referral Service at 333 W. Roosevelt St., Phoenix, AZ 85003, (602) 257-4434; or the Pima County Lawyer Referral Service at 177 N. Church Ave., Tucson, AZ 85701 (520) 623-4625.

BAD CHECKS • Writing a bad check in Arizona isn't just bad manners; it's a misdemeanor. Rubber check writers who don't make good within 12 days may be fined and/or jailed, in addition to having to cover the check.

BICYCLING ● Bicycles are subject to the same basic traffic regulations as motor vehicles, and must travel in the same direction as street traffic. They are required to have brakes (we should hope!), plus a front light and rear reflector if they are ridden at night.

BOAT REGISTRATION ● Pleasure boats moored or used on public waterways must be registered with the Game and Fish Department, which will issue numbers that must be displayed prominently. For other specifics and tips about boating safety, get the *Arizona Boating Guide* from the Arizona Game and Fish Department, 2222 W. Greenway Rd., Phoenix, AZ 85023; (602) 942-3000.

CAMPGROUNDS ● For a directory of more than 250 campgrounds in the state, contact the Arizona Office of Tourism, 1100 W. Washington St., Phoenix, AZ 85007; (800) 842-8257 or (602) 542-TOUR. Also see "Joining the RV clan?" in Chapter seven.

COMMUNITY PROFILES ● Sketches of more than a hundred Arizona towns are available from the Arizona Department of Commerce, 3800 N. Central Ave., Suite 1400, Phoenix, AZ 85017; (602) 280-1321. The price is $15 for the entire package, $18 for the packet in a binder, or 15 cents for profiles of individual communities.

CONSUMER PROTECTION ● These agencies offer consumer protection services:

Arizona Board of Osteopathic Examiners, 1830 W. Colter St., Suite 4, Phoenix, AZ 85015; (602) 255-1747.

Arizona Department of Real Estate, Office of the Commissioner, Consumer Representative, 202 E. Earll Dr., Suite 460, Phoenix, AZ 85012; (602) 255-3232.

Better Business Bureau, phone (602) 264-1721 or check your local phone directory.

Board of Medical Examiners, 2001 W. Camelback Rd., Phoenix, AZ 85015; (602) 255-3751.

Consumer Products Safety (U.S.), (602) 241-2397.

Registrar of Contractors, 800 W. Washington St., Phoenix, AZ 85007, (602) 542-1525; or 416 W. Congress, Tucson, AZ 85701; (520) 628-6345.

Securities Division, Arizona Corporation Commission, 1200 W. Washington St., Suite 201, Phoenix, AZ 85007; (602) 542-4242.

State Department of Insurance, 3030 N. Third St., Suite 1100, Phoenix, AZ 85040; (602) 255-5400.

Superintendent of Banks, 3225 N. Central Ave., Suite 815, Phoenix, AZ 85012; (602) 255-4421.

CONTRACTORS ● They're listed with the Registrar of Contractors in Phoenix and Tucson; see above.

COUNTY GOVERNMENT ● Arizona has 15 counties, each run by a three-member board of supervisors. Elected county officials—all serving four-year terms—are supervisors, county attorney, treasurer, superintendent of schools, recorder, assessor, sheriff and clerk of the superior court.

CROSS-COUNTRY SKIING ● See "Winter sports" below.

DAY CARE ● Anyone who cares for more than four children (not related to them) must be licensed by the Department of Health Services. For the publication *Guidelines for Choosing a Day Care Center,* contact the Arizona Department of Health Services, 1647 E. Morten St., Suite 110, Phoenix, AZ 85020; (602) 255-1109. The office also can tell you if complaints have been lodged against a particular day care center.

These agencies can provide assistance in finding child care: **Association for Supportive Child Care,** 2510 S. Rural Rd., Tempe, AZ 85282, (602) 829-0500; and the **Tucson Association for Child Care,** 1030 N. Alvernon Way, Tucson, AZ 85711, (520) 881-8940.

The Family Service Agency offers assistance in finding child care facilities, as well as providing counseling for family problems, unplanned pregnancies and adoption services. The main office is at 1530 E. Flower St., Phoenix, AZ 85014; (602) 264-9891. Other offices (all 602 area code) are in Tempe (966-0739), Scottsdale (994-0187), Mesa/Chandler (834-9290) and Phoenix Metrocenter (863-1862).

DENTISTS ● Misery with a molar? To find a dentist, contact the Arizona Dental Association, 4131 N. 36th St., Phoenix, AZ 85018; (602) 957-4864.

DIVORCE ● Misery with a mate? Arizona is a no-fault divorce state and a community property state. In ruling on alimony, courts will consider contribution made by one spouse to the other's earning ability, loss of potential earning power by spending years as a homemaker and other factors. The community property law simply means that property acquired by either marital partner during the marriage is considered to be the equal property of both.

DOCTORS ● To find a medical doctor, contact the Arizona Medical Association at 810 W. Bethany Home Rd., Phoenix, AZ 85013, (602) 246-8901; or the Arizona Osteopathic Medical Association at 5057 E. Thomas Rd., Phoenix, AZ 85018, (602) 840-0460. Two county medical societies also provide names of local physicians: the Maricopa County Medical Society, 326 E. Coronado Rd., Phoenix, AZ 85004, (602) 252-2015; and the Pima County Medical Society, 5199 E. Farness St., Tucson, AZ 85712; (520) 795-7985).

DRUG USE ● Arizona gets mean about substance abuse. Possession of a "usable" amount of marijuana will earn you a $750 mandatory fine, plus jail time or community service. If you're found with more of the stuff, or if you're arrested near a school grounds, the penalties get worse. Laws are really tough for heroine, crack and cocaine possession.

ELECTIONS • The state primary is held in September of even-numbered years, followed by the general election in November. You must pick a major party to vote in the primary, but not in the general election. The state doesn't conduct a Presidential primary. Precinct committeemen, who are elected to two-year terms, pick the state's party candidates.

Arizona's elected officials are the governor, secretary of state, attorney general and superintendent of public instruction, who all serve four-year terms; and the state mine inspector, who serves two years. Office holders are subject to recall elections if enough voters sign petitions. Voters also can place statewide initiatives and referendums on the ballot, with sufficient petition signatures. (Also see "Legislature" and "Political parties" below.)

GOLFING • For a list of more than 150 golf courses in the state, contact the Arizona Golf Association at P.O. Box 13236, Phoenix, AZ 85002.

GUN CONTROL • With its Old West attitude, Arizona allows someone to buy a handgun or rifle without a waiting period, and pack it in view. However, you can't own an automatic weapon or sawed-off shotgun. Also, you can't possess any weapon if you have a felony record or a history of mental illness. A legally owned weapon can't be concealed. (You can, however, carry your Swiss army knife in your pocket.)

HEALTH CARE • Persons interested in extended health care can get a directory of state licensed facilities by contacting the Office of Long Term Care of the Arizona Department of Health Services, either at 1647 E. Morten St., Suite 110, Phoenix, AZ 85020; (602) 255-1109.; or at 402 W. Congress St., Suite 116, Tucson, AZ 85701, (520) 628-5870. For information on nursing homes, contact the Arizona Nursing Home Association at 1817 N. Third St., Suite 200, Phoenix, AZ 85004; (602) 258-8996.

HOUSING • The best source for housing information is chambers of commerce and real estate offices, since no single agency compiles data on prices and availability. (We provide pricing information in many of our community listings in Part Two.) If you want to build your own home and need a contractor, contact the Registrar of Contractors, 800 W. Washington ST., Phoenix, AZ 85007, (602) 542-1525; or 416 W. Congress, Tucson, AZ 85701; (520) 628-6345.

HUNTING AND FISHING • Hunting and fishing licenses are required for anyone 14 and older, and are available at most sporting goods stores. Fishing license fees are $6.50 for residents and $25.50 for nonresidents, or $18.50 for a nine-day and $12.50 for a five-day nonresident permit. Trout stamps are $6.50 for residents and $21.50 for out-of-staters. Combined hunting-fishing licenses is $18.50 for residents and $90.50 for nonresidents. For specifics on limits and such, get a copy of fishing and hunting regulations at sporting goods stores or contact the Arizona Game and Fish Department, 2222 W. Greenway Rd., Phoenix, AZ 85023; (602) 942-3000. State licenses aren't required for hunting and fishing on Indian reservations, although most have their own regulations and fees. (See "Other Indian nations" in Chapter seventeen.)

IDENTIFICATION CARDS • ID cards for non-drivers, handy for use in proving your age and identification, can be obtained for a $5 fee from any office of the Motor Vehicle Division.

IMMIGRATION • For matters concerning immigration and naturalization, contact the federal Immigration and Naturalization Service, which as two Arizona offices: 2035 N. Central Ave., Phoenix, AZ 85004, (602) 379-3122; and 301 W. Congress St., Tucson, AZ 85017; (520) 629-6228.

INCORPORATING A BUSINESS • See "Starting a business" in Chapter five.

INSURANCE • As in other states, insurance rates vary from city to city. Auto insurance rates are highest in busy Phoenix, somewhat lower in Tucson and lower still in smaller towns. The Department of Insurance will send you a survey of companies selling automobile and homeowners insurance in the state. It also maintains records of complaints against insurance carriers. To get a copy of the survey, send a self-addressed stamped business-size envelope to: State Department of Insurance, 3030 N. Third St., Suite 1100, Phoenix, AZ 85040. The phone number is (602) 255-5400. (Also see "Auto insurance" above.)

LEGISLATURE • Arizona is sliced into 30 legislative districts, and each sends one representative and one senator to the capital in Phoenix. Members of both houses serve two-year terms. The legislature convenes in early January and usually stays in session about four months. The Senate Information Desk (255-3559) and the House of Representatives Information Desk (255-4221) can tell you the status of a bill.

LIQUOR • See "Alcohol" above.

LOTTERY • The Arizona Lottery sells chances at $1 each and conducts computer drawings on Wednesdays and Saturdays. The jackpot often tops a million dollars; grand prize winners are paid over a 20-year period. About two thirds of the money collected goes to prizes and the rest is used for programs such as public transportation, street maintenance and senior vans.

MAJOR LEAGUE SPORTS • Tickets for the *Phoenix Suns* of the National Basketball Association are available by calling (602) 379-SUNS; they play at Arizona Veterans Memorial Coliseum at 1826 W. McDowell Road. The *Arizona Cardinals* of the National Football League play at Arizona State University's Sun Devil Stadium and tick-

CACTUS LEAGUE: SUN COUNTRY BASEBALL

Every March, shouts of "play ball!" echo among the Southwest's sunny deserts as several members of the majors launch their spring training. The Valley of the Sun is the focal point, hosting the California Angels, Chicago Cubs, Milwaukee Brewers, Oakland A's, San Diego Padres, San Francisco Giants and Seattle Mariners. The Colorado Rockies work out in Tucson, and the new Arizona Diamondbacks of Phoenix also may take the short trip south to play their Cactus League games in Tucson.

Fans like the informality and vigor of Cactus League baseball, and the intimacy of the small stadiums. It's baseball played with enthusiasm, gusto and mistakes; the way we played as kids on America's sandlots. They like the ticket prices, too: $5 to $10 for the best seats in the stands. The communities also like spring training; one survey indicated that Cactus League play generates as much as $150 million to host cities each year.

Many people come to Arizona specifically to watch these exhibition games, particularly the Snowbirds. If you're one of these baseball junkies, here's where you can catch the action. Tickets for the Angels, Athletics, Brewers and Cubs Cactus League games are available through Dillard's Box Office, (800) 638-4253 or (602) 678-2222. For others, contact the individual teams at the numbers below. All games start at 1 p.m.

The new **Arizona Diamondbacks** of Phoenix likely will host their Cactus League games at Tucson's Hi Corbett Field in Reid Park, East Broadway and Randolph Way; (602) 514-8400.

California Angels play at Tempe's Diablo Stadium, 48th Street and Broadway; (602) 438-9300. They work out at Gene Autry Park, 4125 E. McKellips in Mesa.

Chicago Cubs play at HoHoKam Park, 1235 Center St. (near Brown Road) in Mesa; (602) 964-4467.

Colorado Rockies play at Tucson's Hi Corbett Field in Reid Park, East Broadway and Randolph Way; (520) 327-9467.

Milwaukee Brewers play at Compadre Stadium, 1425 W. Ocotillo Rd. (off Arizona Avenue), in Chandler; (602) 895-1200.

Oakland A's play at Phoenix Municipal Stadium, 5999 E. Van Buren (near Galvin Parkway in Papago Park), Phoenix; (602) 392-0217. They practice at Scottsdale Community College, 9000 E. Chaparral Road, Scottsdale.

San Diego Padres play at Peoria Stadium, 10601 N. 83rd Dr.; (602) 486-2011.

San Francisco Giants play at Scottsdale Stadium, 7408 E. Osborn Rd., Scottsdale; (602) 990-7972. They work out at Indian Bend Park, 4289 N. Hayden Road in Scottsdale, and in Scottsdale Stadium.

Seattle Mariners play at Peoria Stadium, 10601 N. 83rd Drive; (602) 878-4337.

ets are available at (602) 379-0102. The new *Arizona Diamondbacks* major league baseball expansion team plays at the new Bank One Ballpark at Jefferson and Fourth Streets in Phoenix; call (602) 514-8500. The *Phoenix Roadrunners* of the International Hockey League play at Veterans Memorial Coliseum; call (602) 340-0001.

MAPS • State highway maps are available for a dollar from the **Arizona Office of Tourism**, 1100 W. Washington St., Phoenix, AZ 85007; (800) 842-8257 or (602) 542-TOUR. They're also available at many chambers of commerce in the state and at visitor information centers in Phoenix and Tucson. For a list of various city, county and other maps, get a brochure from the Department of Transportation, Engineering Records Service, 206 S. 17th Ave., Room 134-A, Phoenix, AZ 85007; (602) 255-7011.

The Arizona Automobile Association also has state maps, plus maps of several communities, available to AAA members only.

National Forest maps are sold for $2 each at forest service offices throughout the state, and at the Southwest Regional Office, **U.S. Forest Service**, 517 Gold Ave. S.W., Albuquerque, NM 87102; (505) 842-3292. Designate the particular national forest you want. Maps of BLM areas are available from the **Bureau of Land Management**, 3707 N. Seventh St., Phoenix, AZ 85014; (502) 650-0504. Topographical maps can be purchased from the **U.S. Geological Survey**, Denver Federal Building 41, Denver, CO 80225; (303) 236-7477.

MARRIAGE LICENSES • Although it isn't noted as a marriage mill, Arizona makes it easy to take the plunge. A license can be secured from any justice court for $22 and there's no waiting period or blood test requirement. Anyone from 18 to 22 years old must provide proof of age (a birth certificate or driver's license), and those 16 and 17 need parental consent. Those under 16 need the court's consent, given only in special circumstances. To learn the location of the nearest justice court, dial (602) 262-3361 in the Phoenix area or (520) 792-8041 in Tucson and vicinity.

MEXICO • See "Exploring south of the border," Chapter eighteen.

MOBILE HOME PARKS • See "RV parks" below.

NO SMOKING AREAS • Most cities restrict smoking to certain areas and many require restaurants to designate no smoking sections. Many employers, either voluntarily or by local ordinance, provide no smoking areas in the workplace.

NURSING HOMES • See "Health care" above.

ORGAN DONORS • You can indicate on your state driver's license if you want to donate organs or other usable parts in case of death. The program has a nice name: the Anatomical Gift Act.

PASSPORTS • No, you don't need a passport to enter Arizona, although you'll need one to go overseas from there. Call (602) 262-3369 in Phoenix or (520) 740-8333 in the Tucson area for details. Proof of citizenship such as a birth certificate or naturalization certificate is required, along with passport photos. Allow a week or more to obtain a passport; longer if you're applying by mail.

POLITICAL PARTIES ● Despite its conservative reputation, Arizona has more registered Democrats than Republicans. To become involved—should you wish—contact the Democratic State Headquarters at 1509 N. Central Ave., Suite 100, Phoenix, AZ 85004, (602) 257-9136; or the Arizona Republican Party at 3501 N. 24th St., Phoenix, AZ 85016-6607; (602) 957-7770. The state has the usual splinter parties, plus a rather active Libertarian Party; contact it at Libertarian State Headquarters, P.O. Box 501, Phoenix, AZ 85001; (602) 248-8425.

PRIVATE SCHOOLS ● Contact the Arizona Private School Association at 420 W. Roosevelt St., Phoenix, AZ 85003; (602) 265-8974.

PROFESSIONAL ORGANIZATIONS ● See Chapter five.

PUBLICATIONS ● Copies of Arizona laws and other state publications may be obtained from the Publications Office, Secretary of State, 1700 W. Washington St., Phoenix, AZ 85007; (602) 542-4086. If you don't know what to ask for, the office will send you a list.

RAINFALL ● See individual community listings in Part Two.

RENTING ● If you're a winter visitor looking for rentals, local chambers of commerce can be helpful, or check the Yellow Pages under "Rentals." Average apartment rentals in 1996 were about $500 per month in Phoenix and $477 in Tucson.

Regulations governing rentals are set down in the Arizona Residential Landlord and Tenant Act, and a copy is available from the Secretary of State's office. Among its provisions are these:

● Final month's rent and deposits can't exceed one and a half times the monthly rent.

● A rental agreement must state which deposits are refundable and which are not.

● Either the tenant or landlord must give 30 days notice prior to the rental due date before terminating a tenancy agreement.

● Tenants must be told within two weeks of their departure from a rental of the disposition of all deposits. In other words, deposits must be returned within that time or reasons must be given for their forfeiture.

● Landlords are required to provide trash removal containers, and to keep the property in compliance with building codes that affect health and safety.

● If a landlord neglects or refuses to make repairs affecting health and safety—or repairs called for in the rental agreement—the tenant has several options. They include terminating the rental agreement, seeking temporary quarters and billing the landlord, or having the work done by a licensed contractor and deducting the cost from the rent. Generally, after receiving written notice from the tenant, the landlord has 14 days to make repairs.

• Landlords can't add surcharges to utility bills; they may collect only the actual amount of the bill from the tenant.

• Landlords must give two days notice of intention to enter the tenant' unit. However, they can enter immediately in the case of an emergency.

RETIREMENT COMMUNITIES • Dozens of retirement communities are located throughout the Arizona sunbelt, and we discuss them in greater detail in Chapter six. Retirement communities can require that one member of a household (not necessarily the head of household) be a particular age or older. The right to set age limitations is covered by law, spelled out in Arizona Revised Statutes 9-46201 A11.

RV PARKS • Towns and cities with RV parks that cater to long-term winter visitors are listed in Chapter seven. For a list of mobile home parks, send a $5 check to the Arizona Mobile Housing Association, 2540 E. Thomas Rd. Suite I, Phoenix, AZ 85016; phone (602) 955-4440. This doesn't include all of the state's mobile home parks. It lists more than 200 that are members of the association, describing their amenities, location and number of spaces.

SCHOOLS • For information on the state's public schools, contact the Arizona Department of Education, 1535 W. Jefferson St., Phoenix, AZ 85007. The department publishes a directory of all schools in the state, and results of periodic student testing. For details on the state's education system, see Chapter four.

SENIOR COMMUNITIES • See "Retirement communities" above.

SENIOR SERVICES AND HEALTH CARE • See "Senior service agencies" listed in Chapter six.

SMALL BUSINESSES • See Chapter five under "Starting a business."

SMALL CLAIMS • Residents can file for debt-collection for amounts up to $500 in Small Claims Court for a modest fee. Lawyers aren't required or permitted in Small Claims Court unless both sides agree to legal representation. Although a judgment may be granted, courts do not assist in collecting. The ruling only confirms the legitimacy of the debt. Contact the Small Claims Division of local courts for specifics.

SKIING • See "Winter sports" below.

SOCIAL SECURITY OFFICES • For Social Security assistance, call (800) 234-5772. Offices are located in these Arizona communities: 397 Malpais Lane, **Flagstaff**, AZ 86001; 5955 W. Myrtle Ave., **Glendale**, AZ 85301; 1050 Main St., Mesa, AZ 85201; 1150 E. Washington Street, **Phoenix**, AZ 85034; 3738 N. 16th St., Suite D, **Phoenix**, AZ

85016; 11000 N. Scottsdale Rd., **Scottsdale,** AZ 85254; 4601 E. Broadway, **Tucson,** AZ 85711; and 2716 S. Sixth Ave., **Tucson,** AZ 85713.

SPEED LIMITS ● See "Things automotive" above.

TELEPHONE SERVICE ● Area codes are (602) for the greater Phoenix-Valley of the Sun area and (520) for the rest of the state. Most of Arizona is served by USWEST communications. To order phone directories, call (800) 422-8793.

TIME ZONES ● All of Arizona is in the Mountain time zone and it doesn't go on Daylight Saving Time in the summer. Why? Because those desert summer evenings are already long enough, thank you. The Navajo Reservation, however, does observe Daylight Saving Time.

TRADE ORGANIZATIONS ● See Chapter five.

VETERANS' ASSISTANCE ● The Veterans Administration regional center is at 3225 N. Central Ave., Phoenix, AZ 85012; (602) 263-5411. Arizona has three veterans' hospitals: at Seventh Street and Indian School Road in Phoenix, 3601 S. Sixth Street in Tucson and on Highway 89 North in Prescott. Call (800) 352-0451 for details on the hospitals and other VA assistance.

VOTING ● Arizona makes it easy to vote. You can register at any city clerk or county recorder's office, department of elections office, driver's license examining station, justice of the peace, political party headquarters or with any deputy registrar. The state embraces all federal voting requirements: You must be an 18-year-old American citizen who hasn't been convicted of treason or other felony, and you must be sane and not under mental guardianship. The state residency requirement is 50 days. (Also see "Political parties" above.)

Absentee ballots are available to anyone who lives more than 15 miles from the polls, or will be absent from their precinct on election day, or is 65 or older, or has a vision or physical defect.

WAGES ● See Chapter five for details on wage ranges for various occupations.

WEATHER ● Arizona's legendary sunshine is perhaps the single most important factor in the state's growth. For weather reports, tune 162.4 or 162.55 on the VHF band, or phone (602) 957-8700. (Also see "Weather or not" in Chapter one.)

WILLS AND THE RIGHT TO DIE ● If you're 18 or older, you can make out a will, which must be witnessed by two parties who aren't beneficiaries of the will. However, if it's hand-written, witnesses aren't required. Out-of-state wills are recognized, although you should check with an attorney to confirm that provisions of your will conform to Arizona law, bearing in mind factors such as the $600,000 inheritance tax exemption. Property should be placed in joint tenancy, so the surviving partner inherits it.

Arizona is a "right to die" state, which means that you can establish a living will that sets forth procedures for dealing with a terminal illness. Based on a 1987 court ruling, patients can refuse treatment if they are terminally ill. If patients are medically or mentally unable to make that decision and no living will has been made, courts can appoint a guardian to act on their behalf.

WINTER SPORTS • Arizona offers these downhill ski areas: **Arizona Snowbowl** above Flagstaff, (800) 842-7293 or (520) 779-1951; **Mount Lemmon Ski Valley** above Tucson, (520) 576-1321; **Sunrise Ski Area**, an Apache-owned year-around resort on the White Mountain reservation, (800) 55-HOTEL or (520) 735-7676; and the small **Williams Ski Area** above Williams, (520) 635-9330.

Groomed cross-country trails are available at the **Flagstaff Nordic Center**, (520) 774-6216; **Mormon Lake Ski Center** near Flagstaff, (520) 354-2240; **Montezuma Nordic Ski Center,** also near Flagstaff, (520) 354-2221; and the **Williams Ski Area,** (520) 635-9330.

Chapter four

SCHOOL DAYS
ARIZONA'S EDUCATION PICTURE

If you're moving a family to Arizona, you'll be concerned about the quality of education in your future hometown. You'll be pleased to know that—overall—Arizona rates at or above the national average in most student test scores. It ranks among the highest states in the nation in per capita student expenditures, and the student-teacher ratio is 18.4 per classroom, also higher than the national average.

The state requires that all elementary and high school students be tested annually for their scholastic proficiency in reading, language and math. Elementary students take the Iowa Test of Basic Skills, while high school kids take either the Stanford Achievement Test (freshmen) or Stanford Test of Academic Skills (sophomores through seniors).

In the most recent tests administered, nearly all school districts in the state scored higher than the national norm. Statewide, most grades (one through 12) scored higher than the U.S. average in language skills. Most intermediate and high school grades also topped national scores in reading, while grades one through five scored slightly below. In math, most Arizona students scored at or near the national average. Significantly, reading, language and math test scores for virtually all grades have shown improvement in recent years.

To encourage continued student proficiency, outstanding elementary and secondary schools are honored in an annual School Recognition Program. The program is sponsored by the Arizona Educational Foundation and Department of Education. For more information on public schools and specific school districts, contact the **Arizona Department of Education** at (602) 542-3652. To learn more about higher education, contact the **Arizona Commission for Post-Secondary Education** at (602) 229-2590.

School attendance

Arizona's school attendance laws are pretty much the same as in other states. Parents or guardians of any child between eight and 16 must ensure that the kid attends classes. Youngsters can leave school before age 16 only if they have finished the tenth grade or are employed in a vocational or work training program.

The following immunization shots are required for school-age children: measles, mumps, rubella, diphtheria, tetanus and polio. Proof of immunization must be provided by parents or guardians within 15 days after a child starts classes.

Private schooling

For a list of accredited private schools, contact the **Arizona Private School Association**, 420 W. Roosevelt St., Phoenix, AZ 85003; (602) 265-8974.

Children can be taught at home if someone in the household has passed the Arizona Teacher Proficiency Examination within six months of the beginning of instruction. The child still must take state-required achievement tests. For specifics on home teaching, contact the Teacher Testing Unit, Arizona Department of Education, 1535 W. Jefferson St., Phoenix, AZ 85007.

Some of the top public schools

Generally speaking, schools in the Phoenix and Tucson suburbs are among the state's leaders, based on results of annual student achievement tests. As a rule, suburban kids outscored their city center and rural peers. According to recent test results, these were among Arizona's top-rated public schools. (This is not a precise analysis, but a general comparison of scores. And of course, testing result often change from year to year, so this is only a rough guide.)

Elementary (grades one through eight)

Cochise County

St. David Unified District—St. David School.

Coconino County

Flagstaff Unified District—Knoles Elementary School.

Maricopa County (Phoenix area)

Mesa Unified District—Alma School, Field School, Franklin School, Washington School, MacArthur School, Jordan School, Sirrine School, Ishikawa School, Kino Junior High, Poston Junior High, Rhodes Junior High, Taylor Junior High and Hendrix Junior High.

Peoria Unified District—Oakwood School, Kachina School, Heritage School, Pioneer School, Desert Palms School, Sahuaro School, Skyview Elementary School and Desert Valley School.

Scottsdale Unified District—Cochise School, Kiva School, Hopi School, Cherokee School, Anasazi School, Laguna School, Sequoya School, Zuni School, Mohave Middle School, Ingleside Middle School and Cocopah Middle School.

Paradise Valley Unified District—Mercury Mine School, Liberty School, Sandpiper School, Desert Springs School and Desert Shadows Middle School.

Chandler Unified District—Goodman Elementary School.

Washington Elementary District—Lookout Mountain School, Richard E. Miller School and Desert Foothills Middle School.

Alhambra Elementary District—Alhambra Traditional School.

Pima County (Tucson area)

Tucson Unified District—Fruchthendler School, Whitmore School, Gale School, Lineweaver School and Wrightstown School.

Tanque Verde Unified District—Tanque Verde School.

Catalina Foothills Unified District—Sunrise Drive School, Manzanita School, Canyon View School and Orange Grove Junior High.

Sonoita Elementary District—Elgin Elementary School.

Secondary schools (grades nine through 12)
Coconino County
Flagstaff Unified District—Coconino High School.
Maricopa County
Mesa Unified District—Mountain View High School and Dobson High School.

Scottsdale Unified District—Arcadia High School, Saguaro High School and Chaparral High School.

Tempe Union High School District—Corona del Sol High School and Evening High School.
Pima County
Tucson Unified District—University High School and Sabino High School.

COLLEGES AND UNIVERSITIES

Arizona boasts some of America's leading institutes of higher education. They include the three-campus University of Arizona and a campus of America's only aeronautical university.

Since joining the Pacific Ten several years ago, Tucson's University of Arizona and Arizona State University in Tempe have earned national attention for their athletic teams, particularly in football and basketball. For instance, UA won the national collegiate basketball title in 1997. But such achievements are mostly for fun and television coverage. More importantly, they rank scholastically among America's leading state universities, and the Northern Arizona campus at Flagstaff is regarded as one of the country's finer small universities.

The state also supports a network of 19 community colleges. These two-year schools provide broad-based science and liberal arts courses for high school graduates who've not yet decided on a major, or who need to tidy up their grades for four-year school admission. Equally important, they are "terminal education facilities," providing vocational studies and career-change training to prepare students for the job market.

In the listings that follow, tuition, fees and room and board figures are per school year, unless indicated otherwise. These are for general guidance only and are subject to change—invariably upward.

The state universities

University of Arizona • *Tucson, AZ 85721; (520) 621-3237.* ◻ Arizona's oldest university, founded in 1885, it offers a broad base of undergraduate and graduate programs. Its colleges include agriculture, architecture, arts and science, business and public administration, education, engineering and mines, law, medicine, nursing and pharmacy. Special programs include anthropology, astronomy, classical archaeology, management information studies and arid land studies. Admission requirement: 3.0 or in the top 25 percent of high school class. Tuition: $1,937 for residents and $7,805 for nonresidents. On-campus housing available, including family units; room and board $4,190. About 33,400 students.

Arizona State University • *Tempe, AZ 85287; (602) 965-9011.* ◻ The state's largest university, ASU offers programs in a variety of fields. It specializes in architecture and environmental design (the campus theater was designed by Frank Lloyd Wright), engineering and applied sciences, accounting, graphic design, journalism and telecommunications, plus fine arts programs such as dance, theater, art and music. Admission requirements: 2.5 for residents and 3.0 for nonresidents. Tuition and fees: $1,590 for residents and $6,996 for nonresidents. On-campus housing available; room and board averages $3,900 per year. About 43,000 students.

Northern Arizona University • *P.O. Box 4084, Flagstaff, AZ 86001; (520) 523-5511.* ◻ Several years ago, NAU was rated by *Money Magazine* as one of the ten top university values in the country, based on its quality of education for a relatively low tuition. Its nine colleges offer programs in arts and sciences, business, education, forestry, health professions, the hospitality industry, engineering, social and behavioral sciences and creative and communications arts. Admission requirement: 3.0 grade point average. Tuition: $1,005 for residents and $3,761 for nonresidents. On-campus housing available; room and board $1,648 per semester. About 13,000 students on the Flagstaff campus; 17,000 statewide.

Other four-year colleges and universities

Arizona College of the Bible • *2045 W. Northern Ave., Phoenix, AZ 85021; (602) 995-2670.* ◻ This small campus offers bachelor of arts degrees in pre-seminary and various Christian studies. Admission requirement: 2.0 grade point average. Tuition: $54746. On-campus housing available; lodging (no meals) $1,600.

DeVry Institute of Technology • *2149 W. Dunlap Ave., Phoenix, AZ 85021; (602) 870-9201.* ◻ This technical school offers courses in electronics engineering technology, electronics technician, computer information systems, business operations and accounting. Admission requirement: high school diploma or GED equivalent. Tuition: $6,580 per academic year for residents and nonresidents. No on-campus housing; about 2,700 students.

Embry Riddle Aeronautical University • *3200 Willow Creek Rd., Prescott, AZ 86301; (520) 708-3728; or contact the Florida campus at Daytona Beach, FL 32114-3900; (800) 222- ERAU.* ◻ America's only university- level aeronautical school, Embry Riddle offers majors in aviation technology, aerospace engineering, aerospace science, aviation administration and related fields. The school has its own fleet of training planes at nearby Ernest A. Love Field and offers training in single and multiple engine craft. Tuition and fees: $9,200 per year. Campus housing available; room and board $4,000 per year. About 1,500 students.

Grand Canyon University • *3300 W. Camelback Rd., Phoenix, AZ 85017; (800) 800-9776 or (602) 249-3300.* ◻ A private Christian liberal arts school, it offers degrees from eight colleges: business, Christian studies, communications and fine arts, continuing studies, education, liberal arts, science and allied health, and nursing. Graduate programs are available in business and education. Tuition and fees: $8,040. On-campus housing available; room and board $3,400. About 2,100 students.

Prescott College • *220 Grove Ave., Prescott, AZ 86301; (520) 778-2090.* ◻ A small liberal arts school, it emphasizes experimental learning programs and field studies. Majors are environmental studies, cultural and religious studies, humanities, human development and adventure education. The school also has undergraduate, masters and teacher certification programs. Admission requirements: individual analysis, essay and review of transcripts. Tuitions range from $6,279 to $10,448, depending on the program. No on-campus housing; 711 students.

Southwestern College • *2625 E. Cactus Rd., Phoenix, AZ 85032; (602) 992-6101.* ◻ A Conservative Baptist school, it focuses on biblical studies, elementary education, pastoral studies, theology and related subjects. Admission requirements: high school diploma or equivalent, plus a written essay. Tuition and fees: $3,720. On-campus housing; room and board about $1,700.

University of Phoenix • *4615 E. Elwood St., Phoenix, AZ 85040; (602) 921-5332.* ☐ This highly regarded proprietary upper level institution offers undergraduate and graduate courses in business administration, management, information systems and nursing. Admission requirements: 2.5 GPA and at least two years of degree-related work experience. Tuition: $6,500 for business courses and $7,050 for nursing. No on-campus housing.

Western International University • *10202 N. 19th Ave., Phoenix, AZ 85021; (602) 943-2311.* ☐ This small school offers graduate and undergraduate business oriented programs to employed professionals who want to further their education. Fields of study include marketing, international business management, accounting, finance and management. Admission requirement: 3.0 for masters programs and 2.75 for bachelor studies. Tuition: $120 per unit for bachelor programs and $145 for masters programs. No on-campus housing; about 1,500 students.

Two-year colleges and technical schools

Arizona's community college program is open to anyone 18 years or older who "demonstrates evidence of potential success" in taking college classes. For some courses of study, there are additional requirements, such as a high school diploma, GED equivalency or college transfer credits. For more information, contact the Arizona Community College Board at 3225 N. Central Ave., Phoenix, AZ 85012; (602) 255-4037.

Arizona Western College • *Yuma, AZ 85364; (520) 726-1050.* ☐ Part of the state community college system, it offers associate of arts degrees in a variety of liberal arts and science subjects, plus vocational and continuing educational programs. Open enrollment. Tuition and fees: $408 for residents and $3,768 for nonresidents. No on- campus housing; 5,200 students.

Central Arizona College • *Coolidge, AZ 85228; (520) 726-4444 or 723-4141.* ☐ A member of the Arizona Community College system, it offers university transfer and associate degree programs in 52 areas of study. Admission requirements: open enrollment except for nursing program, which has prerequisites. Tuition and fees: $658 for 24 credits per year for residents, $4,330 for nonresidents. On-campus housing available; room and board $1,510 per semester. About 14,000 students.

Chaparral College • *4585 E. Speedway, #204, Tucson, AZ 85712; (520) 327-6866.* ☐ This small school offers a four- year course with a bachelor's degree in business administration, two-year courses with associate degrees in accounting, business administration, administrative assistant and legal assistant. Admission requirements: high school graduate or GED equivalency; 2.0 grade average. Fees vary with the programs. No housing on campus; 400 students.

Cochise College • *4190 W. Highway 80, Douglas, AZ 85607; (800) 466-7943 or (520) 364-7943.* ◻ This community college offers AA degrees in a variety of subjects. Specialties include pilot training, aviation maintenance, computer sciences and nursing, plus vocational and continuing education programs. Admission requirement: high school diploma or GED equivalency. Tuition: $26 per semester unit for residents, $158 for out-of-state students. Men's and women's dorms and family apartments available; room and board $1,503 per semester. About 5,000 students.

Eastern Arizona College • *600 Church St., Thatcher, AZ 85552-0769; (520) 428-8233.* ◻ This community college offers AA degrees in several subjects, plus occupational and continuing education programs. Admission requirements: high school graduate or GED equivalency. Tuition: $314 per semester of 12 units or more for residents, $2,718 for nonresidents. On-campus housing: $630 for fall semester and $420 for spring semester, plus $900 to $1,025 for meals. About 2,200 students.

Gateway Community College • *108 N. 40th St., Phoenix, AZ 85034; (602) 392-5000.* ◻ Part of the Maricopa College District, Gateway offers AA degrees in several subjects, plus vocational and continuing education courses. Open admission; requirements for some courses of study. Tuition: $34 per credit unit for Maricopa County residents; higher for out of area and out of state. No on-campus housing; about 6,800 students.

Glendale Community College • *6000 W. Olive Ave., Glendale, AZ 85302; (602) 435-3000.* ◻ This large community college offers the usual variety of lower division academic programs, plus occupational courses in automotive technology, administration of justice, business, emergency medical technology, computer-aided design, semiconductor manufacturing and other fields. It's noted for its high tech programs. Open admission. Tuition: $34 per credit unit for residents and $159 for nonresidents. No on-campus housing; 18,500 students.

ITT Technical Institute • *4837 E. McDowell Rd., Phoenix, AZ 85008; (602) 231-0871. Second campus at 1840 E. Benson Highway, Tucson, AZ 85714; (520) 294-2944.* ◻ This technical school offers one- year courses in computer science, electronics and computer engineering, drafting and computer-aided design. Admission requirements: high school graduate or GED equivalency. Tuition: $11,217 full year for resident or nonresident. No on-campus housing, although roommate assistance is available. About 315 students. Job placement assistance offered during school and after graduation.

Lamson Junior College • *Campuses at 1980 W. Main St., Mesa, AZ 85201; 2701 Bethany Home, Phoenix, AZ 85017; 1548-A W. Montebello, Phoenix, AZ 85015; and 4425 W. Olive, Glendale, AZ 85302.* ◻ This multi-campus junior college offers several lower division academic courses, plus trade and technical programs. Open enrollment, although some courses require a high school diploma or equivalent.

Tuition varies, about $15.50 per semester unit for Maricopa County residents, higher for out of area and out of state students.

Mesa Community College • *1833 W. Southern Ave., Mesa, AZ 85202; (602) 461-7000.* ❑ It offers a variety of lower division programs, plus trade and technical courses; it's the primary transfer institution for Arizona State University. Open enrollment. Tuition: $34 per semester credit unit for Maricopa County residents and $159 per semester credit unit for out of county and out of state residents. No on-campus housing, although the Office of Student Activities provides a free housing directory and roommate service.

Mohave Community College • *Kingman, AZ 86401; (520) 757-4331.* ❑ Mohave offers two-year degrees and certificates in a variety of programs as well as personal interest courses. The college serves residents of Mohave County with campuses in Kingman, Bullhead City and Lake Havasu City, plus the North Mohave Center in Colorado City. All four are linked via a microwave system that enables teaching of classes simultaneously. Call the Kingman campus for details on admission and tuition. About 10,000 students on the four campuses.

Navajo Community College • *Tsaile, AZ 86556; (520) 724-6600.* ❑ This is a federally supported college on the Navajo Reservation, offering a variety of lower division liberal arts programs, including Native American studies. Admission requirements: high school diploma or equivalent. Tuition and fees: $620 per semester. On-campus housing; room and board $2,940. About 1,800 students; 96 percent are Native American.

Northland Pioneer College • *Admission information: (520) 524-6111.* ❑ This community college serves about 9,000 students throughout Navajo and Apache counties, with campuses in Winslow, Holbrook, Snowflake/Taylor and Show Low. Satellite centers are in Keams Canyon, Kayenta, Heber/Overgaard, Whiteriver, St. Johns and Springerville/Eagar. Associate degrees are offered in nearly 50 different areas, ranging from computer and industrial technology to turf grass management, building trades, photography, fire science, law enforcement and medical technician. NPC's Cultural Anthropology program takes advantage of nearby ancient Native American sites for field studies. Tuition: Northland has the lowest in the state—$22 per credit hour for general education transfer courses, continuing education and vocational training. Residence halls are located on the Painted Desert campus in Holbrook.

Phoenix College • *1202 W. Thomas Rd., Phoenix, AZ 85013; (602) 264-2492.* ❑ A campus of the Maricopa Community College system, it offers a variety of lower division academic courses, plus trade, technical and continuing education programs. Open admission. Tuition and fees: $24 per semester unit for residents, $118 for out of county and $149 for out of state residents. No on-campus housing. About 12,000 students.

Pima Community College • *4905 E. Broadway Blvd., Tucson, AZ 85709; (520) 748-4571.* ◻ One of Arizona's largest community colleges, Pima offers certificates and two-year degrees in 63 program areas, including academic studies transferable to universities, trade, technical, continuing education and corporate and community education. Specialties include aviation technology, dental lab and assistant programs, landscaping, legal assistant, nursing, radiological and emergency medical technology, and respiratory care. Pima has the only EPA-approved environmental training center in the southwest. Open admission. Tuition $377 ($31 per credit hour) for residents and $1,975 for nonresidents. No on-campus housing. About 53,000 credit and non- credit students.

Rio Salado Community College • *640 N. First Ave., Phoenix, AZ 85003; (602) 223-4000.* ◻ Part of the Maricopa Community College district, it offers assorted lower division programs, continuing education and technical courses. Open admission. Tuition: $24 per credit unit for county residents and $126 for out of county and out of state students. About 14,000 students.

Scottsdale Community College • *900 E. Chaparral Rd., Scottsdale, AZ 85256; (520) 423-6000.* ◻ Part of the Maricopa Community College District, it offers a variety of liberal arts, technical and continuing education programs. Open admission; tuition and fees: $34 per credit unit for county residents, $159 for out of state students. No on-campus housing; 10,050 students.

South Mountain Community College • *7050 S. 24th St., Phoenix, AZ 85040; (602) 243-8000.* ◻ A Mariposa Community College District school, it offers AA programs in business administration, commerce, management and computer information systems. Open admission. Tuition and fees: $656 for county residents, $3,472 for other Arizona residents and $4,432 for out of state. No on-campus housing; about 3,000 students.

Yavapai College • *1100 E. Sheldon St., Prescott, AZ 86301; (520) 445-7300.* ◻ This small community college offers several science and liberal arts programs, with transfers targeted to the three Arizona state universities. It's noted for its national championship soccer team. Tuition: $333 for 12 credit hours for residents, $2,500 for out of state. On-campus housing and meals; $1,620. About 6,000 students. Second campus in Clarksdale and extension programs throughout Yavapai County.

Chapter five

THE JOB-SEEKERS
ARIZONA'S EMPLOYMENT BASE

Arizona's economy is booming as it rushes toward the millennium, after recovering from a recession in the late Eighties and early Nineties. Between 1985 and 1995, the statewide unemployment rate dropped from 7.3 percent to 5.1 percent.

However, this current growth surge doesn't necessarily mean that good jobs are easy to find. Landing that good paying position still requires a lot of effort. Many professional and semi-skilled positions were in over-supply during the recession, although the job situation is improving rapidly as the economy picks up steam. This is particularly true in the high-tech sector, which accounts for more than half of all manufacturing jobs.

Wages in general are lower in Arizona than the national average, although that gap is closing rapidly. Per capita income went up 55.4 percent from 1985 to 1995.

Arizona's job growth chugged along at two percent a year toward the end of the Eighties, then it passed three percent and continued to gain into the Nineties. In Phoenix, Arizona's economic bellwether, job growth is out-gaining population and this is expected to continue into the next century. This guesstimate comes from Arizona State University's highly regarded Center for Business Research. Particularly significant is the fact that the state's per capita income rose from $12,901 to $20,044 between 1985 and 1995. Total personal income more than doubled during that period.

Tourism and other service industries lead the Arizona job market, employing half a million people and accounting for more than one of every four paychecks. The retail trade follows, comprising a fifth of the employment force. Manufacturing accounts for only 11 percent of Arizona's jobs, although most are generated by highly desirable smokeless industries. The state continues to be successful in attracting high tech plants, which provide more than half of the manufacturing payroll. That number is expected to increase into the next century.

The highest paying blue collar job? It's mining, paying more than $850 a week. However, it's the smallest segment of the state's industry, employing less than one percent of the work force. This, despite the fact that Arizona produces 60 percent of the nation's copper.

Twin plant manufacturing

One curious aspect of the Arizona job market is the so-called "twin plant" or "offshore" manufacturing program. Working in concert with the Mexican government, several American firms have set up manufacturing plants near the Arizona-Mexico border to draw from Mexico's cheap labor pool. Often, plants are located on both sides of the border; thus, the twin plant reference.

This helps American manufacturers compete with cheap overseas labor and it boosts Mexico's economy. However, it offers little for Arizona-bound job hunters, other than a few management positions. Among twin-plant communities are San Luis below Yuma, Naco south of Bisbee, the twin cities of Nogales south of Tucson and Douglas-Agua Prieta in southeastern Arizona.

Offshore manufacturing obviously has a major impact on the south side of the border. Agua Prieta's population leaped from 18,000 to more than 70,000 in ten years. Another example: With more than 100,000 residents, Nogales, Mexico, is nearly ten times as large as Arizona's Nogales. Those twin cities' twin plants employ 24,000 workers. Nearly 50,000 Mexican nationals cross the border each day to work and shop. Because of low wages and intense competition from hardworking Mexicans, we don't recommend job hunting along the border.

Right to work

Arizona is a "right to work" state, which means that mandatory union membership is prohibited. Thus, there are no closed shops. Right to work laws create mixed blessings: They tend to attract business but they suppress wages in fields that are generally unionized elsewhere. Predictably, union membership in Arizona is rather low—seven percent of the work force, compared with a national rate of 17 percent.

Employee rights

On the other side of the coin, Arizona is pro-labor when it comes to employee rights. If you switch jobs, the law requires that you receive copies of all communication between your present and prospective employer.

Blacklisting to prevent someone from getting a job is forbidden. Employers can exchange only specific information on job performance, qualifications, past experience, education and training.

WHERE THE JOBS ARE

Direct contact is the best way to get work, and we discuss it toward the end of this chapter, under "Finding that job." Employment agencies, and trade and professional organizations are useful tools as well.

A good starting point is the Arizona Job Service, which has offices throughout the state. Like other employment offices, they offer lists of local job openings, and they provide counseling to job-seekers. You'll find a complete list of Job Service offices later in this chapter.

The Arizona Department of Economic Security has a variety of publications to aid your job search, including the *Occupational Employment Forecasts, Finding a Job in the Want Ads, Helpful Hits for Job Seekers, Finding Government Jobs* and current employment profiles for each county. Particularly useful is the monthly *Labor Market Information Newsletter*, with statistics and up-to-date articles concerning the job market. For a list of the department's publications, contact the **Arizona Department of Economic Security**, Occupational Employment Statistics, Dept. 733A, P.O. Box 6123, Phoenix, AZ 85005; (602) 542-3871.

When we last checked, the statewide unemployment rate was a modest 5.1 percent, although these conditions change constantly. The two most populous counties had the lowest rates: Mariposa (Phoenix) and Pima (Tucson), both with 4.7 percent. Also low were Yavapai (Prescott), 5.4 percent; and Coconino (Flagstaff-Sedona) with 7.1 percent.

Highest unemployment rates were in Santa Cruz County (south central, including Nogales), 13.1 percent; and Yuma (southwest corner), 24.2 percent.

An excellent job-finding source is the Yellow Pages of the local phone directory, since it lists businesses and firms by type. USWest provides phone service for all Arizona communities except for a few hamlets, and you can order local directories by calling (800) 422-8793.

Phoenix obviously is the core of Arizona's employment market. The Valley of the Sun provides homes and jobs for more than half the state's population. Several major corporations are based here, including Greyhound, America West Airlines, Ramada Inns, U-Haul and Circle K Corporation. If you're seeking a large and diversified employment base, the Valley of the Sun is your best bet.

Phoenix

A useful job source for greater Phoenix is *The Book of Lists*, published annually by the *The Business Journal*. Although it doesn't provide specific job listings, it publishes names, phone numbers and addresses of the area's largest firms. Listings include the type of work they do, what products they create and names of company principals. Other useful lists in the book include leading radio and TV stations, scheduled airline service, car rental agencies, hotels and resorts, colleges and even women-owned firms. For a copy, send a check for $28 plus $3 shipping to: **The Business Journal**, 2910 N. Central, Phoenix, AZ 85012; for information, call (602) 230-8400.

For more information on the Valley of the Sun employment situation, try these contacts:

City of Phoenix, Public Information Office, 251 W. Washington St., Phoenix, AZ 85003; (602) 262-7176.

Phoenix Economic Growth Group, 400 N. Fifth St., Room 1625, Phoenix, AZ 85004; (520) FOR-PHNX or (602) 253-9747.

Greater Phoenix Economic Council, Two N. Central, Suite 210, Phoenix, AZ 85004; (602) 256-7700.

Community and Economic Development Office, City of Phoenix, 200 W. Washington St., 20th Floor, Phoenix, AZ 85003-1161; (602) 262-5040.

Phoenix Chamber of Commerce, 201 N. Central, Suite 2700, Phoenix, AZ 85073; (602) 495-2183.

Tucson

Arizona's number two city, Tucson obviously offers its second largest job market. Major employers include the University of Arizona, Davis-Monthan Air Force Base, Hughes Aircraft and National Semiconductor.

To learn more about the city's economic and employment situation, contact:

Tucson Metropolitan Chamber of Commerce, P.O. Box 991 (465 W. St. Mary's Rd.), Tucson, AZ 85702; (520) 792-2250.

Greater Tucson Economic Council, 33 Stone, Suite 800, Tucson, AZ 85701; (520) 622-6413.

City of Tucson, 255 W. Alameda, Tucson, AZ 85726; (520) 791-4204.

Other job markets

Job availability diminishes as you travel farther from these two metropolitan areas. However, some smaller communities still offer fairly good prospects—particularly in tourism and the service sector. If you want to avoid urban congestion, you might try some of the fast growing towns on the edge of the Valley of the Sun. What follows is a list of communities that offer average to better-than-average employment possibilities. You'll find more detail on these communities in Part Two.

Avondale ● This is the largest of several small communities on the western rim of the Valley of the Sun, with about 24,000 residents. It occupies an area originally settled by the Goodyear Tire and Rubber

Company in 1916. With major developments at nearby Phoenix-Goodyear Airport and firms such as Rubbermaid and McKesson in the area, it offers rather good prospects. For information: Tri City West Chamber of Commerce, 501 W. Van Buren, Suite K, Avondale, AZ 85223, (602) 932-2260; and Avondale Industrial Development Authority, City of Avondale, 525 N. Central, Avondale, AZ 85323, (602) 932-2400.

Buckeye • A small town of 5,000, Buckeye is 30 miles west of Phoenix. The growing community is actively promoting light industry and there are several large manufacturing plants, plus new growth at nearby Phoenix-Goodyear Airport. Its labor force jumped about 40 percent in the past ten years. For information: Buckeye Valley Chamber of Commerce, P.O. Box 717, Buckeye, AZ 85326, (602) 386-2727; Town of Buckeye, P.O. Box 175, Buckeye, AZ 85326, (602) 256-2488; and Western Gateway Team, 800 S. Litchfield Rd., Goodyear, AZ 85338, (602) 932-9138.

Bullhead City • Primarily a Snowbird community, Bullhead City sits across the Colorado River from Laughlin, Nevada, a fast-growing gaming center whose casinos employ more than 10,000 people. And that's where most of the jobs are. Bullhead is a rather unlovely town, strung along the banks of the river, but it is growing, with a population topping 27,000. For information: Bullhead Area Chamber of Commerce, 1251 Highway 95, Bullhead City, AZ 86430, (520) 754-4121; and Bullhead City Economic Development Authority, P.O. Box 21179, Bullhead City, AZ 86439; (520) 763-9400.

Casa Grande • Midway between Tucson and Phoenix, this small city is actively seeking light industry, and it has seen a 20 percent gain in its labor force since 1980. Its population is up nearly 30 percent in the last decade, topping 20,000. For information: City of Casa Grande, P.O. Box 15011 (300 E. Fourth St.), Casa Grande, AZ 85230, (520) 421-8600; and Greater Casa Grande Valley Economic Development Foundation, 201 E. Third St., Casa Grande, AZ 85222, (520) 836-6868.

Chandler • A growing city southeast of Phoenix, with a population approaching 130,000, Chandler offers a broad-based job market. Space age firms such as Intel Corporation, Microchip Technology and Space Data Corporation offer potential high tech jobs. Manufacturing accounts for one out of four jobs—one of the highest rates in the state. For information: Chandler Chamber of Commerce, 218 N. Arizona Ave., Chandler, AZ 85224, (602) 963-4571; and City of Chandler, Department of Development & Community Services, 125 E. Commonwealth St., Chandler, AZ 85225, (602) 786-2734.

Flagstaff • One of our favorite Arizona cities, this is a vibrant, growing community 70 miles south of the Grand Canyon and rimmed by ponderosa forests. It has experienced good job growth in recent years. Tourism, science, high tech manufacturing and education are leading industries in this town of 53,000. For information: Flagstaff Chamber of Commerce, 101 W. Route 66, Flagstaff, AZ 86004, (520) 774-9541 or (800) 842-7293 and (800) 217-2367; and Greater Flagstaff Economic Council, 1300 S. Milton Rd., S-125, Flagstaff, AZ 86001-6354; (520) 779-7658.

Gilbert • Half an hour southeast of Phoenix, this bedroom community has doubled its population every five years since 1980, and it's still growing and soon will top 70,000. Most jobs are in manufacturing and a rapidly expanding retail base. It also has one of Arizona's lowest unemployment rates. For information: Gilbert Chamber of Commerce, P.O. Box 527 (202 N. Gilbert St.), Gilbert, AZ 85234, (602) 892-0056; and Economic Development Department, Town of Gilbert, 1025 S. Gilbert Rd., Gilbert, AZ 85234, (602) 545-6865.

Glendale • Northeast of Phoenix, Glendale is another fast growing city, with a population approaching 180,000. It offers job opportunities in aerospace, communications, precision metal work, chemicals, electronics and warehousing. Nearby Luke Air Force Base offers potential civil service jobs. For information: Glendale Chamber of Commerce, P.O. Box 249 (7105 N. 59th Ave.), Glendale, AZ 85311, (800) ID-SUNNY or (602) 280-1321; and City of Glendale, 5850 W. Glendale Ave., Glendale, AZ 85301, (602) 930-2800.

Goodyear • Half an hour west of Phoenix, this small community of about 10,000 has diversified from its role as a company town for the Goodyear aircraft facility. It has lured firms such as McKesson, Rubbermaid and the huge new Lockheed Martin complex at Phoenix-Goodyear Airport. Its population has nearly doubled in the past decade, with job availability increasing by more than 40 percent. For more information: City of Goodyear, 119 N. Litchfield Rd., Goodyear, AZ 85338, (800) 872-1749 or (602) 932-3910; and Tri City West Chamber of Commerce, 501 W. Van Buren, Suite K, Avondale, AZ 85223; (602) 932-2260.

Kingman • It's a smaller version of Flagstaff, although in a lower desert altitude, with a population of 34,000. Its labor force has almost doubled in the past ten years. "Kingman has been very successful in job creation in manufacturing and distribution businesses, because of its key location (on I-80 near the California border) and its transportation infrastructure," according to a spokesman. For information: Economic & Tourism Development Commission, City of Kingman, 310 N. Fourth St., Kingman, AZ 86402; (520) 753-8130.

Litchfield Park • With a population of about 3,700, this is a planned community 16 miles west of Phoenix. Like neighboring Goodyear, it offers a growing base of light manufacturing and service jobs, with an employment increase of nearly 45 percent in the past ten years. For information: City of Litchfield Park, 214 W. Wigwam Blvd., Litchfield Park, AZ 85340, (602) 935-5033; Tri City West Chamber of

Commerce, 501 W. Van Buren, Suite K, Avondale, AZ 85223, (602) 932-2260; and Western Gateway Team, 800 S. Litchfield Rd., Goodyear, AZ 85338; (602) 932-9138.

Mesa • East of Tempe and Phoenix, Mesa is a thriving community with a low unemployment rate and a broad economic base. It's Arizona's third largest city, with a population nearing 330,000. Among major employers are McDonnell Douglas Helicopters, Rosarita Foods, General Motors Desert Proving Grounds, TRW and Motorola. For information: Mesa Chamber of Commerce, P.O. Box 5820 (120 N. Center St.), Mesa, AZ 85211-5820, (602) 969-1307; and Planning Department, City of Mesa, 55 N. Center St., Mesa, AZ 85201, (602) 644-2185.

Peoria • Just north of Glendale, Peoria is another growing Phoenix suburb. With a population topping 70,000, it offers employment potential in light manufacturing, the services industry and retailing. Nearly one job in four is in manufacturing. Also, one can commute to civil service work at Luke Air Force Base. For information: Peoria Chamber of Commerce, P.O. Box 70 (8355 Peoria Ave.), Peoria, AZ 85380, (602) 979-3601; City of Peoria, 8401 W. Monroe St., Peoria, AZ 85345, (602) 412-7300; and Peoria Economic Development Corporation, 10601 N. 83rd Dr., Peoria, AZ 85435, (602) 486-2011.

Prescott • Handsomely situated in the pines of central Arizona, Prescott offers a mix of history (as the first territorial capital), culture and steady economic growth. The job base in this attractive town of 31,000 has increased more than 35 percent in the past ten years. Its economic mix includes mining, ranching, light manufacturing and education—with two small colleges and an aeronautical university. For information: Prescott Chamber of Commerce, P.O. Box 1147 (117 W. Goodwin St.), Prescott, AZ 86302, (520) 445-2000; and City of Prescott, P.O. Box 2059 (201 S. Cortez St.) Prescott, AZ 86302, (520) 445-3500.

Sierra Vista • This is an Arizona surprise—a significant population center in the otherwise sparsely populated southeast. Located southeast of Tucson, with a population of about 38,000, it offers a mild climate and a relatively large employment base. Nearby Fort Huachuca Army base has nearly 12,000 military and civilian personnel. Sierra Vista itself is working to attract more light industry. It offers the best job potential in southeastern Arizona, although it isn't as strong as the Phoenix, Tucson or Flagstaff areas. The work force has increased 25 percent in the past ten years. For information: Sierra Vista Chamber of Commerce, 21 E. Wilcox Dr., Sierra Vista, AZ 85635, (800) 288-3861; or (520) 458-6940; Sierra Vista Economic Development Foundation, P.O. Box 2380, Sierra Vista, AZ 85636, (520) 458-6948; and City of Sierra Vista, 2400 E. Tacoma St., Sierra Vista, AZ 85635, (520) 458-3315.

Tempe ● With a people count of 156,000, Tempe is home to Arizona State University, the largest school in the state and one of the town's largest employers. Manufacturing provides about one in five Tempe jobs, with 200 companies producing electronics, clothing, processed foods, prefabricated housing and machine products. Tempe is considered the high tech capitol of Arizona, with 20 percent of the state's companies located within its borders. For information: Tempe Chamber of Commerce, P.O. Box 28500 (909 E. Apache Blvd.), Tempe, AZ 85285, (602) 967-7891; and City of Tempe, 31 E. Fifth St., Tempe, AZ 85281, (602) 967-2001.

WHAT THE JOBS ARE

Arizona's five leading job-producers are the services sector, with 28 percent of the total work force; retail trades, 19.42 percent; government, 16.39 percent; manufacturing (mostly high tech), 10.69 percent; and construction 6.63 percent.

At mid-decade, the total civilian labor force was 2,107,000, up from 1,469,600 in 1985, a gain of 43 percent. Perhaps the most remarkable measure of the state's economic gain in the past ten years was total per capita income, which more than *doubled* from $40.8 billion to $84.8 billion. Personal income made significant gains, as well— up 55.4 percent from $12,901 to $20,044 per capita.

Although the employment numbers look good, it's best to come to Arizona with a skill. Other than mining, there is very little heavy industry, so most of the unskilled jobs are in the service sector and agriculture. Mexican "guest workers" and resident Mexican nationals take most of the farm labor jobs.

The tourist industry absorbs a lot of folks—desk clerks, maids, culinary workers, waiters, tour guides and such. As in the rest of the world, most of these jobs pay little more than minimum wage. And much of this work is seasonal.

THE EMPLOYMENT BASE

	Total employed	Percent
Agriculture	41,280	2.29
Manufacturing	193,071	10.69
Mining	12,500	0.69
Construction	119,821	6.63
Transportation, utilities and communication	85,495	4.73
Wholesale trades	93,793	5.19
Retail trades	350,681	19.42
Finance, insurance and real estate	107,972	5.98
Services	504,870	27.95
Government	296,041	16.39
Non-classifiable	534	0.03

THE 100 MOST-NEEDED JOB SKILLS

According to the Arizona Department of Economic Security, about a hundred different job skills will in most demand in future years. All are expected to increase by more than 20 percent during the next decade. Most of these are in the professional, skilled and semi-skilled occupations.

Jobs with a projected growth rate of 24 percent or more

Artists and related workers
Dentists
Drywall installers
Employment interviewers
Flight attendants
Glaziers
Guards and watchmen
Interviewing clerks
Lathers
Lithographic press setters
Managers
Medical secretaries, techs
Nurses aids and orderlies
Pest controllers
Photo machine operators
Plasterers, stucco masons
Plumbers, pipefitter helpers
Printing press operators
Physical therapists
Respiratory therapists
Retail and counter clerks
Roofers
Transportation agents

Those with increases ranging from 21 to 23 percent

Architects
Assemblers (precision & general)
Bartenders
Bill and account collectors
Brick & stonemason helpers
Bricklayers and masons
Bus drivers
Chemical technicians
Detectives and investigators
Dispatchers (police and fire)
Electrical mechanical workers
Electricians
Electromechanical assemblers
Engineers
Food service, lodging managers
Food and beverage workers
Hairdressers and hair stylists
HVAC installers
Helpers (construction trades)
Home health aides
Hostesses, restaurants & lounges
Housekeepers
Insulation workers
Interior designers
Laundry machine operators
Legal secretaries
Phone solicitors
Mail machine operators
Manicurists
Medical assistants
Health service managers
Nurses
Office machine operators
Opticians
Painters and paperhangers
Paralegal personnel
Pharmacists, pharmacy techs
Photographers
Physical therapy assistants
Physicians and surgeons
Pilots and flight engineers
Plumbers and pipefitters
Property estate managers
Radiological technicians
Receptionists, infor clerks
Reporters, correspondents
Restaurant cooks
Sales agents and reps

Service supervisors
Sheet metal installers
Social workers
Statistical clerks
Street vendors
Structural metal workers
Switchboard operators
Tax preparers

Taxi drivers and chauffeurs
Technical writers
Travel agents
Typesetting and composing
machine operators
Waiters and waitresses
Word processing typists
Writers and editors

A useful book called *The Phoenix Job Bank* describes the employment situation and salary ranges for dozens of occupations in Arizona. It lists major employers in Phoenix and Tucson, and tells readers which job skills are in most demand. The book can be ordered through most book stores, or contact **Bob Adams, Inc.**, 260 Center St., Holbrook, MA 02343; (800) USA-JOBS or (617) 767-8100. The price is $16.95, plus $4.50 shipping.

White collar jobs

According to a recent edition of the *Phoenix Job Bank*, white collar jobs are expected to outpace overall job growth in Arizona in future years. Among the white collar jobs showing rapid growth are (some of these are duplicated in the list above):

Accountants and auditors
Advertising personnel
Architects
Attorneys
Bank officers and managers
Dietitians and nutritionists
Economists
Engineers
Financial analysts
Hotel managers and assistants
Industrial designers
Insurance actuaries

Insurance agents and
claims adjusters
Managers of retail stores
and factories
News reporters, editors
Physicists
Public relations personnel
Statisticians
Systems analysts
Teachers
Underwriters and other
insurance personnel

The wage picture

The average weekly wage in Arizona, while not as high as some urban areas of America, is higher than the national average. Predictably, agriculture is the lowest, at $277.15 a week. Average wages in mid-decade, according to the Arizona Department of Economic Security, were:

Agriculture—$277.15
Construction—$500.62
Finance, insurance—$610.23
Government—$515.15
Manufacturing—$686.62
Mining—$852.85

Retail trades—$292
Services (including
tourism—450.54
Transport, communications
and utilities—$627
Wholesale trade—$622.23

Starting a business

Perhaps you're interested in creating jobs instead of getting one. With its pro-growth attitude, Arizona is very supportive of people and corporations wanting to go into business. Its corporate tax is relatively low—nine percent.

If you want to set up shop, begin by sending for the *Guide to Establishing a Business in Arizona*. It's available from the **Arizona Department of Commerce,** 3800 N. Central Ave., Suite 1400, Phoenix, AZ 85017; (602) 280-1321. The same department offers *Arizona Industrial Profiles*, which are comprehensive studies of various communities interested in attracting new businesses. It also has demographic profiles for 141 Arizona communities, available as a complete set for $15, or $18 with a binder.

For information on business licenses and taxes, contact the **Arizona Department of Revenue,** 1600 W. Monroe St., Phoenix, AZ 85007; (602) 255-3381.

If you want to incorporate, contact the office of the **Secretary of State,** 1700 W. Washington St., Phoenix, AZ 85007; (602) 255-4285. For specific requirements on incorporation, check with the **Arizona Corporation Commission,** which has two offices: 1200 W. Washington St., Suite 102, Phoenix, AZ 85007, (602) 542-3135; and 402 W. Congress St., Tucson, AZ 85701; (520) 628-5284.

A particularly useful organization for new businesses is the **Arizona Small Business Association,** 301 W. Osborn Rd., Room 104, Phoenix, AZ 85013; (602) 265-4563 or 248-8856. It's a nonprofit group set up to assist small business owners. Among its services are legislative representation, group medical and dental plans, a credit union and a group legal and accounting referral plan.

Types of businesses

What business to open? Restaurants are the most common new businesses in the state, although they also have the highest failure rate. In a growing state, there's obviously room for new construction and contracting firms, housing developers, mortgage companies and real estate firms. Surveys show that these are among the businesses most in demand:

Accounting firms	Insurance agencies
Attorneys	Investment firms
Auto dealers (new and used)	Laundries and dry cleaners
Beauty parlors	Management consulting firms
Clothing stores	Mortgage companies
Computer stores	Physicians
Furniture stores	Printers and copy shops
General contractors	Real estate companies
Housing developers	Travel agencies

Job service offices

The Department of Economic Security's Job Service offices are located in these communities:

Bisbee • 209 Bisbee Rd., Bisbee, AZ 85603-1193; (520) 432-5703.

Bullhead City • 813 Hancock Rd., Bullhead City, AZ 86442-5083; (520) 763-4154.

Casa Grande • 401 N. Marshall St., Casa Grande, AZ 85222-5244; (520) 426-3529.

Coolidge • 1155 N. Arizona Blvd., Coolidge, AZ 85228-3294; (520) 723-5351.

Cottonwood • 1645 E. Cottonwood St, Suite E, Cottonwood, AZ 86326-4500; (520) 634-3337.

Douglas • 1140 F Ave., Douglas, AZ 85607-1988; (520) 364-4446.

Flagstaff • 397 Malpais Lane, Suite 9, Flagstaff, AZ 86001-6281; (520) 779-4513.

Fort Defiance • P.O. Box 589, Fort Defiance, AZ 86504-0589; (520) 729-5076.

Glendale • 666 W. Peoria Ave., Suite 101, Glendale, AZ 85302-7015; (602) 486-9891.

Globe • 605 S. Seventh St., Globe, AZ 85501-0630; (520) 425-3101.

Kingman • 301 Pine St., Kingman, AZ 86401-5661; (520) 753-4333.

Lake Havasu City • 1990 McColloch, Suite 104, Lake Havasu City, AZ 86403-4647; (520) 680-6005.

Mesa • 225 E. Main St., Suite 110, Mesa, AZ 85201-7409; (602) 834-7777.

Nogales • 480 N. Grand Ave., Nogales, AZ 85621-2736; (520) 287-4635.

Payson • 122 E. Highway 260, Suite 110, Payson, AZ 84441-4925; (520) 474-4521.

Phoenix • four offices:
4635 S. Central Ave., Phoenix, AZ 85040-2148; (602) 276-5587.
9801 N. Seventh St., Phoenix, AZ 85020-1701; (602) 861-0208.
3406 N. 51st Ave., Phoenix, AZ 85031-3002; (602) 247-3304.
438 W. Adams St., Phoenix, AZ 85003-1607; (602) 252-7771.

Prescott • 234 N. Grove Ave., Prescott, AZ 86302-2912; (520) 445-5100.

Safford • 1938 W. Thatcher Blvd., Safford, AZ 85546-3318; (520) 428-2911.

Show Low • 40 St. 11th St., Show Low, AZ 85901-6001; (520) 537-2948.

Sierra Vista • 2981 E. Tacoma St., Sierra Vista, AZ 85636-1398; (520) 458-4005.

Tuba City • P.O. Box 1140, Tuba City, AZ 86045-1140; (520) 283-4510.

Tucson • three offices:
316 W. Fort Lowell Rd., Tucson, AZ 85703-3816; (520) 293-1919.
7750 E. Broadway, Tucson, AZ 85701-3901; (520) 886-2145.
195 W. Irvington Rd., Tucson, AZ 85714-3097; (520) 741-7188.

Willcox • 265 S. Curtis Ave., Willcox, AZ 85643-2115; (520) 384-3583.

Winslow • 319 E. Third St., Winslow, AZ 86047-3901; (520) 289-4644.

Yuma • 201 S. Third Ave., Yuma, AZ 85634-2294; (520) 783-1221.

LICENSED OCCUPATIONS

Nearly a hundred professions require licensing or certification in Arizona. Some may have reciprocity with other states; check this out before starting your job hunt. These are the agencies that oversee the state's various regulated occupations:

Accounting • Arizona State Board of Accountancy, 3110 N. 19th Ave., Suite 140, Phoenix, AZ 85015; (602) 255-3648.

Architect • Arizona State Board of Technical Registration, 1951 W. Camelback Rd., Suite 250, Phoenix, AZ 85015; (602) 255-4053.

Assayer • Arizona State Board of Technical Registration, 1951 W. Camelback Rd., Suite 250, Phoenix, AZ 85015; (602) 255-4053.

Attorney • Executive Director, State Bar of Arizona, 111 W. Monroe St., Phoenix, AZ 85003; (602) 252-4804.

Auctioneer • License and Registration Section, Department of Revenue, 1600 W. Monroe St., Phoenix, AZ 85007; (602) 542-4576.

Aviation • (commercial pilots, flight instructors, crop-dusters, aviation mechanics, etc.) Federal Aviation Administration, Flight Standards Office, 15041 N. Airport Dr., Scottsdale, AZ 85260; (602) 640-2561.

Bail bondsman • Department of Insurance, 2910 N. 44th St., Suite 210, Phoenix, AZ 85018; (602) 912-8470.

Boxer or wrestler • Arizona State Boxing Commission, 1645 W. Jefferson St., Room 212, Phoenix, AZ 85007; (602) 255-1417.

Barber • Arizona Board of Barbers, 1645 W. Jefferson St., Phoenix, AZ 85007; (602) 542-4498.

Chauffeur • Motor Vehicle Division, Department of Transportation, 1801 W. Jefferson St., Phoenix, AZ 85007; (602) 255-7011, extension 7451.

Chiropractor • Board of Chiropractic Examiners, 5060 N. 19th Ave., Room 317, Phoenix, AZ 85015; (602) 255-1444.

Collection agent • State Banking Department, 2910 N. 44th St., Suite 310, Phoenix, AZ 85018; (602) 255-4421.

Contractor • Registrar of Contractors, 800 W. Washington St., Phoenix, AZ 85007, (602) 542-1525; and 416 W. Congress St., Tucson, AZ 85701; (520) 628-6345.

Cosmetologist • (including manicurist and hairdresser) Board of Cosmetology, 1645 W. Jefferson St., Room 125, Phoenix, AZ 85007; (602) 255-5301.

Dentist and dental hygienist • Board of Dental Examiners, 5060 N. 19th Ave., Suite 406, Phoenix, AZ 85015; (602) 255-3696.

Driving instructor (private) • Motor Vehicle Division, Department of Transportation, 1801 W. Jefferson St. Phoenix, AZ 85007; (602) 255-7011, extension 7451.

Driving instructor (high school) • Teachers Certification Office, State Board of Education, 1535 W. Jefferson St., Room 126, Phoenix, AZ 85007; (602) 542-4367.

Emergency medical technician • Emergency Medical Services, Arizona Department of Health Services, 1647 E. Morten St., Suite 110, Phoenix, AZ 85020; (602) 255-1109.

Engineer • Arizona State Board of Technical Registration, 1951 W. Camelback Rd., Suite 250, Phoenix, AZ 85015; (602) 255-4053.

Escrow agent and mortgage broker • 2910 N. 44th St., Suite 310, Phoenix, AZ 85018; (602) 255-4421.

Funeral director and embalmer • Board of Funeral Directors and Embalmers, 1645 W. Jefferson St., Phoenix, AZ 85007; (602) 542-3095.

Geologist • Arizona State Board of Technical Registration, 1951 W. Camelback Rd., Suite 250, Phoenix, AZ 85015; (602) 255-4053.

Homeopathic medicine • Board of Homeopathic Medical Examiners • 1645 W. Jefferson St., Phoenix, AZ 85007; (602) 542-3095.

Insurance agent • (also broker and adjustor) Department of Insurance, 2910 N. 44th St., Suite 210, Phoenix, AZ 85018; (602) 912-8470.

Midwife • Office of Maternal and Child Health, Arizona Department of Health Services, 1647 E. Morten St., Suite 110, Phoenix, AZ 85020; (602) 255-1109.

Naturopath • Board of Examiners, Naturopathic Physicians, 1645 W. Jefferson St., Phoenix, AZ 85007; (602) 542-3095.

Notary public • Secretary of State, 1700 W. Washington St., Phoenix, AZ 85007; (602) 255-4285.

Nurse • Arizona State Board of Nursing, 1651 E. Morten Ave. Phoenix, AZ 85020; (602) 255-5092.

Nursing care administrator • Board of Administrators, Nursing Care Institution, 1645 W. Jefferson St., Phoenix, AZ 85007; (602) 542-3095.

Occupational therapist • Occupational Therapy Examiners Board, 1645 W. Jefferson St., Phoenix, AZ 85007; (602) 542-6784.

Optician • (including opthamologist and optometrist) Board of Optometry, 1645 W. Jefferson St., Phoenix, AZ 85007; (602) 542-3095.

Osteopath • Arizona Board of Osteopathic Examiners, 1830 W. Colter St., Suite 4, Phoenix, AZ 85015; (602) 255-1747.

Pawnbroker • License and Registration Division, Department of Revenue, 1600 W. Monroe St., Phoenix, AZ 85007; (602) 542-4576.

Pest control (agricultural) • Arizona Department of Agriculture, 1688 W. Adams St., Phoenix, AZ 85007; (602) 542-4373.

Pest control (structural) • Structural Pest Control Commission, 9545 E. Doubletree Ranch Rd., Scottsdale AZ 85258; (602) 255-3664.

Pharmacist • State Board of Pharmacy, 5060 N. 19th Ave., Room 101, Phoenix, AZ 85015; (602) 255-5125.

Physician and surgeon • (also physicians' assistants) Board of Medical Examiners, 1651 E. Morten Ave., Phoenix, AZ 85020; (602) 255-3751.

Physical therapist • Board of Physical Therapy Examiners, 1645 W. Jefferson St., Phoenix, AZ 85007; (602) 542-3095.

Physicians assistant • State Board of Medical Examiners, 1651 E. Morten Ave., Phoenix, AZ 85020.

Podiatrist • Board of Podiatry Examiners, 1645 W. Jefferson St., Phoenix, AZ 85007; (602) 542-3095.

Private investigator and polygraph examiner • Department of Public Safety, 2102 W. Encanto Blvd., Phoenix, AZ 85009; (602) 223-2300.

Psychologist • Psychologists Board of Examiners, 1645 W. Jefferson St., Phoenix, AZ 85007; (602) 542-3095.

Racetrack worker • Investigations and Licensing Division, Arizona Department of Racing, 800 W. Washington St., Room 500, Phoenix, AZ 85007; (602) 542-5151.

Radiology worker • Medical Radiological Technology Department, Board of Examiners, 4814 S. 40th St., Phoenix, AZ 85040; (602) 255-4845.

Real Estate broker and agent • Department of Real Estate, 2910 N. 44th St., Phoenix, AZ 85018; (602) 468-1414.

Respiratory therapist • Arizona Board of Respiratory Care Examiners, 1645 W. Jefferson St., Phoenix, AZ 85007; (602) 542-5995.

Sanitation worker • Arizona Department of Environmental Quality, 3033 N. Central Ave., Phoenix, AZ 85012; (602) 257-2300.

Securities dealer • Securities Division, Arizona Corporation Commission, 1200 W. Washington St., Suite 201, Phoenix, AZ 85007, (602) 542-4242; or 402 W. Congress St., Tucson, AZ 85701, (520) 628-5284.

Security guard • Department of Public Safety, 2102 W. Encanto Blvd., Phoenix, AZ 85009; (602) 223-2300.

Surveyor and assayer • Arizona Board of Technical Registration, 1951 W. Camelback Rd., Suite 250, Phoenix, AZ 85015; (602) 225-4053.

Teacher (community college) • Community College Board, 3225 N. Central Ave., Suite 810, Phoenix, AZ 85012; (602) 255-5582.

Teacher (elementary and high school) • Teachers Certification Office, State Board of Education, 1535 W. Jefferson St., Room 126, Phoenix, AZ 85007; (602) 542-4367.

Travel agent • Department of Insurance, Department of Insurance, Department of Insurance, 2910 N. 44th St., Suite 210, Phoenix, AZ 85018; (602) 912-8470.

Veterinarian and veterinary technician • Veterinary Medical Examining Board, 1645 W. Jefferson, Phoenix 85007; (602) 542-3095.

Water treatment plant operator • See "Sanitation worker" above.

Weighmaster • State Department of Weights and Measures, 9535 E. Doubletree Ranch Rd., Scottsdale, AZ 85258; (602) 255-5211.

Well driller • Department of Water Resources, 500 N. Third St., Phoenix, AZ 85004; (602) 417-2400.

TRADE & PROFESSIONAL ORGANIZATIONS

For union locals, check the Yellow Pages of various communities under "labor organizations."

Accounting • Arizona Society of Certified Public Accountants, 426 N. 44th St., Suite 250, Phoenix, AZ 85008; (602) 273-0100.

Society of Practicing Accountants, 6103 E. Grant Rd., Tucson, AZ 85715; (520) 886-5793.

Air conditioning contractors • See "Construction" below.

Advertising and public relations • Public Relations Society of America, 200 W. Washington, Phoenix, AZ 85003; (602) 258-7772.

Appraisers • American Society of Appraisers, 3134 E. Camelback Rd., Phoenix, AZ 85017; (602) 265-5001.

Architects • American Institute of Architects, 802 N. Fifth Ave., Phoenix, AZ 85003; (602) 252-4200.

Automobile service • Service Station Dealers of America, 1030 E. Guadalupe Rd., Tempe, AZ 85283; (602) 491-1301.

Aviation • Association of Flight Attendants, 1600 W. Broadway Rd., Tempe, AZ 85282; (602) 966-1231.

Banking and savings institutions • Arizona Bankers Association, 2700 N. Central Ave., Suite 620, Phoenix, AZ 85005; (602) 222-5717.

American Institute of Banking, 201 N. Central Ave., Phoenix, AZ 85004; (602) 254-3621.

Broadcasting • Arizona Broadcasters Association, 3101 N. Central Ave., Phoenix, AZ 85005; (602) 274-1418.

National Academy of TV Arts & Sciences, 1101 E. Monte Cristo Ave., Phoenix, AZ 85023; (602) 866-2144.

Business • See "Small businesses" below.

Chambers of commerce • Arizona Chamber of Commerce, 1221 E. Osborn Rd., Phoenix, AZ 85014; (602) 248-9172.

Computers and data processing • Data Processing Management Association, Phoenix; (602) 234-3098.

Construction and contractors • District Council of Carpenters, 1401 N. 29th Ave., Phoenix, AZ 85009; (602) 272-2700.

American Society of Plumbing Engineers, c/o Jonathan Lundstrom, 12675 N. 73rd Ave., Peoria, AZ 85345; (602) 371-1333.

Associated General Contractors of America, 1825 W. Adams St., Phoenix, AZ 85007, (602) 252-3926.

Associated General Contractors, Arizona Building Chapter, 2702 N. Third St., Phoenix, AZ 85004; (602) 274-8222.

Home Builders Association of Central Arizona, 2111 E. Highland Ave., Phoenix, AZ 85016; (602) 274-6545.

National Electrical Contractors Association, 4315 N. 12th St., Phoenix, AZ 85014; (602) 263-0111.

Plumbing and Air Conditioning Contractors, 1783 W. University Drive, Tempe, AZ 85281; (602) 966-0377.

Data processing • See "Computers and data processing" above.

Education • Arizona Education Association, 100 W. Clarendon Ave., Phoenix, AZ 85013; (602) 264-1774.

Arizona Federation of Teachers, 4035 N. Reddell, Scottsdale, AZ 85251; (602) 949-8261.

Arizona School Administrators, 2526 W. Osborn Rd., Phoenix, AZ 85017; (602) 252-0361.

Electronics • Arizona State Electronics Association • 340 E. Carol Ann Way, Phoenix, AZ 85022; (602) 942-0040.

Engineering • (also see "Construction" above) Arizona Society of Professional Engineers, 24 W. Camelback Rd., Suite 100, Phoenix, AZ 85013-2530; (602) 264-4871.

Structural Engineers Association of Arizona, Scottsdale; (602) 994-9193.

Financial services • American Society of Appraisers, 3134 E. Camelback Rd., Phoenix, AZ 85016; (602) 265-5001.

National Association of Credit Management, 2024 N. Seventh St., Phoenix, AZ 85006; (602) 252-8866.

Food production and distribution • Dairy Council of Arizona, 2008 S. Hardy Dr., Tempe, AZ 85282; (602) 966-7211.

Health care • Arizona State Association of Physician Assistants, 3210 W. Camelback Rd., Phoenix, AZ 85017; (602) 589-1099.

Arizona Medical Association, 810 W. Bethany Home Rd., Phoenix, AZ 85013; (602) 246-8901.

Arizona Pharmacy Association, 1845 E. Southern Ave., Tempe, AZ 85282; (602) 838-3385.

Arizona Physical Therapy Association, 3900 E. Camelback Rd., Phoenix, AZ 85018; (602) 912-5310.

Hotels and motels • Arizona Hotel and Motel Association, 2201 E. Camelback Rd., Phoenix, AZ 85016; (602) 553-8802.

Interior design • American Institute of Interior Design, 16855 E. Parkview Ave., Fountain Hills, AZ 85269; (602) 946-9601.

American Society of Interior Designers, 3900 E. Camelback Rd., Phoenix, AZ 85018; (602) 912-5304.

Jewelers • Arizona Jewelers Association, 2323 N. Central Ave., Phoenix, AZ 85004; (602) 254-3328.

Legal services • State Bar of Arizona, 111 W. Monroe St., Phoenix, AZ 85003; (602) 252-4804.

Optometry • Arizona Optometric Association, 3625 N. 16th St., Suite 119, Phoenix, AZ 85016; (602) 279-0055.

Osteopaths • Arizona Osteopathic Medical Association, 5057 E. Thomas Rd., Phoenix, AZ 85018; (602) 840-0460.

Pharmacy • See "Health care" above.

Plumbing • See "Construction" above.

Public relations • See "Advertising and public relations" above.

Real estate and property management • Arizona Association of Realtors, 4414 N. 19th Ave., Phoenix, AZ 85041; (602) 248-7787.

Building Owners and Managers Association, 3900 E. Camelback Rd., Phoenix, AZ 85018; (602) 912-5337.

National Association of Independent Fee Appraisers, 3747 N. 24th St., Phoenix., AZ 85016; (602) 381-0809.

National Association of Real Estate Appraisers, 8383 E. Evans Dr., Scottsdale, AZ 85260; (602) 948-8000.

Phoenix Association of Realtors, 5033 N. 19th Ave., Phoenix, AZ 85015; (602) 246-1012.

Tucson Association of Realtors, 1622 N. Swan Rd., Tucson, AZ 85712; (520) 327-4218.

Restaurants • Arizona Restaurant Association, 2701 N. 16th St., Phoenix, AZ 85006; (602) 234-0701.

Small businesses • Arizona Small Business Association, 1500 E. Bethany Home Rd. Phoenix, AZ 85014; (602) 265-4563.

National Association of the Self Employed, 4110 N. Scottsdale Rd., Scottsdale, AZ 85251; (602) 947-8008.

Structural engineers • See "Construction" and "Engineers" above.

Technology • American Institute of Technology, 440 S. 54th Ave., Phoenix, AZ 85034; (602) 233-2222.

Trucking • Arizona Motor Transport Association, 2111 W. Mc-Dowell Rd., Phoenix, AZ 85009; (602) 252-7559.

Veterinarians • Arizona Veterinary Medical Association, 5502 N. 19th Ave. Phoenix, AZ 85015; (602) 242-7936.

Women's professional groups • National Association of Women Business Owners, 5050 N. 19th Ave., Phoenix, AZ 85015; (602) 246-2926.

National Association of Women in Construction, Phoenix; (602) 220-1441.

HOW TO LAND THAT JOB

The day after I graduated from a small rural high school in Idaho, I hit the road, seeking fortune, if not fame. With only a high school diploma and no specific skills, I found neither. However, I did find out how to get a job. After wandering around the western states for several months, I took shelter at the home of a favorite uncle in southern Oregon. I was broke and needed work.

Uncle Clark took me to a pear packing shed and asked the foreman if he could use a hard-working, skinny 17-year-old kid. Unfortunately, all the jobs were taken. My uncle then pointed to a stack of pallets.

"I'm gonna sit this kid over there," he told the foreman. "Sooner or later, one of your crew will get mad and quit, or he'll get lazy and you'll fire him. And when that happens, here's his replacement."

I was put to work shortly after lunch.

My point is simple. To find a job, go where the jobs are. Direct contact with a prospective employer is the best way to get work, whether you're looking for something glamorous, highly skilled or mundane. I realize that my pear packing plant experience is a bit simplistic. You'll want to be more professional than that—developing a list of prospective companies, finding out who to contact, and then making appointments to see them.

Even with today's emphasis on college degrees and vocational skills, employers still admire job-seekers with drive and spunk. It suggests that they'll be enterprising and hard working once they get the job. If two people are equally qualified for a position, the one who makes a good personal appearance—and shows a bit of grit—often gains the edge.

The key is timing

Besides, there's the advantage of timing. If you wait for a job opening to show up in the want-ads, several people will have applied by the time you send in your resume. However, if you canvas the industry with resumes, and then follow up with phone calls and personal visits, you just might wind up in the right place at the right time.

That's how it worked after I'd gone from pear packing to a stint in the Marine Corps to newspaper reporting. When I decided I was ready to advance to a better job, I'd write to every newspaper in the area where I was interested in working. I'd include a resume and cover letter saying that I'd be in the area in a few days. Then I'd follow up with a phone call, asking if I could make an appointment—at a time convenient for the editor, of course.

A couple of times, I got a job almost before an editor knew he had an opening.

According to *The Phoenix Job Bank,* job seekers who use direct contact are twice as successful as those who rely on the want-ads or an employment agency.

That isn't to suggest that you should ignore the other two sources. The best approach is to employ all three. Incidentally, the Sunday edition of a newspaper generally has the most help wanted ads. Also, some trade and professional organizations offer employment services for their members.

Finding prospective employers

But how do you determine which employers to contact? Several resources are available to you. Trade and professional groups and unions may have lists of affiliated companies. The *Phoenix Job Bank,* the book we mentioned above, is particularly useful. To get a copy, check the nearest bookstore, or contact Bob Adams, Inc., 260 Center St., Holbrook, MA 02343; (800) USA-JOBS or (617) 767-8100. The price is $16.95, plus $4.50 shipping.

Also useful is the Phoenix Business Journal's *Book of Lists,* which lists many of the city's largest firms. To get one, send a check for $28 plus $3 shipping to: The Business Journal, 2910 N. Central, Phoenix, AZ 85012; for information, call (602) 230-8400.

As we also mentioned above, try the good old Yellow Pages. Call USWEST at (800) 422-8793 to order directories for various Arizona communities. You'll find addresses but not ZIP codes, so pick up a copy of the *U.S. Postal Service Zip Code Directory* for complete mailing address. They're available for a fee at post offices. (The ZIP directory now comes in two editions; Arizona cities are listed in volume one.)

The news source

Other possible sources are the business pages of local newspapers. You may encounter stories about businesses that are expanding, have a product breakthrough or are opening branches—all strong indicators of potential jobs. Further, companies on a major hiring binge may place a display add in the business section instead of using the classifieds.

Generally, you can find daily newspapers of major cities in the reference department of the library. Arizona's major dailies are the *Arizona Republic* and *Phoenix Gazette* in Phoenix, both (602) 271-8000; the *Tucson Citizen*, (520) 573-4560, and *Arizona Daily Star* in Tucson, (520) 573-4400; and the *Arizona Daily Sun* in Flagstaff, (520) 774-4545. Other city newspapers are listed in the communities section of Part Two.

Once you've compiled a list of prospective employers, narrow it down to the firms that interest you, and those most likely to be hiring. Next, find out who to contact. A simple phone call to the company personnel department should work. Never send a job query without addressing it to a specific person. If you do, it'll likely end up in the wastebasket with the rest of the junk mail.

COVER LETTERS AND RESUMES

Now, armed with a list of companies and a contact at each, prepare your cover letter and resume. Both should be brief, yet complete, convincing and to the point. Don't give a busy personnel manager or foreman too much to read. Also, avoid corporate doublespeak, redundancy and verbosity. Write about yourself confidently without sounding pompous. Don't brag; let the facts of your background make your case. And avoid clichés like the plague.

Neat appearing resumes can be produced at a copy shop, although the cover letter should be personalized. This doesn't mean that each individual letter must be painfully pecked out by hand on your trusty L.C. Smith typewriter. If you have access to a computer with a word processing program, you can use the automatic mail merging feature that allows you to personalize a mass-produced letter. If you don't own a computer with word processing software, some copy shops will provide personalized multiple mailing service. Also, many firms specialize in preparing and producing resumes and cover letters.

Above all else, neatness counts. From the look of your cover letter to the style of your tie and the shine on your shoes when you appear for an interview, you will be judged by appearance. When you go in for an interview, you go in as a stranger. Your prospective employer can evaluate you only by the facts you present and the way you present yourself.

A well organized presentation and neat personal appearance suggest a competent, organized individual. In reality of course, this isn't always true. In the writing business, it tends to be the exception. Some of the best, most creative and ambitious writers and photographers I've known usually came to work looking as if they'd just fallen out of bed. (Some probably had.) Still, the reality is that first impressions are extremely important. Get the job and prove your worth before revealing your penchant for grooming yourself like a Neanderthal.

Writing a cover letter

Experts disagree on the style and content of cover letters and resumes. In reality, there is no best style, since the personalities of the recipients differ. Some personnel managers get off on symphonic prose that oozes buzz words and corporate jargon. Others are no-nonsense types who want you to present your case directly and precisely. One point upon which they all agree: Say positive things about the company; leave the impression that you *want* to work for such an outstanding firm!

I've found that a simple, to-the-point style works best. Save the details and adjectives for the job interview.

Here's a final tip: In your letter, write as if you know the territory. It suggests that you've done your homework; that you've studied up on your future hometown. Use words and phrases familiar to locals, such as "Valley of the Sun" instead of "Phoenix and vicinity." However, don't overdo it. Only guidebook authors are supposed to say "the glorious Grand Canyon state."

Writing a resume

Like cover letters, resumes can have a variety of styles, as long as they're simple and to the point. If the job you seek is skill-intensive, the resume should emphasize your qualifications and work experience. If you're seeking management opportunities, a chronological resume would best, showing how you've worked up through the ranks. If you're just starting out, the resume should stress your educational accomplishments, preparedness for the particular kind of work and your career goals. On any resume, toss in a little "Mister Good Citizen" community service stuff.

Although some resume writers disagree, I prefer to give a reason for leaving each job—a positive reason, obviously. On the pages that follow are a sample cover letter, and the kind of resume I'd write if I were applying for work at Pine Cone Press, and my wife and I didn't already own the company.

SAMPLE COVER LETTER

Robin R. Righteous
1494 Confidence Lane
North Chicago, IL 60064
Phone (708) 123-4567

January 14, 1999

Scrooge McTaxbite, Personnel Manager
Moneygrub and Nickelsqueeze, Inc.
1010 Taxshelter Way
Phoenix, AZ 85007

Dear Mr. McTaxbite:

After several years as an accountant with a major Chicago firm, I have decided to move my family to the Valley of the Sun. My research tells me that Moneygrub and Nickelsqueeze is one of Arizona's more aggressive and successful accounting firms. And that's the kind of company I'm seeking.

You will note in my enclosed resume that I have considerable experience in tax accounting, payroll, slush fund concealment and money laundering. These are skills that can be useful in your operation. I thrive in a competitive work environment and I'm seeking the kind of challenge offered by an aggressive company in a growing state such as Arizona.

I'm coming to your area in early March. Can we set up an appointment to discuss job possibilities? You can contact me at the above phone number and address.

Thank you for your attention.

Robin R. Righteous

Robin R. Righteous

SAMPLE RESUME

Don W. Martin
1649 Dust Devil Drive
Henderson, NV 89015
(702) 123-4567

PROFESSIONAL EXPERIENCE

April 1988 to present: Founder and co-owner (with my wife) of Pine Cone Press. Using the motto of "Remarkably useful guidebooks," we research, write and publish regional guides. We currently have 16 on the market, with total sales exceeding 200,000. Primary subjects are travel, wine appreciation and small ship cruising. I do much of the research and writing, and work with my wife in planning, designing and producing the books.

March 1979 to March 1988: Associate editor of *Motorland*, the travel magazine of the California State Automobile Association. I was responsible for much of the editorial operation, working with staff writers and editorial assistants in planning, writing and editing copy. Also researched and wrote travel stories, along with articles on traffic safety, anti-smog programs and other auto-related technical subjects. Left to start my own publishing company.

March 1978 to February 1979: Managing editor of the Petaluma (California) *Argus-Courier,* a small daily newspaper north of San Francisco. Directed a news, sports, society and photo staff of eight. I was responsible for the planning and layout of the newspaper, and I wrote some copy. Left to enter the field of travel magazine editing and writing.

June 1963 to February 1977: Staff member of the Oxnard *Press-Courier*, a mid-sized daily newspaper in southern California. Began as a copy editor on the city desk, then spent four years as editor of the Sunday feature magazine and daily entertainment page. Left to accept the challenge of newspaper management.

May 1960 to May 1963: Various editorial posts on the Oceanside *Blade-Tribune,* a small daily newspaper in southern California. Began as a police beat reporter, then was promoted to assistant sports editor, then copy editor and editorial page editor. Left to accept a post on a larger newspaper.

Other employment: 1950 to 1960: Began my career as a printer's devil for the weekly Wilder (Idaho) *Herald* at age 16, while still in high school; also was editor of the high school newspaper. Served in the Marine Corps Public Information Service as an editor of several base newspapers and as a correspondent in Korea, Japan and Taiwan.

Related experience: I have sold dozens of freelance articles and photos to newspapers and magazines.

PROFESSIONAL SKILLS

Familiar with Word Perfect, WordStar and Ventura 7 desktop publishing. Comfortable with computers and can surf the Internet with ease. Proficient with professional-level 35mm cameras.

EDUCATION

Wilder (Idaho) High School, graduated in 1951.
Naval Journalists' School, Great Lakes, Ill., graduated in 1956.
Have taken several college courses in English, journalism, political science and history.

AWARDS AND COMMUNITY SERVICE

Member of the Society of American Travel Writers.
Four photo layouts prepared by myself and my photographer at the Oxnard *Press-Courier* won California Press Photographers Association awards.
Was awarded the Ventura County (California) Diane Seeley Award for promoting the arts.
Served as founding president of the Ventura County Theater Council and as a board member of the Ventura County Forum of the Arts.
Former member of the Petaluma (California) Kiwanis Club and Daly City (California) Junior Chamber of Commerce.
Won two Department of Defense awards and one Marine Corps Journalism Award for excellence in editing military newspapers.

PERSONAL INFORMATION

In excellent health, non-smoker; married to Betty Woo Martin, pharmacist, co-author of guidebooks and former real estate broker.
Born April 22, 1934, in Grants Pass, Oregon.
Listed in Marquis' *Who's Who in the World, Who's Who in the West* and *Who's Who in California.*
Listed in *Gale's Contemporary Authors.*

REFERENCES

Personal and professional references available on request.

Chapter six

THE RETIREES

A PLACE UNDER ARIZONA'S SUN

Contrary to what you may have seen on the evening news, most retired folks aren't spending their golden years in a home for the aged, or sitting in a creaking rocking chair on the front porch.

Many of them are upbeat, active people who've saved their money and perhaps paid off their homes. They look forward to some of the best years of their lives.

Our average life expectancy is approaching 70 for men and 75 for women. Further, the life expectancy for people who have achieved age 60 is even higher—into the 80s. More than 30 million Americans are now retired and that number will increase dramatically as the Baby Boomers, children born between 1946 and 1966, reach retirement age. Statistics reveal that one third of all living Americans were born during that period. Further, many people are retiring at a younger age, adding more numbers to these growing ranks. (However, this trend may reverse if the retirement age is increased to help save the heavily impacted Social Security system.)

With the current emphasis on physical fitness and the decrease in heart attack rates, many older people today are healthier than their parents. (This despite the growing popularity of junky fast foods and the fact that more than half of all American adults are overweight! Many of those, of course, don't make it to retirement age.)

We are creating a new socio-economic order—a great legion of people who retire earlier and live longer. Some spend as many years in retirement as they did raising their families. A recent survey indicated that more than 70 percent of retirees feel that they are secure economically. This security leads to disposable income and mobility. And that leads us into this chapter of *Arizona in Your Future.*

Today's seniors are less inclined to keep the old family roost after the last kid has flown the coop and the dog has died. Further, the kids tend to scatter more, leaving their home towns in search of greener pastures and greener paychecks, so parents don't feel the need to maintain a family base.

Since the brood has left and old Fido is in the Pet Sematary, why put up with another frigid February or urban traffic jam? Why worry about high crime rates and higher taxes? Why deal with all that gardening and house cleaning? With the current emphasis on physical fitness, todays retirees want to get out and do things. They don't want to trudge through snow to reach indoor tennis courts or be chased off the golf course by a chilling rain. So why not go someplace that's warm, safe, secure and affordable?

Like Arizona, for instance.

Arizona attracts more migrating seniors than any other state except Florida and California. It's ahead of Texas and New Mexico, the two other leading sunbelt states, and if current trends continue, it will pass crowded and tax-expensive California.

Shedding the Midwest

Where are these folks drawn from? Although migration figures aren't broken down by age, most sunbelt newcomers are from the Midwest. Illinois loses more citizens to Arizona than any other state—more than 10,000 a year. Ohio is a distant second, with about half as many migrants going south. An equal number comes from Michigan.

Surprisingly, California sends nearly as many emigrants to Arizona as does Michigan, although they aren't necessarily retirees. Job opportunities and lower housing prices lure many Californians to the state next door. Other leading sources for migrants—in order of numbers—are Colorado, New York, Wisconsin, Minnesota, Iowa and Indiana.

Like most states, Arizona permits apartment, condo and subdivision owners to designate a minimum age for residents. This, of course, defines the "retirement complex." They range from full-care apartments and assisted living facilities to condos and planned developments with golf courses, swimming pools, tennis courts and other active-life amenities.

Mobile home parks are popular with year-around retirees, as well as wintertime Snowbirds. In fact, one in ten Arizona residents lives in mobile housing—one of the highest ratios in the Nation. Adults-only parks are particularly numerous along the Colorado River corridor and in and about Phoenix and Tucson.

If you're considering the purchase of a home or condo in a retirement community, remember that the age requirement limits your market and thus may inhibit the unit's resale value. Further, although it can be willed to your children when you pass on, they can't occupy it unless they meet that age requirement, and some retirement complexes limit renters. Except in a few highly desirable communities, retirement units tend to bring less on the resale market than comparable family homes. Also, mobile homes generally *depreciate* while "stick built" houses increase in value.

However, since you probably plan to spend all of your remaining years in your retirement home, condo or double-wide, why worry about resale value?

The Phoenix Yellow Pages contains several pages of listings for "Retirement & Life Care Communities & Homes." Tucson's phone book has a three and a half page section. Both have extensive adult mobile home park listings as well.

WHAT KIND OF RETIREMENT?

Once you've made the decision to move to Arizona, you need to determine which retirement facilities best suit your needs. Basically, they fit into five categories. In the first two, one usually has the option of purchasing, leasing or renting, while the final three are usually on a month-to-month basis, with the cost of care and perhaps meals included. Some advanced care units can be purchased, however.

Independent living • As the name suggests, this is retirement in a conventional family community. Some seniors, particularly active ones, prefer this. They like the mix of young and old, which is more akin to the city or town they left behind. Arizona offers a host of planned all-age communities with the same amenities as retirement villages—golf, tennis, swimming and scheduled activities. Some of these colonies have both senior and family sections, with separate-but-equal facilities for each age group.

Planned adult community • Like any planned complex, the adult village offers a variety of activities, plus the advantage of facilities geared to older people. Ease of mobility is taken into account in room layouts. And you don't need to worry about a teen-age rap party next door. Dwellings range from detached homes and townhouses to condos and apartments.

Independent retirement complex • These facilities, usually offered on a lease plan, are for fully ambulatory people who don't want the bother of housekeeping. They usually offer maid service, planned activities and outings. Meals may be included, or they can be an option offered at a central dining area. One might compare it to living in a hotel, or perhaps a motel with a kitchenette. These complexes are usually set up as townhouses, condos or apartments.

Assisted living facility • These offer a higher level of care than the independent complex. Full housekeeping and meal service generally are provided, and aides are on hand to help with mobility problems and perhaps monitor medications. However, they generally don't have on-site nursing care. Most are apartments or condos. Group outings are offered for those who are unable to drive or who prefer not to.

Life care facility • These complexes are best for those with impaired mobility or a debilitating illness. Also, some still-ambulatory seniors prefer to turn all of their day-to-day decisions and responsibilities over to someone else. Facilities range from apartments to furnished rooms.

On-site medical care is part of the program at a life care facility, and all housekeeping and meals are furnished. Full time nursing care is available for those in need. The most comprehensive level of life care facilities are nursing homes and—despite their rather misleading names—convalescent hospitals.

Senior service agencies

Several agencies in Arizona offer advice, assistance and information for seniors. If you're interested in extended health care, the **Office of Long Term Health Care** of the Arizona Department of Health Services will send you *A Guide to Selecting Long Term Health Care Services for the Elderly and Disabled.* Contact either of these offices:

Phoenix area • Arizona Department of Health Services, Assurance and Licensure Services, 1647 E. Morten St., Suite 110, Phoenix, AZ 85020; (602) 255-1109.

Tucson area • Arizona Department of Health Services, Assurance and Licensure Service, 400 W. Congress St., Suite 116, Tucson, AZ 85701; (520) 628-6991.

For a directory of nursing homes and related services, contact the **Arizona Nursing Association,** 1817 N. Third St., Suite 200, Phoenix, AZ 85004; (602) 258-8996. Another useful organization is the **Governor's Advisory Council on Aging**, P.O. Box 6123-A, Phoenix, AZ 85005.

Offices of Arizona's **Agency on Aging** provide a variety of services for people 60 and over. They function as activity and information centers for seniors, and they even offer delivery services for those who can't get about. Offices are in these communities:

Phoenix area • 1366 E. Thomas Rd., Suite 108, Phoenix, AZ 85014; (602) 264-2255.

Northwestern Arizona • P.O. Box 57, Flagstaff, AZ 86002; (520) 774-1895.

Southwestern Arizona • 100 Maple Ave., Yuma, AZ 85364; (520) 782-1886.

Central Arizona • P.O. Box 1129 (512) E. Butte St.), Florence, AZ 85232; (520) 868-4166.

Tucson area • 2955 E. Broadway, Tucson, AZ 85716; (520) 795-5800.

Southeastern Arizona • 118 Arizona St., Bisbee, AZ 85603; (520) 432-5301.

THE RETIREMENT TOWNS

Planned retirement communities were invented in Arizona, although the well-known Sun City wasn't the first. A place appropriately called Youngtown is the nation's—and probably the world's—oldest retirement village. Located just west of Phoenix, it was created in 1954 by the Youngtown Land and Development Company. It still thrives today as a busy little city of about 2,600 residents.

Del E. Webb started Sun City, next door to Youngtown, in 1960. It has become America's largest retirement community, with a population around 45,000. A satellite, Sun City West, was started in 1978 and it now has more than 25,000 residents. A third Del Web retirement complex, Sun City Vistoso, is just north of Tucson. Sun City communities also are located in several other states.

We offer below a list of some of Arizona's major planned retirement villages. A letter or phone call to each will earn you a quick packet of information. (Incidentally, some of these commercial retirement villages have evolved into incorporated communities, so they also may be listed elsewhere in this book.)

Fountain of the Sun • 8001 E. Broadway, Mesa, AZ 85208; (602) 984-0165.

Leisure World • 908 S. Power Rd., Mesa, AZ 85026; (602) 832-3232.

SaddleBrooke Country Club • 64518 E. Saddlebrooke Blvd., Tucson, AZ 85737; (800) 733-4050 or (520) 791-7464.

SunBird Golf Resort • 6250 SunBird Blvd., Chandler, AZ 85249; (800) 523-6664 or (602) 732-1000.

Sun City Vistoso • 13990 N. Desert Butte Dr., Sun City Vistoso (Tucson), AZ 85704; (800) 442-8483.

Sun City • Del E. Webb Development Company, 13323 W. Meeker Blvd., Sun City, AZ 85375, (602) 975-2270; and Northwest Valley Chamber of Commerce, 12211 W. Bell Rd., Suite 204, Surprise, AZ 85374; (602) 583-0692.

Sun City West • 13323 W. Meeker Blvd., Sun City, AZ 85375; (800) 341-6121 or (602) 546-5126.

Westbrook Village • 9721 W. Rockwood Dr., Peoria, AZ 85345; (602) 933-0181.

WHERE THE SENIORS LIVE (by percentage)

Source: Population Statistics Unit, Arizona Department of Economic Security

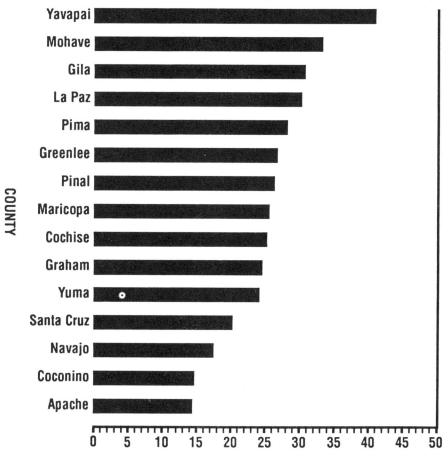

PERCENTAGE OF POPULATION OVER 50

Yavapai County, which contains Prescott and south Sedona, has Arizona's highest ratio of residents over fifty--more than 40 percent. They aren't all retired, of course, but the county is very popular with retirees. Mohave County on the Colorado River Corridor is second in senior ratio.

Retirement areas

Maricopa (Phoenix) and Pima (Tucson) counties are home to most of Arizona's retirees. Not all of these folks live in planned retirement villages like Sun City, of course. Smaller senior complexes are scattered throughout the Valley of the Sun and greater Tucson.

About one in four Maricopa and Pima County residents are over fifty, and incoming Baby Boomers are bound to elevate that figure. However, several other counties have more seniors per capita. Yavapai

County, whose main city is Prescott, has Arizona's highest ratio of folks over fifty—41 percent. Mohave County along the Colorado River is second with 33 percent.

The Colorado River corridor ranks third behind Phoenix and Tucson in the total number of retirees. Most are in the communities of Yuma, Parker, Lake Havasu City and Bullhead City. The river towns offer two big advantages—access to water sports and housing that's less expensive than in the Phoenix and Tucson areas. They have disadvantages, as well. For one thing, it can get hotter than the hinges of Hades along *Rio Colorado* in summer. Phoenix and Tucson, at higher elevations, are cooler (which doesn't mean cool in July and August). Also, the river towns offer little in the way of cultural lures—unless you count the London Bridge at Lake Havasu City, or the casino shows at Laughlin, Nevada, across the river from Bullhead City.

If you're considering an Arizona retirement, don't restrict yourself to the sunbelt. Communities such as Flagstaff, Sedona and Prescott to the north and Sierra Vista in the southeast have retirement facilities as well. Small mountain towns north and east of Phoenix such Payson, Pinetop and Show Low also offer a mix of retirement and recreational opportunities.

Nippy but not harsh

Most of these places are more than 4,000 feet high, so some of them get winter snow (particularly around Flagstaff), although the weather is never harsh. Compared with Toronto, Buffalo or Chicago, winters are downright mild. Annual snowfall in Prescott, for instance, is 24 inches. Sierra Vista's is a mere ten inches and the average January low temperature is 35 to 40 degrees.

Some retirees are drawn to these higher elevation towns because they miss the four season back home. In Prescott, Payson, Flagstaff and Sedona, you even get piney woods and fall color.

If we were considering going to Arizona as retirees, we'd pick one of the places listed below. We don't suggest heavily urbanized Phoenix, since there's no reason for a retiree to become entangled in crowds or commuter traffic. However, if you don't mind a little congestion and want to be close to downtown Phoenix with its many cultural and shopping lures, you might consider suburban towns such as Mesa, Tempe (with Arizona State University at your doorstep), Glendale or Peoria.

CENTRAL ARIZONA

Folks who want to be near the business, economic and social hub of Arizona should set their sights on the Valley of the Sun. Although the basin is beginning to resemble Los Angeles with its sprawl, you still can find your own personal cactus patch on the fringes and escape the congestion. Phoenix is served by a growing network of freeways and the heart of the city is easily reached during off-commute hours.

Even during the morning rush, delays are nothing compared with those you'll encounter in large Eastern and Midwestern cities or the Los Angeles and San Francisco Bay areas. When we were exploring the Phoenix-Scottsdale area for our tour book, *Arizona Discovery Guide,* we stayed at an RV park near Goodyear, about 20 miles west. By 9 a.m., we could breeze into the heart of town within half an hour.

Scottsdale and Paradise Valley were once difficult to reach because of the Phoenix suburban sprawl, although a new cross-town freeway has penetrated that northeastern edge of the Valley of the Sun.

If you'd like to get a bit further out and still be within dinner range, we'd recommend places such as Apache Junction on the eastern edge of the valley, Sun City to the west or Arizona City and Florence to the south. The latter two are near the busy north-south Interstate 10 corridor, providing easy access to both Phoenix and Tucson.

Apache Junction • This city of about 20,000 is set against the rough backdrop of the Superstition Mountains, southeast of Phoenix. It offers several mobile home parks and a few planned developments. It's within a short drive of Phoenix, yet well beyond its urban congestion. We particularly like its topography. The terrain is high desert and, for outdoor lovers, the forested hills and reservoirs scenic of Salt River Canyon are a short drive away. *For information: Apache Junction Chamber of Commerce, P.O. Box 1747, Apache Junction, AZ 85217; (520) 982-3141.*

Arizona City • The agricultural setting isn't particularly stimulating, although the weather's nice and so is the location—midway between Phoenix and Tucson. This planned community of 2,700 was established in 1960, and it offers amenities such as a fake lake, golf course and several parks. *For information: Arizona City Chamber of Commerce, P.O. Box 5, Arizona City, AZ 85223; (520) 466-5141.*

Carefree and Cave Creek • Take your pick of these two small towns, located in the rugged desert northeast of Scottsdale. Carefree, with about 2,000 residents, is a somewhat upscale planned community. Larger Cave creek, with nearly 3,000 folks, is on the rustic side, preserving remnants of an old mining town. They both offer good locations—close to Phoenix and Scottsdale, yet on the uncluttered outer edge of the Valley of the Sun. *For information: Carefree/Cave Creek Chamber of Commerce, 748 Easy St. (P.O. Box 734), Carefree, AZ 85377; (602) 488-3381.*

Florence • You don't hear much about it, although Florence is a fine place for retirement, with an historic Western style downtown section and some modern subdivisions around the edges. Located in Pinal County midway between Phoenix and Tucson, it has a rather mild climate and a population of 11,500. It's in an agricultural valley, so you won't find any desert or mountain scenery. *For information: Florence Chamber of Commerce, P.O. Box 929 (291 Bailey St.), Florence, AZ 85232; (520) 868-9433.*

Fountain Hills • This planned community is on the northeastern rim of the Valley of the Sun, with a population of about 14,000. Established in 1970 by the creators of Lake Havasu City, it's a modern town set in attractive high desert terrain. It offers a mix of planned subdivisions and shopping centers. There's no London Bridge, although it does have the world's highest fountain, squirting from a park-rimmed lake as the town centerpiece. *For information: Fountain Hills Chamber of Commerce, P.O. Box 17598 (16838 E. Palisades Ave., #2), Fountain Hills, AZ 85269; (602) 837-1654.*

Paradise Valley • If you can afford it, Paradise Valley is a retirement paradise, desert style. Just beyond the reach of Phoenix and Scottsdale's congestion, it's a community of elegant homes set in a ruggedly handsome desert and surrounded by equally rugged mountains. Most lodgings are individual homes; there are few planned retirement complexes. It's a stable, slow growing community with a population of about 13,000, a gain of only 2,000 in the past 15 years. Expect summers to be hot here, although if you can afford Paradise Valley, you can afford to keep the air conditioner running. *For information: Greater Paradise Valley Chamber of Commerce, 16042 N. 32nd St., Paradise Valley, AZ 85032; (602) 482-3344.*

Scottsdale • Upscale and expensive, this community of 170,000 sits against dramatic Camelback Peak in the high desert on the edge of Phoenix. Although pricey, it's homes are somewhat less expensive than those in next-door Paradise Valley. Scottsdale has become rather urbanized and has lost much of its early Western charm, although the rustic flavor of Old Scottsdale has been preserved. The town offers some of Arizona's finest planned developments, upscale shopping centers and luxury resorts. *For information: Scottsdale Chamber of Commerce, 7343 Scottsdale Mall, Scottsdale, AZ 85251, (602) 945-8481; and City of Scottsdale, P.O. Box 1000 (3939 Civic Center Rd.), Scottsdale, AZ 85251, (602) 945-8481.*

Sun City and Sun City West • Large Sun City offers a complete assortment of leisure amenities. Lodgings range from detached homes and townhouses to condos. Sun City West is newer, smaller and a bit more modern. With a combined population of more than 70,000 the twin communities provide ample shopping and other commercial facilities. They're on the western edge of the Valley of the Sun, convenient to Phoenix yet beyond the sprawl. *For information: Sun City, Del E. Webb Development Company, 13323 W. Meeker Blvd., Sun City, AZ 85375, (602) 975-2270; Sun City West, 13323 W. Meeker Blvd., Sun City, AZ 85375, (800) 341-6121 or (602) 546-5126; and Northwest Valley Chamber of Commerce, 12211 W. Bell Rd., Suite 204, Surprise, AZ 85374, (602) 583-0692.*

Wickenburg • This town among rough desert hills just loves to play cowboy. Western shops line its streets, half a dozen dude ranches are nearby and real cowboys herd dogies in the surrounding desert. It's 50 miles northwest of Phoenix and well beyond that suburban scatter. Indeed, it feels like another place in another time—"out Wickenburg way." There are few planned retirement facilities in this peaceful town of 5,000 folks. However, if you love old Roy Rogers movies, this is your place. *Wickenburg Chamber of Commerce, 216 N. Frontier St., Wickenburg, AZ 85390, (520) 684-5479; and Town of Wickenburg, 155 N. Tegner St., Suite A, Wickenburg, AZ 85390, (520) 684-5451.*

Youngtown • This is where it all began, in America's first planned retirement town. It has the requisite senior leisure facilities—a club-house, fake lake, tennis and six golf courses. Another 18 courses are within five miles. No longer isolated in the desert, Youngtown is now rimmed by Sun City, Peoria and El Mirage. Although it preceded Sun City as a retirement community, it's much smaller, with a population of about 2,700. *For information: Town of Youngtown, 12030 Clubhouse Square, Youngtown, AZ 85363, (602) 933-8286; and Northwest Valley Chamber of Commerce, 12211 W. Bell Rd., Suite 204, Surprise, AZ 85374, (602) 583-0692.*

NORTH CENTRAL ARIZONA

If you want pine trees and four seasons in your retirement picture, pick one of these north central Arizona towns. Some, such as Flagstaff and Prescott, are more than a mile high. They offer occasional winter snows but severe storms are rare. The Sedona-Oak Creek Canyon-Verde Valley areas are noted for their fall color, so transplanted New Englanders will feel right at home.

Cottonwood • Although it's a rather ordinary looking town with-out fancy subdivisions, this town of 6,545 people offers a fine location, just below beautiful Oak Creek Canyon and Sedona. A relatively mild climate, proximity to a variety of tourist attractions and low housing costs have lured many retirees. One of four residents is over 65. *For in-formation: Verde Valley Chamber of Commerce, 1010 S. Main St., Cot-tonwood, AZ 86326; (520) 634-7593.*

Flagstaff • One of our favorite Arizona communities, Flagstaff has a balance of cultural offerings, educational facilities and an appealing location. It sits at the base of the towering San Francisco Peaks, about 70 miles southeast of the Grand Canyon. With a population of about 53,000, it offers all the services and amenities a retiree would need, plus the cultural lures of Northern Arizona University. It can get cold in winter, however. Not Chicago cold, although the average January low is 15 degrees, and it gets about 84 inches of winter snowfall. *For information: Flagstaff Chamber of Commerce, 101 W. Route 66, Flag-staff, AZ 86004; (520) 774-9541 or (800) 842-7293.*

Lake Montezuma are • Lake What? Lake Montezuma, Rimrock and McGuireville are little known outside Arizona. They are three planned villages in the higher reaches of the Verde Valley, with terrain

Weekend sailors who retire to Page will enjoy the water sports and the beauty of Glen Canyon National Recreation Area. Here, a narrow side canyon casts a perfect reflection of itself in Lake Powell.

ranging from prairie to forest. These hamlets, with a combined population of 2,200, are popular with retirees who like the surrounding national forest and don't mind chilly weather in winter. Snowfall is rare. *For information: Cottonwood-Verde Valley Chamber of Commerce, 1010 S. Main St., Cottonwood, AZ 86326; (520) 634-7593.*

Page and Lake Powell ● If you're a weekend sailor and want to float your boat, Page may be your retirement answer. This desert town of 8,000 people is located adjacent to Lake Powell, which offers unlimited water sports opportunities. Although not a particularly handsome community, Page—the former construction town for Glen Canyon Dam—does offer a well-planned downtown core. A few subdivisions are cropping up in its desert outskirts, although it's not considered a major retirement community. *For information: Page/Lake Powell Chamber of Commerce, P.O. Box 727 (106 S. Lake Powell Blvd.) Page, AZ 86040; (520) 645-2741.*

Payson ● This is another woodsy place, a town of 11,000 sitting a mile high, 78 miles northeast of Phoenix. The Chamber of Commerce says it offers a mix of "Swiss alpine, Old West and contemporary ambiance," which is something of an exaggeration, since the heart of town is mostly an unplanned commercial strip. It *is* a popular senior community; 60 percent of its residents are retired and it sponsors several senior programs. You'll get the four seasons although winters are mild, with perhaps two feet of total snowfall. *For information: Payson Chamber of Commerce, P.O. Box 1380, Payson, AZ 85541, (800) 6-PAYSON or (520) 474-4515; and Town of Payson, 303 N. Beeline Highway, Payson, AZ 85547; (520) 474-5242.*

Pine and Strawberry • Essentially vacation and retirement towns, these villages with a combined population of 3,800 are in the east-central Arizona woods north of Payson. Many Valley of the Sun residents spend weekends here to escape desert heat; some maintain second homes among the pines. The area is more than a mile up, so winters are chilly but not harsh. Figure on a couple of feet of total snowfall. *For information: Pine-Strawberry Chamber of Commerce, P.O. Box 333, Pine, AZ 85544; (520) 476-3547.*

Prescott • Like Flagstaff, Prescott offers a mix of culture, education and scenery, located in the west central Arizona pines. This small city of 30,606 residents has extensive senior programs and good medical facilities; one in four residents is retired. This is four-seasons country, getting splashes of fall color and about two feet of winter snow. The ambiance and attitude are Old West, although the town has a sturdy and attractive red brick New England look. Incidentally, it's pronounced "PRESS-kit," partner. *For information: Prescott Chamber of Commerce, P.O. Box 1147 (117 W. Goodwin St.), Prescott, AZ 86302; (520) 445-2000.*

Sedona • If we could afford the tariff, we'd be tempted to retire in Sedona and watch those glorious sunups and sundowns against the red rock peaks of Oak Creek Canyon. One of the most dramatically located towns in America, this community of 9,000 is a haven for tourists, artists, well-heeled retirees and an occasional music festival. Shops, galleries and boutiques abound. Several planned communities extend south; some are tucked into their own awesome red rock niches. At 4,300 feet, Sedona offers mild year-around climate and glorious fall color. *For information: Sedona/Oak Creek Canyon Chamber of Commerce, P.O. Box 478, Sedona, AZ 86336; (800) 228-7336 or (520) 282-7722.*

Verde Village • This planned complex, next door to Cottonwood, has about 8,600 residents and two-thirds of them are retired. It's in an agricultural valley, between the imposing setting of Oak Creek Canyon and the pine forests of the Prescott area. *For information: Verde Valley Chamber of Commerce, 1010 S. Main St., Cottonwood, AZ 86326; (520) 634-7593.*

COLORADO RIVER CORRIDOR

Prepare for extreme summer heat if you choose the Colorado River corridor as your retirement refuge. This area is noted mostly as a Snowbird haven, although many people crank up their air conditioners and stay the year-around. The Colorado River has so many dams that it's now a virtual chain of lakes, so cooling water sports are always available.

The transplanted London Bridge lures both tourists and retirees to the planned community of Lake Havasu City.

Bullhead City • Sprawled over 43 square miles along the river corridor, Bullhead is an unlovely city, although it offers great winter climate. Further, if you like one-armed bandits and green felt games, the Nevada gaming center of Laughlin is just across the pond. Summers get very hot here, sometimes topping the national charts. With a growing population approaching 27,000, Bullhead has many mobile home parks and a few planned residential communities. *For information: Bullhead Area Chamber of Commerce, 1251 Highway 95, Bullhead City, AZ 86430; (520) 754-4121.*

Lake Havasu City • This community of 36,285 was started by developer Robert P. McCulloch in the 1960s; he had the London Bridge hauled over here (in pieces, of course) as a focal point. Reassembling England's historic stone bridge in the desert got him the headlines he wanted and his planned community grew quickly. It offers a good mix of retirement villages, all-age subdivisions and mobile home parks. The lake provides water sports and a gimmick English village has been built around the bridge. The only negative: the countryside ain't very pretty. *For information: Lake Havasu Area Chamber of Commerce, 1930 Mesquite Ave., Suite 3, Lake Havasu City, AZ 86403; (800) 242-8278 or (520) 453-3444.*

Yuma • If you like living far from the rest of civilization while still enjoying some of its amenities, consider Yuma. With a population topping 60,000, it offers all the basic essentials and an abundance of water recreation on the adjacent Colorado River. Not a fancy place, it's an honest workingperson's town. It is rich in history, as the site of Yuma Crossing on the first trail to California, and the Yuma Territorial Prison; both are now visitor attractions. That early trail to California is now Interstate 8, so access to this remote mini-metropolis is easy. Like the other Colorado River corridor towns, Yuma's biggest disadvantage for year-around retirement is summer heat. *For information: Yuma County Chamber of Commerce, P.O. Box 10230 (377 S. Main St.), Yuma, AZ 85366-8230; (520) 783-2567.*

SOUTHERN ARIZONA

The Tucson-to-Nogales corridor is rapidly gaining favor with all-year retirees. Averaging more than a thousand feet higher than Phoenix, the region's towns aren't quite as hot in summer. Another choice is southeastern Arizona, the state's undiscovered corner. Far from Arizona's urban and suburban mainstream, it offers a mix of high desert, prairie country and mountains. Winters are relatively mild and the area's largest community, Sierra Vista, is said to have the most temperate year-around climate in America.

Bisbee • This old copper mining town of 6,500 people isn't well known as a retirement haven. However, we like its funky look and sense of history, and the year-around climate is quite mild. Summer highs are in the upper eighties and winter lows are in the middle thirties; there's virtually no snowfall. Bisbee is about six miles from the Mexican border—a plus for lovers of things Latino. *For information: Bisbee Chamber of Commerce, P.O. Box BA (Seven Main St.), Bisbee, AZ 85603, (520) 432-5421; City of Bisbee, 118 Arizona St., Bisbee, AZ 85603, (520) 432-5446.*

Catalina • Twelve miles north of Tucson, Catalina is home to a pair of major retirement communities, Sun City Vistoso and Saddle-Brooke, which house many of its 5,529 residents. Established in the 1950s, the town is situated in the foothills of the Catalina Mountains, giving it a pleasing backdrop. Although it's in the desert, the elevation is 3,000 feet, so summers are relatively mild—five to ten degrees cooler than Tucson. *For information: Catalina/Golder Ranch Village Council, P.O. Box 8674 CRB, Catalina (Tucson), AZ 85738; (520) 791-2265.*

Green Valley • Like Sun City, this town of 25,000 was planned as a retirement community, so it offers extensive senior facilities, plus golf, tennis, swimming and such. We like its location midway between Tucson and the Mexican border at Nogales. The terrain is rolling desert, not really attractive, although the climate's great in winter. Temperatures routinely top 100 degrees in summer, but that's why air conditioning was invented. *For information: Green Valley Chamber of Commerce, P.O. Box 566 (270 W. Continental, Room 100), Green Valley, AZ 85622; (520) 625-7575*

Sierra Vista • Looking more like a suburb than a city, Sierra Vista is an orderly sprawl of subdivisions and shopping centers southeast of Tucson. The elevation is 4,623 feet, creating a very temperate year-around climate. While not really handsome, this community of nearly 38,000 is clean, well planned and easy to navigate, with several modern housing developments. Historic Fort Huachuca, a still-active Army post, is just to the south. *For information: Sierra Vista Chamber of Commerce, 21 E. Wilcox Dr., Sierra Vista, AZ 85635, (800) 288-3861 or (520) 458-6940; and City of Sierra Vista, 2400 E. Tacoma St., Sierra Vista, AZ 85635, (520) 458-3315.*

Tubac • If you like history and artistic funk with your retirement, check out this weathered little town 40 miles south of Tucson and 23 miles north of Nogales. With a population of 1,146—two-thirds of them retired—Tubac offers several galleries and boutiques and a very laid-back lifestyle. Tubac State Historic Park and Tumacacori Mission National Monument are in the neighborhood. *For information: Tubac Chamber of Commerce, P.O. Box 1866, Tubac, AZ 85646; (520) 398-2704.*

Tucson • Since we didn't recommend bustling and sprawling Phoenix as a retirement town, why Tucson? Because it's less than half the size, not quite as sprawling and less congested. While the greater Valley of the Sun has more than two million residents, Tucson only about half a million. (Only?) Further, it's higher and slightly cooler than Phoenix in summer, and it's in a dramatic setting, surrounded by craggy desert mountains. Finally, it offers cultural and historic lures and it is home to the University of Arizona. *For information: Tucson Convention and Visitors Bureau, 130 S. Scott Ave., Tucson, AZ 85701, (800) 638-8350 or (520) 624-1817, and Tucson Metropolitan Chamber of Commerce, P.O. Box 991 (465 W. St. Mary's Rd.), Tucson, AZ 85702.*

Chapter seven

THE SNOWBIRDS

FEATHERING YOUR WINTER NEST

While hundreds of thousands of retirees snip their roots and nestle here permanently, an even larger number of seniors head for Arizona each year only to enjoy its winter sunshine.

They embrace the best of both worlds—heading south before the snow flies, and then returning home in the spring to keep their ties with family and friends. It's no wonder that they've earned the nickname Snowbirds. Arizona ranks second to Florida and ahead of California and Texas as America's leading Snowbird retreat. It draws more than a million winter visitors each year.

A recent Arizona State University survey of winter visitors in the Valley of the Sun indicated that the largest number arrives in November and departs in April. Chambers of commerce in other areas report a similar pattern. The ASU survey revealed some surprising statistics. Despite the typical Snowbird's image as an RV enthusiast, at least half of Arizona's winter visitors check into apartments or condos, and many own winter homes here. Of those who do occupy RV or mobile home parks, 70 percent leave their rigs in Arizona the year-around. Only 30 percent tow a trailer or drive an RV to the state. So it's evident that most of these visitors, like other migrating birds, like to return to the same nest year after year.

And Snowbirds definitely are migrants. While the state lures tens of thousands of permanent retirees each year, 95 percent of winter visitors responding to the ASU survey said they planned to return home in the spring. The average length of a winter stay is between four and five months. Two-thirds of those questioned had been doing the Snowbird bit for five or more years.

Where do most of the Snowbirds roost? Along the Colorado River corridor and in the greater Phoenix area. Some *Rio Colorado* towns see their populations increase many-fold each winter. The Phoenix Convention and Visitors Bureau estimates that as many as 200,000 Snowbirds flock into the Valley of the Sun.

Where do they come from? A surprising 20 percent are from Canada, despite the fact that its total population is only one tenth that of the U.S. Most American Snowbirds come from the chilly Midwest, but not from Michigan, although that state sends the largest number of permanent retirees to Arizona. In fact, Michigan doesn't even finish in the top ten. After Canada, Minnesota sends the most winter visitors, with 13 percent of the total; Iowa and Washington are tied in second place with 11 percent. North Dakota is next with seven percent, an amazing figure, since it has a total population of less than 700,000. Others in the top ten are Colorado, six percent; Illinois, four percent; and California, Oregon and Wisconsin, each with three percent.

Winter visitors don't just come for suntans and golf. Three out of four of Arizona's Cactus League Baseball ticket buyers are from out of state (although not all are long-term winter visitors). Two-thirds of these fans say they head south *specifically* for spring hardball. (See Cactus League box in Chapter three.)

For those interested in finding winter apartments and condos, Tucson, Phoenix and a few other cities list short-term lodgings in their accommodations guides.

Most Arizona RV parks offer special rates for long-term visitors. Many of these parks are elaborate resorts with swimming pools, golf courses, marinas, recreation centers, social programs, group outings and other amenities.

A chill in the air?

Incidentally, whether you plan to winter in Arizona for two weeks or six months, remember to bring your sweater—perhaps even a down jacket. Compared with Bismark, North Dakota, and Edmonton, Ontario, much of Arizona is a balmy winter paradise. However, nighttime temperatures sometimes dip to freezing in the Phoenix and Tucson areas. Days generally are in the 60s, often climbing into the 70s. Tucson is more than a thousand feet higher than Phoenix and therefore slightly cooler the year around.

If you require toastier winter nights, the Colorado River corridor is warmer than the higher desert interior. Bullhead City, for instance, boasts an average low of just 37 degrees and a high of 80 in January. Yuma, Parker and Bullhead often report the nation's highest temperatures, both in winter and summer.

Although higher elevation places such as Flagstaff, Sedona, Prescott and the mountain regions northeast of Phoenix attract many year-around retirees, few Snowbirds choose to fly to these areas. Therefore, our list of recommended roosts is focused on cactus country. Colorado River towns offer a plenitude of RV and mobile home parks, while their selection of condo and apartment rentals is rather limited. So if you want a solid roof over your winter roost, you'll find a much better selection in the Valley of the Sun and Tucson.

THE BEST SNOWBIRD ROOSTS

Our list ranges from cosmopolitan Phoenix to dusty Quartzsite, and it includes some sun-country places you may not be aware of. Some of our selections also are suggested as retirement towns in the previous chapter, so expect to trip over some repetitions.

To learn more about these cities, towns and villages, move along to Part Two of this book. We discuss population growth, advantages and disadvantages, summer-winter climate and many other essentials.

CENTRAL ARIZONA

As we said in the last chapter, central Arizona is the state's beating heart—its business, social and population hub. You can winter in the busy Valley of the Sun or park on the fringes to stay away from the crowds. If we had a choice, we'd probably pick our first listing—Apache Junction; Carefree and Cave Creek would be close seconds.

Apache Junction • Forty miles southeast of Phoenix in the Superstition Mountain foothills, Apache Junction is popular with winter visitors as well as permanent retirees. With more than a hundred RV parks and resorts, this town of 20,000 people draws double that in winter visitors. We particularly like its setting in a handsomely rugged desert. It's a short drive to Salt River Canyon, whose reservoirs offer a bit of aquatic recreation. Pine-clad mountains are just beyond. And Phoenix is less than an hour's drive in the other direction. *For information: Apache Junction Chamber of Commerce, P.O. Box 1747, Apache Junction, AZ 85217; (520) 982-3141.*

Cave Creek and Carefree • These hamlets with a combined population of about 5,000 are 25 miles north of Phoenix. Cave Creek is a deliberately rustic Western style town; the planned community of Carefree is more contemporary. The only disadvantage for Snowbirds is that the area has a limited number of RV parks and winter apartments. However, some are a-building. If you want a Carefree (sorry about that) or Cave Creek winter vacation, you'd better book up early. *For information: Carefree/Cave Creek Chamber of Commerce, 748 Easy St. (P.O. Box 734), Carefree, AZ 85377; (602) 488-3381.*

Casa Grande • Midway between Phoenix and Tucson, this town of 21,000 doesn't attract a big winter flock. It's in a farm belt and the area can get a bit windy. However, if you'd like to be within an hour's

El Pedrigal Marketplace between Scottsdale and Carefree is one of Arizona's more curious architectural creations.

drive of both major urban centers, you might check it out. Winters are temperate with warm days and cool to chilly evenings. A few RV parks are in the area and more are being built. *For information: Greater Casa Grande Chamber of Commerce, 575 N. Marshall, Casa Grande, AZ 85222; (520) 836-2125.*

Mesa-Tempe ● In the southeastern part of the Valley of the Sun, the large communities of Mesa and Tempe offer all your basic needs, with a combined population of nearly half a million. Access to next-door Phoenix and Scottsdale is easy and the towns have their own cultural lures as well. Both offer fine museums and Tempe is home to Arizona State University. They're primarily year-around residential communities although they do have several RV parks and resorts. Apartments may be a bit scarce because of the presence of ASU; all those students need winter roosts, too. *For information: Mesa Convention & Visitors Bureau, 120 N. Center St., Mesa, AZ 85201; (602) 969-1307; and Tempe Chamber of Commerce, 60 E. Fifth St., Suite 3, Tempe, AZ 85281; (602) 894-8158.*

Phoenix-Scottsdale ● You say you want to be in the middle of the action, with a great choice of cultural offerings, shopping, restaurants and classy resorts? Phoenix and Scottsdale *are* the Valley of the Sun, containing most of its population and its finest resorts. Most of the RV parks are on the outskirts, while apartment and condo rentals are scattered throughout the area. The Yellow Pages can help you find a place to roost. If you're a pre-season baseball fan, fly no further. Several Cactus League clubs conduct spring training in and about Phoenix. Ironically, the Phoenix expansion team, the Arizona Diamondbacks does its training elsewhere. Expect Phoenix-Scottsdale accommodations to be on the pricey side, compared with much of the rest of Arizona. *For in-*

formation: Phoenix-Valley of the Sun Convention and Visitors Bureau, 400 E. Van Buren, Suite 600, Phoenix, AZ 85073; (602) 262-7176; and Scottsdale Chamber of Commerce, 7343 Scottsdale Mall, Scottsdale, AZ 85251; (602) 945-8481.

COLORADO RIVER CORRIDOR

If you love water sports and balmy January nights, head for the river. Although the mighty Colorado has its roots in the 10,000-foot ramparts of the Rocky Mountains, it has dropped to nearly sea level by the time it reaches the Arizona-Nevada-California border. This is the warmest part of Arizona—too hot for some in summer but great for just about everyone in winter.

Bullhead City • Fast growing Bullhead offers toasty winter climate and less than four inches of rain a year. An added bonus is the busy Nevada casino town of Laughlin just across the water. In fact, free shuttles are available to hurry gamblers over from Bullhead City parking lots. Bullhead isn't attractive. It's a poorly planned and hastily assembled town of 29,000 residents, scattered along a dozen miles of Lake Mojave shoreline. However, it offers an abundance of water recreation. Dozens of RV parks rim the river, mostly on the Arizona side, with a few on the Nevada shore. *For information: Bullhead Area Chamber of Commerce, 1251 Highway 95, Bullhead City, AZ 86430; (520) 754-4121.*

Lake Havasu City • The home of the displaced London Bridge is the first and still the largest of the Colorado River's planned winter resort communities, with a population of 36,285. Adjacent Lake Havasu offers an aquatic bounty. Many RV parks are in the area, including a full service resort on Lake Havasu Peninsula. *For information: Lake Havasu Area Chamber of Commerce, 1930 Mesquite Ave., Suite 3, Lake Havasu City, AZ 86403; (800) 242-8278 or (520) 453-3444.*

Lake Mead National Recreation Area • This isn't a community in the normal sense; it's a federal recreation area covering Arizona and Nevada shorelines of Lake Mead and Lake Mohave. If you're a water sports buff, this is the place; Lake Mead is America's largest reservoir. For those impressed by statistics, Mead and Mohave combined have more total shoreline miles than California.

There's no town on the Arizona side of the lake, although Boulder City, Nevada (population 14,000), offers all the essentials. It's an attractive community laid out in the 1930s as the construction town for Hoover Dam, and its downtown area has been preserved as an Art Deco historic site. Curiously, Boulder City is the only town in Nevada that prohibits gambling. However, there are plenty of casinos nearby, including one between Boulder City and the Arizona border. Las Vegas is a mere 30 miles away. Lake Mead NRA is primarily RV country, unless you want to check into a motel room or resort for the winter. Nine marinas occupy Lake Mead and Lake Mojave shorelines. Most have

NRA-operated campgrounds, plus RV parks with long-term rental spaces. Some offer lodge resorts as well. In addition, there are several motels in Boulder City. Incidentally, RV facilities book up very early in the winter season, so act accordingly. The climate at lakeside is similar to Bullhead City. Winters are warm and dry with cool evenings, and rainfall is less than four inches a year; most falls in summer. *For information: Lake Mead National Recreation Area, 601 Nevada Highway, Boulder City, NV 89005; (702) 293-2034 and Boulder City Chamber of Commerce, 1305 Arizona St., Boulder City, NV 89005; (702) 293-2034.*

Parker ● Surrounded by the Colorado River Indian Reservation, Parker is a friendly mix of Native Americans and the rest of us Americans. It has a quiet, small-town aura, with a population around 3,000. While not a fancy resort town, it's one of the least expensive places on the river. The area offers a huge selection of RV parking spaces. The 20-mile "Parker Strip" between the town and Parker Dam to the north is practically wall-to-wall rec vehicle parks and resorts. They line both the Arizona and California shores. *For information: Parker Area Chamber of Commerce, P.O. Box 627, Parker, AZ 85344; (520) 669-2174.*

Quartzsite ● This curious settlement is 21 miles east of the Colorado River, on Interstate 10. The good news is that it has the cheapest RV parks in the state—probably in the country. The bad news is that it's hound-dog homely. Quartzsite is a scraped-away patch of desert that has become one huge RV facility. Permanent dwellings are limited to a few houses, service stations, cafés and stores. Thousands of temporary shops are set up in tents during huge annual swap meets held from late January into February. They lure the world's largest gathering of RVers, swelling the town's population from 2,000 to several hundred thousand. The nearest normal community is Blythe, California, 25 miles west. *For information: Quartzsite Chamber of Commerce, P.O. Box 85, Quartzsite, AZ 85346, (520) 927-5600.*

Yuma ● Snowbirds nearly double Yuma's population of 60,475 each winter. It's not a fancy resort town, but more of a Main Street USA that happens to sit in the middle of the desert. The town is rich in history, occupying the site of Yuma Crossing, on the first cross-country trail to California. The area is being developed as a historical park. The southernmost of the Colorado River corridor towns, Yuma also is the driest, with an annual rainfall of less than three inches. Although it rims the river, most of its RV resorts are inland, along I-8 to the east. Others are across the stream, in Winterhaven, California. *For information: Yuma County Chamber of Commerce, P.O. Box 10230 (377 S. Main St.), Yuma, AZ 85366-8230; (520) 783-2567.*

SOUTHERN ARIZONA

Tucson and the area south to Nogales offer fine Snowbird climes. We also recommend Sierra Vista, a bit farther east. It's located in a rather interesting area, often overlooked by Arizona visitors:

Sierra Vista • This sprawling yet well-planned community of 38,000 is an appealing winter roost if you don't mind chilly evenings. January nights can get frosty and you may get a rare dusting of snow. We like its location in Arizona's "Cowboy Corner," near historic sites such as Tombstone, Fort Huachuca and Chiricahua National Monument. Several mountain wilderness areas are nearby. Tucson is but 70 miles away, and the Mexican border is close as well. Seasonal apartments are scarce; most winter accommodations are in RV parks, which are rather inexpensive. Several are concentrated in nearby Huachuca City, which is a bit on the scruffy side. *For information: Sierra Vista Chamber of Commerce, 21 E. Wilcox Dr., Sierra Vista, AZ 85635; (800) 288-3861 or (520) 458-6940.*

Tubac • A bit warmer than Sierra Vista, Tubac is a tiny, weather-worn art colony about 40 miles south of Tucson. It's rich in history as Arizona's oldest non-Indian settlement. Assuming you like historic-artistic funk, Tubac has only one major drawback for potential Snowbirders. Its winter visitor facilities are minimal. There are a few RV parks in the surrounding area; apartment/condo rentals are rare. *For information: Tubac Chamber of Commerce, P.O. Box 1866, Tubac, AZ 85646; (520) 398-2704.*

Tucson • With fine cultural offerings, good restaurants, desert gardens, excellent museums and galleries, Tucson is a great Snowbird roost. Think of it as a flat San Francisco with warm sunshine. It offers a good assortment of RV parks and resorts, winter apartments and condos. Another plus: Arizona's best Mexican bordertown shopping is just 63 miles south, in Nogales. Tucson is cooler than the Colorado River corridor; January nights can be chilly although the average daytime high is a pleasant 66. *For information: Tucson Convention and Visitors Bureau, 130 S. Scott Ave., Tucson, AZ 85701; (800) 638-8350 or (520) 624-1817.*

JOINING THE RV CLAN?

If retirement is just down the road, you may be considering the purchase of a travel trailer, fifth-wheel unit or motorhome. They're a great boon to Snowbirds, offering most of the comforts of home in a more or less portable package.

Virtually every sunbelt chamber of commerce has lists of RV parks and mobile home resorts that cater to long-term visitors. Incidentally, the best place to find RV park and campground guidebooks is in rec vehicle and camper supply stores, not in book stores.

The *Arizona Travel Planner* published by the state's tourist office lists scores of RV parks. For a free copy, contact the **Arizona Office of Tourism,** 1100 W. Washington St., Phoenix, AZ 85007; (800) 842-8257 or (602) 542-TOUR.

The **American Automobile Association** lists assorted Arizona campgrounds and RV parks in its *Southwestern CampBook.* Woodalls

North American Campground Directory and Trailer Life's *Campground/RV Park Directory* are thick, comprehensive guides listing camping facilities in Arizona and elsewhere. Also useful is the Trailer Life book, *RVing America's Backroads: Arizona.* It's not a campground directory but a full-color hard cover travel guide. The text is tilted toward the RV set, with travel tips, attractions, activities and maps of suggested tours.

You probably know that mobile home parks are set up primarily for permanently parked units while RV parks are more for short-term visitors. In Arizona, however, both types often make exceptions to accommodate RVers and trailer-travelers for the winter. Many are combined mobile home and RV parks.

IMPORTANT: Many RV parks with long-term rates—particularly those near metropolitan areas—book up early for winter, so make your plans as soon as possible.

If you intend to be a somewhat mobile Snowbirder, you might pick a copy of our *Arizona Discovery Guide,* a comprehensive statewide guidebook with a strong focus on RV travel. It lists scores of campgrounds and RV parks and special "RV Advisories" point out road conditions and help RVers find parking places in congested areas. It's available in book stores, or it can be ordered directly from the publisher. See details in the back of this book.

TYPES OF REV VEHICLES

We've had considerable experience with RV living, since we use a 21-foot "Minnie-Winnie" named *Ickybod* to research our travel guides. Of course, *Ick* would be a bit snug for your four to six month stay under the Arizona sun. You'll likely want something more roomy.

Rec vehicles come in seven basic types and we'll review each to help you make your choice. A major consideration is mobility once you get to your Snowbird roost. Some folks tow a "tag-along" vehicle that becomes their runabout after they're parked at an RV park. Others lean toward travel trailers or fifth-wheel units so they can use the towing rig to get about.

If you plan to buy a tag-along, check with the car dealer about its tow-ability. Some vehicles' drive trains are lubricated only when the engine is running. A solution is to get a two-wheel towing dolly that keeps the drive wheels off the ground.

IMPORTANT: Most states, including Arizona, require that occupants wear safety belts whenever the vehicle is in motion, and this includes RVs. A belted seating position must be available for every occupant. It's legal in most states to ride in the back of a motorhome, fifth-wheel or camper if belts are available, but not in a towed travel trailer. Obviously, it's unsafe to be unbelted in any vehicle, and particularly to be moving about in an RV that's underway.

Now, a review of your RV choices:

Pickup-mounted campers

This was America's original mass produced motor home—a housing shell mounted on a pickup or truck bed.

Advantages • Obviously, it's your best buy if you already own a pickup. Some camper units are equipped with jacks so you can drive out from under the shell and have use of your vehicle. (However, the support legs on most aren't very substantial; they're designed mostly for shedding and storing the camper shell at home.) Today's fancy pickups come with all the trimmings and are fairly easy to handle. They have a reasonably short wheelbase and they aren't too difficult to park.

Disadvantages • You can't move between the driving and passenger compartment without stopping, although emergency access is now required on campers sold in most states. Campers have a rather high center of gravity and tend to be unstable in winds. Also, most are a bit small for long-term residence.

Motorhomes

These are built from the wheels up, onto a ready-made chassis. Most have long rear overhangs to provide more interior room on a relatively short wheelbase.

Advantages • Motorhomes are the vehicles of choice for most Snowbirds and other RVers. They come in all sizes from little 18-footers to 50-foot castles on wheels with all the amenities. They offer direct access between the driving and living area. They're easy to set up and most are self-contained. Pull up and park, and you're home.

Disadvantages • The larger and more comfortable they are, the more difficult they are to maneuver. Of course, they have power steering and brakes and the better ones have adequate horsepower. Still, the long wheelbase makes them tricky to maneuver. And forget about parallel parking! Because of long rear overhangs, the driver has to be careful not to swat a sign or passer-by when making a tight turn. Motorhomes generally are the most expensive RV rigs, foot for foot.

Chassis mount

They're similar to motorhomes, although the unit is built onto the body of a van or pickup, utilizing the original cab.

Advantages • They're usually less expensive than a motorhome, since the builder buys mass-produced chassis-cab units. Otherwise, they offer the same advantages.

Disadvantage • The van wheelbase limits their size, and some of the larger rigs have ridiculously long rear overhangs, increasing the risk of slapping something in a tight turn.

Travel trailers

These are the oldest RVs, tracing their ancestry back hundreds of years to horse-drawn gypsy carts and shepherd wagons.

Advantages ● If you like to nest in the same place all winter, travel trailers may be your best bet. They're much less expensive, since you aren't buying a motor vehicle, and they generally offer more room per lineal foot. And of course, you have your towing rig free once you get settled in.

Disadvantages ● Speed limit is 55 miles per hour for towed vehicles in most states. Also, most states prohibit carrying passengers in trailers. The rigs tend to be unstable in high crosswinds and winding roads. Your ride up front will be rougher, since the hitch telegraphs bumps to the towing vehicle. Finally, they're really tough to park.

Fifth-wheel unit

This is a hybrid between a travel trailer and a camper. The rig is attached to a special hitch mounted in the bed of a pickup. Fifth-wheelers cost about the same, foot-per-foot, as a travel trailer.

Advantages ● They're more stable than a travel trailer and some states allow belted passengers to ride in them. They're easy to unhook and set up at a campground, although perhaps not quite as easy as a travel trailer. You can get very large rigs with all of the comforts, providing you have a pickup hefty enough to pull it. Fifth-wheelers are easier to maneuver than trailers.

Disadvantages ● Once you've parked the rig, you're stuck with a truck for transportation. Also, fifth-wheelers share a trailer's disadvantages in maneuvering and parking.

Tent trailers

If you're on a tight budget, or if you have a light-duty towing vehicle, folding tent trailers may be the way to go.

Advantages ● They're a cut above a tent, and relatively cheap. Some of the better tent trailers even have bathrooms and showers, plus full kitchens. They tow much easier than travel trailers. Their compact, fold-down design offers little wind resistance and the lower ones don't block your rear vision.

Disadvantages ● They offer little insulation from temperature and campground noises. Although they're *relatively* easy to set up, all other types of RVs are easier.

Van conversion

This is similar to a chassis mount, except that the living area is built into the original body shell of the van.

Advantages ● They're small enough to maneuver and park in town. We researched our earlier guidebooks in the original *Ickybod*, a Volkswagen pop-top, and really appreciated its maneuverability. Van conversions get better gas mileage than bigger rigs. Pop-top versions are reasonably comfortable, once you get settled in a campground.

Disadvantages ● Face it, folks. Do you want to live for several months in a van without an onboard pottie or full kitchen? (Some have tiny bathrooms, although that sacrifices what little storage space is available.) Vans have limited living space and the bed has to be put up or folded away every day. They're not practical for long-term use, except for a person who doesn't mind padding to a campground pottie.

TRAILER REGULATIONS

All rec vehicles require special handling skills, particularly trailers and fifth-wheel units. Because of the inherent instability of towed vehicles, most states have special laws governing them. They are fairly uniform from state to state and usually include these requirements:

• Safety chains are mandatory. They should be long enough to permit turning, yet short enough to keep the trailer tongue from digging into the ground if the hitch fails.

• Passengers aren't allowed to ride in travel trailers in most states.

• Size limits vary from state to state. In Arizona, a trailer can't be more than 40 feet long, eight feet wide and 13.5 feet high. Combined length of a trailer and towing vehicle can't exceed 65 feet.

• Outside mirrors are required on both sides of a towing vehicle if the trailer obstructs rear vision—which all but small tent trailers do.

• Towed rigs must have the same lighting system as any other vehicle—taillights, stoplights and turn indicators.

• Towing more than one vehicle, such as a travel trailer and a boat, is a no-no.

• The speed limit for towed vehicles is the same as for large trucks, which in most states is 55 mph.

• In Arizona, separate braking systems are required on trailers with a gross weight over 1,500 pounds. It varies from 1,500 to 3,000 pounds in other states. Trailer brakes are always a good idea, whether required or not. They help prevent jackknifing and they keep the trailer from shoving the towing vehicle ahead in a sudden stop.

HANDLE WITH CARE

Whether you're driving a motorhome or towing a trailer or fifth-wheel, follow these tips to ensure that your new home on the road stays there:

• If you're a first-timer, practice stopping and turning on familiar roads before you head out. An RV has a wider turning radius and most have long rear overhangs. They also have higher centers of gravity and they're sluggish in acceleration. Give yourself plenty of leeway when passing. RVs require longer stopping distances than cars, particularly trailers and fifth-wheel units. Incidentally, most states require all slow moving vehicles to pull over and let faster traffic pass, and many require that RVs and trailers stay to the outside lane of multiple lane highways and freeways, except when passing.

• Downshift when you're going downhill. The added weight will push you faster than you think.

• When you approach a speed bump, *crawl* over it. If you hit a speed bump at an angle, your land yacht will rock and pitch like a boat in a storm.

- **VERY IMPORTANT!** RV's behave very badly on muddy roads. Unlike cars and trucks, most of an RV's weight is over the rear wheels and this can act as a pendulum on a slippery surface. Dual rear wheels don't help much. You may be less likely to bog down in the mud with duals, but you'll fishtail very quickly on a slippery surface. As for snow and ice, you'd best stay in the RV park or campground until conditions improve.

- If you're pulling a heavy trailer, get a special towing package that includes a beefed-up rear suspension and load-leveler. Otherwise, the trailer tongue will push down on your vehicle's rear, making it less stable. Also, it can tilt your headlights into the eyes of oncoming drivers. Larger trailers should have independent braking systems to avoid jackknifing in a sudden stop; most states require them.

- Remember that your rear vision is restricted when you're driving an RV or pulling a trailer, and side-view mirrors usually have blind spots. (A combined regular and concave mirror will help solve this problem.) Signal well in advance and change lanes slowly, to give vehicles around you time to react.

- Don't overload your rig. Water and fuel weigh about eight pounds per gallon, adding hundreds of pounds to the vehicle weight. Check with the dealer for the gross vehicle weight rating, which is the maximum allowable load, including people and cargo. If you exceed this, lots of things can happen and they're all bad. You may have a blowout; your rig may lurch drunkenly on curves and accelerate on downgrades; and you won't have adequate pickup for safe passing.

- Balance your load and keep your RV's center of gravity as low as possible. Don't put heavy objects in higher cabinets or cab-over bunks.

- Be very careful of fire! Check all gas fittings and carry dry chemical extinguishers. Bear in mind that you're traveling with several gallons of Propane and gasoline. Check evacuation routes. RVs are required to have at least two exits. One may be a break-away window, so learn where it is.

- Don't give your RV and headache. The average car is just over four feet high but most RVs top out at seven feet or more.

- Keep an eye on your tail. Most RVs have long rear overhangs, and it's easy to swat something on a tight turn, or back into an object that's closer than it appears in your mirrors. Also, the distance between your rear view mirror and rear window creates a tunnel vision effect; you usually can't see a vehicle that's riding on your tail. To correct this problem, install one of those fish-eye lenses on the rear window.

- If your rig has dual wheels, periodically check the air pressure of both the inner and outer tires by pressing your thumb hard into the sidewalls. You can't always tell by the tire profile if one has gone flat, since one holds the other up. It's extremely dangerous to travel at high speeds if both duals aren't sharing the load. Also, remember that RV tires are rated to carry more air than passenger car tires; keep them at the proper pressure.

● Finally—and this is for courtesy as well as safety—stay in the right hand lane except to pass. On two-lane roads, pull over whenever possible to let faster traffic go by. An RV's width makes it difficult for those behind to see oncoming vehicles. Further, motorists following too closely may not realize that you can't see them in your side view mirrors or through your rear window.

Nothing is more exasperating than trundling behind a big motor-home or trailer rig on a two-lane highway. Drivers *do not* have the right to arbitrarily set speed limits for those behind them by poking along. And no, we're not amused by those bumper stickers that read: "I may be slow, but I'm ahead of you."

Don't force an impatient motorist into an unsafe pass. You may be the first at the scene of the accident—as a participant.

RV SUPPORT GROUPS

When you join the RV set, you join a fraternity that has its own jamborees, caravans and clubs. You'll find that its members are a gregarious lot, quick to share information, opinions, advice, assistance and friendship. Making friends at an RV park or campground is easy; just stop by and borrow a cup of coffee. Many RV parks, particularly those catering to long-term visitors, sponsor dances and other social functions.

Incidentally, we encountered a discomforting statistic a few years ago: Ninety-six percent of all RVers are couples. The vast majority of those who have lost a mate or are single apparently stay at home. That's a shame. If you're single or widowed, don't be shy about hitting the road alone. Many second-time-around romances and good friendships have bloomed over a campground barbecue pit or bingo party.

Some rec vehicle makers, such as Airstream, promote social programs and RV gatherings for their vehicle owners. Camping groups such as Thousand Trails do the same.

A particularly useful organization for Snowbirds is the **Good Sam Club,** operated by TL Enterprises. A modest annual membership fee provides a ten percent discount on Good Sam-rated RV parks, plus free trip routing service, and a newsletter that lists upcoming caravans, camporees and other news of the RV world. Other services include RV insurance and towing, a travel agency, and mail forwarding and messenger service (for a fee). Thick directories listing Good Sam member and non-member RV parks and campgrounds can be purchased. For information, contact: Good Sam Club, 3601 Calle Tecate, Camarillo, CA 93012-5040, (800) 234-3450.

If all this sounds like a paid commercial, it isn't. Sam probably doesn't even know that he's getting a free plug. As a matter of fact, we aren't Good Sam members because many participating RV parks won't extend the ten percent discount if you pay by credit card. Since we're often on the road for months at a time, we don't want to carry a pocket full of cash, so Sam isn't as useful as he might be.

PART TWO
THE COMMUNITIES

We've already touched on several communities that offer good job prospects, retirement opportunities or winter roosts. What follows is a more detailed look at the state's cities and towns. We don't attempt to cover every hamlet. We review only those which we feel offer potential—and appeal—for those contemplating Arizona in their future.

In the lists that follow, property taxes were supplied by the Arizona Department of Commerce or by individual communities. Population figures are the most recent we could find, from the last census or from community estimates.

ARIZONA'S COUNTIES

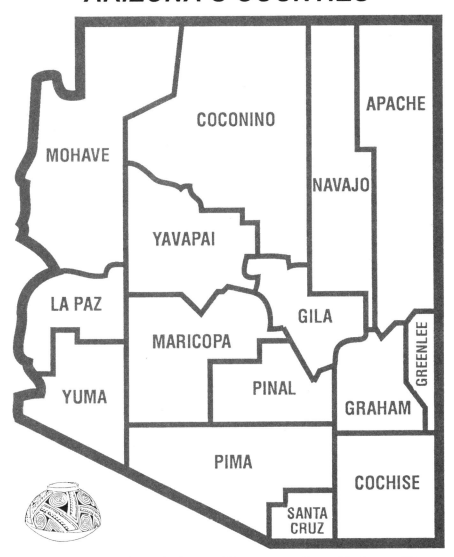

Arizona's population is focused in two counties—Maricopa (Phoenix) and Pima (Tucson). More than two-thirds of the state's residents live in one or the other. Both counties also have extensive wilderness areas. Phoenix in Maricopa County is surrounded by rugged mountains, and Pima County stretches west across untracked desert, nearly reaching the California border. Huge Coconino County, covering 18,629 square miles, embraces much of the Grand Canyon and the ponderosa uplands above the Mogollon Rim. Its seat is Flagstaff, the largest community in northwestern Arizona, with 43,780 residents.

Chapter eight

THE WESTERN EDGE
THE COLORADO RIVER CORRIDOR

This section covers communities bordering on the Colorado River, that watery divide between Arizona, Nevada and California. We also mention two towns that are a few miles inland.

Rio Colorado isn't really a river in this area, however. With seven dams between the Grand Canyon and the Mexican border, it's more of a chain of lakes. These reservoirs may disturb environmentalists, although they provide unlimited water recreation, and that's one of the area's chief lures.

THE WAY IT WAS ● The Colorado is one of the most harnessed and harassed rivers in the world. Indeed, its much-diverted muddy water is the lifeblood of southwestern Arizona and much of southern California and Nevada.

It ran wild and free for untold centuries, carving the majestic Grand Canyon above and carrying rich red soil into the Gulf of California. Like all wild things, *Rio Colorado* was unpredictable. For centuries, Native Americans tried to farm along its rich bottomlands, only to be flooded out one year and wilted by drought the next.

European and American explorers began coming upriver from the Gulf of California in the early 1800s; others passed this way overland during the 1849 California gold rush. Some chose to stay; they pushed the native inhabitants off their land and took up farming. Suffering

Wedged into rugged Black Canyon, Hoover Dam put the mighty Colorado into harness and quickly became—from the ground and from the air—a major tourist attraction

from the same water flow frustrations as their predecessors, these newcomers decided that the great river needed to be put into harness.

The first efforts came in 1901, when water was diverted into the Imperial Canal near Yuma to irrigate the dry but rich soils of California's Imperial Valley. However, the river didn't take to harness easily. A flood breached the canal in 1905 and the wild river changed course. For 16 months it flowed unchecked into the Salton Basin, which was 235 feet below sea level. By the time the breach finally was closed in 1907, the Salton Basin had become the 40-mile-long Salton Sea, which still exists.

Men were more determined than ever to control Big Red. In 1909, the Laguna Dam was completed just north of Yuma. It provided desert irrigation, and it also brought an end to river navigation. Until this time, paddlewheelers had chugged as much as 300 miles upstream from the Gulf of California to serve riverside communities.

No more river mischief

Laguna Dam was too far downstream for effective flood control, and spring thaws continued bringing muddy overflows. To put an end to *Rio Colorado's* mischief, the U.S. Bureau of Reclamation launched history's most challenging dam project, in the narrow and rocky walls of Black Canyon. In 1935, the completion of Hoover Dam—the world's highest—marked the end of the free-flowing Colorado.

Meanwhile, in another time and place, air conditioning was being perfected. In 1906, Willis S. Carrier of Buffalo, New York, developed a "dew-point control air washer," passing air through water-cooled pipes. Better refrigerants were developed in the 1920s and the true air conditioner was born. The first public use of air conditioning was in a movie theater in 1922. By the 1930s, small and relatively efficient units were being produced.

In Arizona, they couldn't have come at a better time.

THE WAY IT IS ● Air conditioners and reservoirs have spawned a string of skinny communities along the banks of the Colorado River. They stretch from Hoover Dam south to Yuma and into Mexico.

Most of the riverside towns are unplanned and not very pretty. The subtle beauty of the desert suffers under the weight of asphalt and the glare of neon. These towns are lively places, however, where glossy speedboats skim over placid reservoirs and retirees live out their American dream of a winter place in the sun.

The corridor isn't strictly for Snowbirds. Thousands of folks crank up their air conditioners and live here the year-around. However, the area is much more popular with winter visitors. Yuma, the largest of the river towns, nearly doubles its population in winter, and scruffy little Quartzsite balloons from a couple of thousand to about 200,000. If you plan to settle permanently along Arizona's western edge, stay close to your air conditioner in July, when the average daytime high is around 108!

BULLHEAD CITY

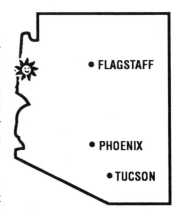

Named for a promontory now submerged into Lake Mohave, Bullhead City sits just above the triangle where the Arizona, Nevada and California borders merge. It's a low-rise scatter of housing tracts, modular homes and mobile home parks. This sun-warmed jumble of hasty settlement is the most northernof the string of towns along *Rio Colorado's* Arizona shorelines.

South along State Route 95, the unincorporated communities of Riviera, Fort Mohave and Golden Shores stretch Bullhead's outskirts to Interstate 40. Much of this area is within the Fort Mohave Indian Reservation.

Bullhead City wasn't incorporated until 1984, although its roots go back to 1945, when it was the construction camp for Davis Dam, immediately to the north. A mere 504 feet above sea level, it often earns the dubious honor as America's summer hot spot. Tourist officials wish people wouldn't talk about that, of course. In winter, thousands of

Snowbirds triple the town's population. About 20 RV and mobile home parks and resorts line the river's shores.

Across the reservoir, Laughlin, Nevada, is another reason for Bullhead's popularity. Back in 1966, entrepreneur Don Laughlin guessed that winter vacationers might like to pass the time pulling a few slot machine handles. He bought a broken-down bait shop and six acres of riverfront and built a small gambling parlor. His Riverside Casino prospered and expanded; more followed and a sudden city blossomed in the desert. Laughlin immodestly named it for himself.

Nearly a dozen gaming halls now line the Nevada side, beguiling Bullhead folks with the seductive glitter of neon. To make things easier, large parking lots have been paved at Bullhead City's north end, where launches provide free casino shuttles.

Elevation ● 504 feet

Location ● In Mohave County on State Route 95.

Climate ● Warm, dry winters with cool evenings; hot, dry summers. July average high is 108.2, low is 79.1; January average high is 62.2, low 41.8. Annual rainfall 4.19 inches; no snowfall.

Population ● 26,940

Population trend ● Gained 22 percent in the past five years.

Property tax ● (assessed at ten percent of real value) $11.74 per $100 assessed valuation.

Economy ● Tourism fuels Bullhead's economic fires, and of course Snowbirds bring their retirement checks. Booming Laughlin employs more than 10,000 people. The Mohave Generating Station, a cooperative of four utilities, also is a major employer.

Job prospects ● The services sector, including tourism, employs nearly 40 percent of Bullhead's work force, and much of that commutes to Laughlin. (There's a bridge as well as river shuttles.) Retail trade is second with 20 percent and construction is third with 14 percent. Job prospects, according to the chamber of commerce, are about average.

Industrial facilities ● A 190-acre industrial park near the airport.

Real estate ● The area has several planned subdivisions with amenities such as pools and tennis courts, along with conventional homes and a few condos. A typical new three-bedroom home averages about $105,000. Much of Bullhead's housing, both permanent and temporary, is in mobile home parks.

The media ● Three newspapers—the tri-weekly *Mohave Valley News*, bi-weekly *Booster/Laughlin Leader* and the weekly *Laughlin Gambler-Bullhead City Bee*. One TV station, plus a cable company.

Medical services ● A 68-bed hospital, a 120-bed extended care facility and a mental health clinic.

Transportation ● Served by Greyhound. Bullhead City Airport has a 5,000 foot runway and scheduled flights by feeder lines.

Education ● Bullhead City campus of Mohave Community College, plus elementary, intermediate and high schools.

Local government ● Incorporated in 1984; mayor, six council members and a city manager.

Places to stay ● Twenty-five motels, 21 RV parks and nine mobile home parks.

Leisure facilities ● Three public parks, one 18-hole and four nine-hole golf courses.

Tourist lures ● The biggest lure, of course, is Lake Mohave, offering assorted water sports. Laughlin's gaming parlors are another major draw. The Black Mountains to the east provide outdoor pursuits such as hiking, picnicking and off-road vehicle areas. The historic mining towns of Oatman and Goldroad are just to the east.

Contacts ● Bullhead Area Chamber of Commerce, 1251 Highway 95, Bullhead City, AZ 86430; (520) 754-4121.

Bullhead City Economic Development Authority, P.O. Box 21179, Bullhead City, AZ 86439; (520) 763-9400.

KINGMAN

This community of more than 32,000 occupies a ruggedly attractive valley of eroded buttes and cliffs at the junction of I-40 and U.S. Highway 93. Dating from 1882, it was named for surveyor Lewis Kingman, who was plotting a rail route between Needles, California, and Albuquerque, New Mexico. However, it was silver and copper discoveries in the surrounding hills that kept the town on the map.

Mining declined during the 1930s and was virtually shut down as a non-essential industry during World War II. The surrounding countryside is dotted with ghost towns and semi-ghost towns worthy of exploring. They include Chloride, Cerbat, Mineral Park, Goldroad, Old Trails and Oatman.

While those towns withered, Kingman survived as a provisioning center for travelers on the Santa Fe Railway and historic U.S. Highway 66. The first path through here dates back to 1859, when Army Lieutenant Edward Beal's construction crew carved a wagon road that eventually led from Arkansas to Los Angeles. It was the first federally funded road in the Southwest. Old Route 66 roughly follows its course, although it eventually veers northeast to Chicago.

Kingman is still an important crossroad and a popular pausing place for motorists hurrying along I-40. The Economic and Development Commission has been successful in attracting light industry and warehousing operations, and the town has seen a population jump of nearly 30 percent in the past decade. Incidentally, the town's favorite son isn't surveyor Kingman. It's the late, gravel-voiced actor Andy Devine, who was born in nearby Flagstaff and grew up here. The main street is named for him, and he's featured in a special exhibit at the local museum. The turn-of-the-century downtown looks a bit sleepy these days, since most of the business has shifted to suburban shopping centers.

Elevation ● 3,225 feet

Location ● In Mohave County on I-40, about 50 miles northeast of the Colorado River.

Climate ● More temperate in summer than the river towns because of its higher elevation. July average high 97.4, low 67.2; January average high 55.3, low 31.4. Rainfall 9.35 inches; snowfall 3.4 inches.

Population ● 32,482, with a similar number in surrounding unincorporated areas.

Population trend ● Gained nearly 30 percent in the past five years.

Property tax ● (assessed at ten percent of real value) $11.83 per $100 assessed valuation.

Economy ● Kingman is the regional trade center for northwestern Arizona. With I-40 and the Santa Fe railway passing through town, it's an important warehousing and distribution area. An airport industrial park has attracted some light manufacturing.

Job prospects ● Fairly good, according to the Economic Development Commission. Kingman has been very successful in job creation in the manufacturing and distribution business, because of its key location and transportation infrastructure. The best prospects are in manufacturing, warehousing, retail sales, tourism and related services. More than one job in four is in wholesale and retail trade, with a similar number in the services sector.

Industrial facilities ● Kingman Airport Industrial Park with 4,000 acres, plus various other industrial and warehousing sites.

Real estate ● The housing market includes a mix of older homes and a few subdivisions, with the average price of a three-bedroom detached home around $70,000.

The media ● One daily newspaper, *The Mohave County Miner* and a weekly, the *Kingman Booster*. One local TV station plus feeds from Phoenix and Las Vegas; also a cable service.

Medical services ● An 83-bed regional hospital, one medical clinic, a mental health clinic, a spinal rehabilitation center and two nursing homes.

Transportation ● Served by Greyhound, Las Vegas-Tonopah-Reno Stage (bus) and Amtrak. Kingman Airport has two 6,800-foot lighted runways, with scheduled air service.

Education ● Mojave Community College, plus elementary, junior high and high schools.

Local government • Seat of Mohave County since 1887. Incorporated in 1952; mayor, six council members and a city manager.

Places to stay • More than 30 motels and several RV parks.

Leisure facilities • Nine public parks, three aerobic centers, a senior center and Elderhostel facility, three public pools and two golf courses, plus tennis, racquetball and shuffleboard courts.

Tourist lures • Hualapai Mountain Park and the Cerbat Mountains offer picnicking, camping and hiking. A downtown historic district includes turn-of-the-century buildings, Locomotive Park, Historic Route 66 monuments and the excellent Mohave Museum of History and Arts.

Contacts • Kingman Area Chamber of Commerce, P.O. Box 1150 (333 W. Andy Devine Ave.), Kingman, AZ 86402; (520) 753-6106.

Economic & Tourism Development Commission, City of Kingman, 310 N. Fourth St., Kingman, AZ 86402; (520) 753-8130.

Kingman 2000 and Mohave County Airport Authority, 7000 Flightline Dr., Kingman, AZ 86402; (520) 757-2005.

LAKE HAVASU CITY

You've likely heard the story. The London Bridge, while not falling down, was too old and narrow to handle modern traffic, so city officials put it up for sale in 1968. They didn't really expect any buyers, but entrepreneur Robert P. McCulloch offered $2,460,000. He said he wanted to move it to the Arizona desert, where he'd purchased a piece of Lake Havasu shoreline.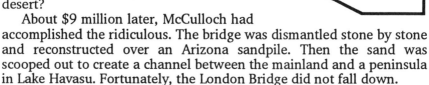

The London Bridge? In the Arizona desert?

About $9 million later, McCulloch had accomplished the ridiculous. The bridge was dismantled stone by stone and reconstructed over an Arizona sandpile. Then the sand was scooped out to create a channel between the mainland and a peninsula in Lake Havasu. Fortunately, the London Bridge did not fall down.

Voile! McCulloch had the centerpiece for his planned city in the desert. Incidentally, there were some bridge pieces left over, and you can buy them at local souvenir shops.

Lake Havasu City is the largest of the new communities along the Colorado River and the fastest growing, with a population increase of nearly 50 percent in the past five years. It's also the best planned. Local officials say "The Bridge" is Arizona's second most-visited attraction, after the Grand Canyon. An adjoining English Village offers such British lures as a London cab, double decker bus and even a proper pub. Much of it, however, is given over to tourist shops and fast food stands and not much of that is veddy British.

Elevation • 482 feet

Location • In Mohave County, 19 miles south of I-40 on State Highway 95.

Climate • Warm, dry winters with cool evenings, hot, dry summers. July average high 108.6, low 78.8; January average high 67.3, low 37.1. Rainfall 3.82 inches; no snowfall.

Population • 36,285

Population trend • Gained more than 40 percent in the past five years.

Property tax • (assessed at ten percent of real value) $9.56 per $100 assessed valuation.

Economy • Tourists and retirees are the main contributors to Havasu's economy. Officials estimate that "The Bridge" lures more than 35 million tourist dollars a year. Light manufacturing is gaining ground, particularly in a city-owned industrial park.

Job prospects • They're average, with rather low wages, according to the local Job Service office. Best possibilities are in light manufacturing, tourism and related service jobs.

Industrial facilities • One city-owned and one private industrial park.

Real estate • Planned subdivisions offer some of the best housing variety along the Colorado River. Prices for a three-bedroom home begin around $70,000.

The media • One daily newspaper, *Today's News Herald*; the area also is served by Kingman's daily *Mohave County Miner*. Two local TV stations and cable feeds of regional stations, plus a cable TV company.

Medical services • A 99-bed hospital and a 120-bed nursing home, plus several resident care and retirement homes.

Transportation • Served by Greyhound and shuttle vans to the Las Vegas airport; America West Express operates out of Lake Havasu Airport.

Education • Lake Havasu campus of Mohave Community College, with extension courses from Northern Arizona University, plus several elementary schools, a middle school and high school.

Local government • Incorporated in 1978; mayor, six council members and a city manager.

Places to stay • More than a score of motels and resort hotels, short-term apartment and condo rentals, several mobile home parks and campgrounds.

Leisure facilities • Four 18-hole golf courses, three public parks, several tennis courts, and swimming beaches on Lake Havasu.

Tourist lures • The bridge and its English Village are the main draws, of course. Water sports are popular and various watercraft rentals are available at the village. Lake Havasu State Park contains several beaches, camping and picnic areas.

Contacts • Lake Havasu Area Chamber of Commerce, 314 London Bridge Rd., Lake Havasu City, AZ 86403; (520) 855-4115.

Lake Havasu City Tourism Bureau, same address as above; (520) 453-3444.

Partnership for Economic Development, same address as above; (520) 505-7333.

PARKER

Parker is a folksy little riverside town surrounded by the Colorado River Indian Reservation. However, it's not exclusively an Indian community, but an affable ethnic mix of Native Americans and the rest of us Americans. The town was founded in 1908 and named in honor of Eli Parker, the first Native American to fight in the Spanish-American War.

While it's not a glamorous resort, Parker offers the advantage of inexpensive home prices and some of the cheapest RV parks in Arizona. In fact, it's the recreatonal vehicle capital of the Colorado River corridor.

The "Parker Strip" stretching ten miles north to Parker Dam is an almost continual swatch of RV parks, on both the Arizona and California shores. The reservoir here has a typical Native American name, Lake Moovalya. It's one of the busiest boating, water-skiing and fishing lakes on the river.

Elevation • 450 feet

Location • On State Route 95 in La Paz County, on Lake Moovalya, about midway between interstates 10 and 40.

Climate • Warm, dry winters with cool evenings; hot, dry summers. July average high 108.6, low 78.8; January average high 67.3, low 37.1. Rainfall 3.82 inches; no snowfall.

Population • 2,950

Population trend • Stable; gained less than a percentage point in the past five years.

Property tax • (assessed at ten percent of real value) $11.42 per $100 assessed valuation.

Economy • Like everything else in Parker, the economy is water oriented. Most of the area's income is derived from tourism, retail sales and retirees. A new Native American casino has added to the local economy.

Job prospects • It's not a good market for job hunters, since growth is rather stagnant. A third of the jobs are in tourism and another fifth are in retail trades.

Industrial facilities • A 100-acre industrial park, owned by the Colorado River Indian tribe.

Real estate • Home prices are a good buy and property taxes are among the lowest in the state. Figure on $50,000 to $60,000 for a three-bedroom house.

The media • One weekly newspaper, the *Parker Pioneer*. Two local TV stations, plus feeds from Yuma and Phoenix, and a cable TV company.

Medical services • One small hospital.

Transportation • Served by Greyhound. Avi-Suquilla Airport has a 4,800-foot lighted runway; no scheduled air service.

Education • Elementary and high schools; extension courses available from Yuma's Arizona Western College.

Local government • Incorporated in 1948; mayor, six council members and a city manager. Parker became the seat of La Paz County when it was separated from northern Yuma County in 1983.

Places to stay • About a score of motels, 49 mobile home and RV parks on the Arizona side and a similar number on the California shore.

Leisure facilities • Six parks, a public swimming pool, a senior citizens' center and an 18-hole golf course.

Tourist lures • Water sports abound, particularly along the Parker Strip. The Colorado River Tribes Indian Museum offers exhibits on Native American culture, plus a gift shop and library. Camping, boat launching, water sports and picnicking are available at Buckskin State Park, 11 miles north; and River Island State Park and La Paz County Park, eight miles north.

Contacts • Parker Area Chamber of Commerce, P.O. Box 627, (1217 California Ave.) Parker, AZ 85344; (520) 669-2174.

Town of Parker, P.O. Box 6509, (1314 11th St.) Parker, AZ 85344; (520) 669-9265.

Colorado River Tribal Council, Parker, AZ 85344; (520) 669-9211.

QUARTZSITE

We probably should be more kind, but let's face it, folks, Quartzsite is the ugliest town in Arizona. Actually, it isn't a normal town, but more of a collection of RV parks in the desert.

It dates back to 1856 when one Charles Tyson built a civilian fortress and stage stop. Not much happened for the next century until a developer built a service station and restaurant and began promoting an annual gem show and flea market called "The Main Event." Today, the town resembles a huge traveling
show that's about to pull up stakes. Although a few businesses are anchored to the desert dirt, most of the trade is conducted out of tents

and shade ramadas. And most of this happens in winter, particularly when three overlapping flea markets and gem shows occur from late January into February. Then, when the mercury starts to rise, Quartzsite shrinks to about 2,000 souls.

The town's mobile population, who's median age is somewhere between Social Security and infinity, reaches hundreds of thousands during peak winter season. They're having the time of their lives with barbecues, potluck dinners and dances. Some merely unfold camp chairs on a swatch of Astroturf beside their RVs and breathe in clean desert air. Some claim that the itinerant population approaches a million during the annual shows. Folks say that you can walk from one end of town to the other over the rooftops of RVs.

Cheap rent is the town's main attraction. With dozens of RV parks competing for customers, space rent is the lowest in Arizona and perhaps in the entire country. Further, the Bureau of Land Management will let RVers park at La Posa Recreation area for just $100 for six months. Located south of I-10, La Posa has no hookups, but you can't beat the rates.

Elevation • 879 feet

Location • In La Paz County, 21 miles west of the Colorado River at the junction of I-10 and Highway 95.

Climate • Warm, dry winters with balmy evenings; sizzling, dry summers. July average high is 108.6 with no nearby reservoir to cool things off, low is 81; January average high 65, low 36.8. Rainfall 4.37 inches; no snowfall.

Population • About 2,000

Population trend • Gained about six percent in the past five years.

Property tax • (assessed at ten percent of real value) $11.78 per $100 of assessed valuation.

Economy • Tourism is the only basis for Quartzsite's economy and most of that comes between November and April.

Job prospects • They're limited to a few government and light manufacturing jobs, plus seasonal retail work. Indicative of the economy, the largest single employer is a truck stop and restaurant.

Industrial facilities • None.

Real estate • Little is happening in the way of housing development; most of the action is in RV parks.

The media • No local publications or TV stations. Television feeds from Yuma and Phoenix, plus a cable system.

Medical services • Part-time medical centers only; the nearest full-scale hospital is in Blythe, California, 22 miles west.

Transportation • Greyhound; nearest airports are in Parker and Blythe.

Education • An elementary school; nearest high school is in Salome, 36 miles east.

Local government • Incorporated in 1989; mayor, town council, and town manager.

Places to stay • Three motels and scores of rec vehicle and mobile home parks.

Leisure facilities • You mean other than sitting on a patch of Astroturf in front of your RV, sipping a martini? There's a nine-hole golf course, a senior center and some shuffleboard courts. Some mobile parks have pools, not open to the public.

Tourist lures • Other than a small, scruffy museum, there isn't much, although hundreds of thousands come for the annual shows. Also, folks are lured into the surrounding hills for excellent rockhounding; the Kofa Mountains to the southwest offers several scenic areas and hiking trails.

Contacts • Quartzsite Chamber of Commerce, P.O. Box 85, Quartzsite, AZ 85346; (520) 927-5600.

Town of Quartzsite, P.O. Box 2812, Quartzsite, AZ 85346; (520) 927-4333; FAX (520) 927-4400.

Quartzsite Economic Development Task Team, P.O. Box 85, Quartzsite, AZ 85346; (520) 927-5600.

YUMA

It isn't handsome, although Yuma is a lively town that offers modest home prices and a lot of history. With a rather high unemployment rate, however, the town appeals mostly to retirees and to Snowbirds, who fly in by the thousands in winter.

Arizona's first explorers saw more barrier than beauty in the Colorado River. Then in 1699, mission-founder Father Eusebio Kino found a fording place where the Gila and Colorado rivers merge. "Yuma Crossing" ultimately became an important link in the first trails west. Kino, incidentally, is credited with naming the Colorado for its reddish, silt-laden waters. (With the many upstream dams, the water now flows more clearly; the silt is slowly filling up all those reservoirs.)

In 1799, Father Francisco Tomas Garcés established two missions along the river. A presidio was built to protect Mission la Purisima Concepcion, on what is now the California side. The entire settlement, including the good padre, was wiped out in a bloody Quechan Indian uprising two years later. That finished things for the Spanish at Yuma Crossing.

Colonel Stephen Watts Kearny and frontier scout Kit Carson forded the river here in 1846, headed west to help snatch California from Mexico. During California's gold rush, many argonauts used this south-

Yuma Territorial Prison is one of that city's many historic attractions; this watchtower was built over the prison reservoir.

ern route to avoid the difficult barrier of the Sierra Nevada range to the north. A few returned to this area, attracted by nearby gold strikes and the agricultural potential along the Colorado River's bottomlands.

The hamlet of Colorado City was established here in 1854. Historians tell us, with a sly grin, that the town's first permanent resident was a shady lady named Sarah Bowman, who ran a combined restaurant and bawdy house. The river flexed its muscles in 1862, washing Colorado City into the Gulf of California, bordello and all. Another town, called Arizona City, was built on higher ground. The name later was changed to Yuma, after the local native tribe.

Water diversion from the Colorado River provided an agricultural base for Yuma's economy and the town took hold. The military was attracted during World War II by the area's cloud-free days and wide open spaces, and several bases were built. Two still remain—a Marine Corps Air Station and the U.S. Army Yuma Proving Ground.

If you approach Yuma from California, you'll pass through a sand dune area right out of *Lawrence of Arabia*. In fact, several films have been shot here, including *Lawrence* footage and desert scenes for a *Star Wars* episode. From fall through spring, hundreds of RVers camp along a frontage road and run their dune buggies over this slice of California Sahara.

Elevation • 138 feet

Location • In Yuma County, on Interstate 8 along the Colorado River, 25 miles north of the Mexican border.

Climate • Warm, dry winters with cool evenings; hot, dry summers. July average high 106.6; low 73.6; January average high 68.4, low 36.8. Rainfall 2.99 inches (the lowest in Arizona); no snowfall.

Population • 60,475

Population trend • Gained ten percent in the past five years.

Property tax • $15.22 per $100 of assessed valuation.

Economy • It's a mixed bag, from military bases to Snowbirds to agriculture. More than 166,000 acres of crops are watered by the Colorado River. The town also is an important stop for cross-country travelers, who pause for a tank of gas and six-pack of Mountain Dew as they hurry through.

Job prospects • They're limited. Our hard-working Mexican neighbors take most of the field work. A few light industries have been drawn here, although this is being offset by government cutbacks in civilian workers at the military bases.

Industrial facilities • Several industrial parks have been built as Yuma pushes to attract more light manufacturing.

Real estate • A typical three-bedroom house ranges from about $60,000 to $85,000.

The media • The *Yuma Daily Sun* and the weekly *Valley Foothills News*. Two local TV stations, plus cable TV.

Medical services • A fully-equipped hospital and an emergency care unit; several extended care facilities.

Transportation • Greyhound and Amtrak stop here. Yuma International Airport is served by scheduled airlines.

Education • Arizona Western College, six vocational schools, five private schools, plus several elementary, junior high and high schools.

Local government • The seat of Yuma County, it was incorporated in 1873; mayor, six council members and a city administrator.

Places to stay • More than 30 motels and a dozen or more RV parks. Some parks are in town; others are along the river, and eastward along I-8.

Leisure facilities • Eight public parks, four golf courses, three public pools, an adult recreation center, plus bowling alleys, tennis courts and such.

Tourist lures • Yuma offers three museums (see Part Three), plus the Yuma Territorial Prison State Park, the newly developed Yuma Crossing Quartermaster Depot Historic Site and Fort Yuma's Quechan Museum on the California side.

Contacts • Yuma County Chamber of Commerce, P.O. Box 10230 (377 S. Main St.), Yuma, AZ 85366-8230; (520) 783-2567.

City of Yuma, 180 W. First St., Yuma, AZ 85364; (520) 783-1271.

Yuma Economic Development Corporation, 1600 S. Fourth Ave., Suite B, Yuma, AZ 85366-1750; (520) 783-0193.

Chapter nine

NORTHWESTERN ARIZONA

BENEATH THE MOGOLLON RIM

If you explore northwestern Arizona in search of a possible future home site, you may think you've taken a wrong turn and wound up in the Pacific Northwest. Approaching Flagstaff, the area's largest city, you'll see great stands of ponderosa pines carpeting Coconino National Forest. On the horizon, the serrated San Francisco Peaks thrust more than 12,000 feet skyward.

The great Colorado Plateau occupies much of northwestern Arizona, lifting it 7,000 feet or more above sea level and pushing much of it into a conifer zone. The Grand Canyon was created when this table-land gradually uplifted while the Colorado River carved down through its layered rock. However, that's a simplistic explanation that won't satisfy any self-respecting geologist. They like to talk about their "stream piracy theory," saying that two rivers flowing in opposite directions began carving the primeval course of the Grand Canyon. Each originated high in a ridgeline of the Colorado Plateau. Then the northbound stream formed a lake. It eventually backed over ridge and the southern stream "pirated" it to form a single southbound Colorado River.

The Colorado Plateau, ranging from 4,000 to 9,000 feet, extends down from the Grand Canyon and drops off abruptly at the 200-mile-long Mogollon Rim. It's a wonderfully mixed land of alpine lakes, volcanic peaks and red rock canyons.

THE WAY IT WAS ● The area's first settlers were drawn to these high, cool pine forests around 15,000 to 20,000 years ago. They shared the land with antelope, bison and a native camel, migrating with the seasons to hunt and forage. About 4,000 years ago, they began rudimentary agriculture, growing a balanced protein diet of corn, squash and beans.

From these early tribes evolved the Sinagua (*si-NAU-wa*), who settled around present-day Flagstaff and south through Oak Creek Canyon around 1000 A.D. Although they occupied much of the forested Colorado Plateau, their name in Spanish means "without water." It was a reference to the dry, porous volcanic soil in the plateau's eastern region, where their abandoned villages were first noted by Spanish explorers. An advanced society, the Sinagua farmed, built irrigation canals and constructed elaborate adobe pueblos above ground and in the niches of protective cliffs and canyons.

Then curiously, by the time those Spanish travelers passed through here in the 16th century, the Sinagua had gone. Were they driven out by drought, disease or the arrival of warlike Athabaskans from the north? Archaeologists can only speculate. Thousands of ruins have been found to prove that they were here; nothing has been found to confirm why they left. It's likely that the present-day Hopi are their descendants.

White migration to the region didn't begin until the middle of the 1800s. Settlers were drawn by minerals, harvestable forests and potentially rich farmlands. The first permanent community was Prescott, selected as the site for Arizona's territorial capital in 1863. Four years later, it lost the capital to Tucson and finally to Phoenix. However, mining and lumbering continued to draw settlers.

From Prescott, settlement spread northward, through the fertile Verde Valley and Sedona's beautiful Oak Creek Canyon to the ponderosa pine fringes of Flagstaff and Williams.

THE WAY IT IS ● Despite its beauty, much of northwestern Arizona is thinly populated. Most of its citizens are focused along a narrow north-south corridor from Prescott through Sedona to Flagstaff. Coconino County, which covers much of this area, has only 100,000 residents and more than half of these live in Flagstaff, the area's largest city. Grand Canyon National Park, national forests and several Native American reservations occupy much of the land.

The Arizona Strip, a region north of the canyon—and therefore isolated by it—is one of the least populated areas of the state. It's occupied by a few hardy Mormon settlements, high prairie and ranches, some fine stands of pine and not much else.

Northwestern Arizona's lower reaches offer good potential for relocating families and year-around retirees who don't mind an occasional snowfall and cold winter nights. Folks who miss the four seasons but don't miss blizzards should like this area's more gentle winters.

CAMP VERDE

If you like small town living, you may like to retire to historic Camp Verde. The oldest settlement in the Verde Valley, it was established in 1865 as an Army fort to protect settlers from Indian reprisals, since they were pushing them off their lands. Remnants of the garrison are preserved in Fort Verde State Historic Park.

The town is rather ordinary looking, although it's in a good location, just off a major interstate highway and within a short drive of several tourist lures. It's popular with the horsy set. Incidentally, non-Spanish speaking folks may like to know that *verde* means green, and it refers to the green swatch of the Verde River flowing through the valley.

Elevation • 3,133 feet

Location • In Yavapai County, just off Interstate 17, about 85 miles north of Phoenix.

Climate • Warm to hot summers; cool winters. July average high 101, low 63; January average high 56.5, low 29. Rainfall 13 inches; no snowfall.

Population • 7,465

Population trend • Gained about 19 percent in the past five years.

Property tax • (assessed at ten percent of real value) $14.40 per $100 assessed valuation.

Economy • Construction, tourism and light industry form Camp Verde's rather limited economic base.

Job prospects • They're about average, according to the Camp Verde Chamber of Commerce. Many residents commute to nearby Cottonwood and Sedona to work, since Camp Verde isn't a significant commercial center.

Industrial facilities • Several small industrial sites are available.

Real estate • Homes are rather inexpensive, perhaps $50,000 for a typical three-bedroom unit. A few new subdivisions are being built in the surrounding Verde Valley. A 42-unit low income senior housing project is available for retirees.

The media • One bi-weekly newspaper, *The Bugle & Journal*. TV via relay from Flagstaff and Phoenix.

Medical services • Hospital in Cottonwood; some medical offices in Camp Verde.

Transportation • Nearby I-17 brings Greyhound and Arizona Central bus lines. Air service is available from Sedona and Flagstaff.

Education • Elementary, middle and high schools, plus a private Montessori school.

Local government ● Incorporated in 1986; mayor, six council members and a town manager.

Places to stay ● Three motels and three campgrounds.

Leisure facilities ● A recreation center, large senior center, tennis courts and a horse arena.

Tourist lures ● Fort Verde State Historic Park, plus the other Verde Valley attractions (see Cottonwood below). Also, it's a short drive to Sedona, Oak Creek Canyon and Flagstaff.

Contacts ● Camp Verde Chamber of Commerce, P.O. Box 1665, Camp Verde, AZ 86322; (520) 567-9294.

Town of Camp Verde, P.O. Box 710, Camp Verde, AZ 86322; (520) 567-6631.

COTTONWOOD

While not very large, Cottonwood is the commercial center of the Verde Valley. It's actually a town with two faces. Newer Cottonwood is a typical collection of small shopping centers and subdivisions, while Old Cottonwood offers as handful of false front stores that house Indian crafts shops, antique stores and a couple of curio shops.

The town dates from the 1870s when soldiers from nearby Camp Verde were stationed here. Settlers followed, and named their hamlet for a nearby stand of cottonwoods along the Verde River.

Clarkdale is a smaller town just to the south, with an old style business district and a more interesting history. It was built as a model company town in 1914 to house workers for a large smelter that processed copper ore from Jerome, which is perched on the side of nearby Mingus Mountain. The smelter has shut down and today's Clarkdale is a quiet little place with an old fashioned "Main Street USA" feel. A much newer model community, Verde Valley Ranch, is being built nearby, with 1,200 homes, a golf course, a lake and river access. It's a project of the Phelps Dodge Corporation, once a major player in Jerome-Clarkdale mining activities.

Elevation ● 3,300 feet

Location ● In Yavapai County, in the heart of the Verde Valley, about 20 miles southwest of Sedona.

Climate ● Warm summers, mild to chilly winters. July average high 98.4, low 66; January average high 58.2, low 28.4. Rainfall 12.21 inches; snowfall five inches.

Population ● Cottonwood 6,700; Clarkdale 2,600

Population trend ● Gaining about four percent a year.

Flagstaff offers several historic sites and museums, such as Riordan State Historic Park, which preserves the estate of a wealthy pioneer family.

Property tax ● (assessed at ten percent of real value) $12.36 per $100 assessed valuation in Cottonwood and $13.47 in Clarkdale.

Economy ● Since Cottonwood is the trade center for the Verde Valley, its economy is rooted in the retail and service areas. Retired people make up 25 percent of the Cottonwood-Clarkdale population.

Job prospects ● Cottonwood offers a rather tepid employment market, according to the local Job Service office. Most positions are in retail sales, tourism and other service areas. The recent arrival of a Wal-Mart boosted things a bit. Many residents commute to motel, restaurant and retail jobs in Sedona.

Industrial facilities ● Two industrial parks near the airport.

Real estate ● This is where folks come when they can't afford Sedona prices. Average cost of a three-bedroom home is $96,000 to $150,000.

The media ● Bi-weekly *Verde Independent*. TV via feeds from Flagstaff and Phoenix, plus a cable TV company.

Medical services ● A 104-bed hospital and several smaller medical clinics.

Transportation ● The Greyhound stops at Camp Verde, 15 miles away. Cottonwood Airport has a 4,250-foot lighted runway; charter service and rental cars.

Education ● Verde Valley campus of Yavapai College, plus the usual elementary, junior high and high schools.

Local government • Incorporated in 1960; mayor, six council members and a city manager.

Places to stay • About ten motels offering an inexpensive alternate to Sedona's pricey resorts; a few campgrounds and RV parks.

Leisure facilities • Four public parks, a recreation center, golf course, public pool and bowling alleys, tennis courts and such.

Tourist lures • Cottonwood is a good base for exploring nearby attractions such as Sedona and Oak Creek Canyon, Tuzigoot National Monument, Montezuma's Castle National Monument, Fort Verde State Historic Park and the rustically historic mining town of Jerome.

Contacts • Cottonwood/Verde Valley Chamber of Commerce, 1010 S. Main St., Cottonwood, AZ 86326; (520) 634-7593.

City of Cottonwood, 827 N. Main St., Cottonwood, AZ 86326; (520) 634-5526.

FLAGSTAFF

Flagstaff is the most versatile small city in Arizona, both for visitors and potential new residents. Northern Arizona University provides cultural opportunities while fine museums and historic buildings preserve the area's past. It's the seat of government for huge Coconino County, Arizona's second largest, covering 18,629 square miles.

Within a day's drive of Flagstaff are seven national parks and monuments, including several intriguing Indian ruins. It gets nippy in winter since it's the highest and most northerly of northwestern Arizona's larger towns. Snow is not unusual although severe storms are rare.

If you like the great outdoors, you'll find it in abundance, since Flagstaff sits at the foot of the San Francisco Peaks, crowned by Mount Humphreys, the tallest mountain in Arizona. The state's largest ski area, the Arizona Snowbowl, is cradled in these ramparts, and the area abounds with hiking trails, fishing lakes and campgrounds.

Downtown Flagstaff is a mix of turn-of-the-century and modern. The historic district along old Route 66 is undergoing a major renaissance, blossoming with trendy cafés, boutiques and specialty shops.

White settlement of the region didn't begin until the 1870s. After several false starts, sheepherder Thomas Forsythe McMillan and family arrived, concluded that it was good sheep country and stayed. By 1880, the area's population had swelled to 67. The railroad came through two years later and Flagstaff's future was assured.

The town's curious name came from a flagpole that may or may not have existed. Some historians say that limbs were stripped from a tall Ponderosa and a flag was hoisted on July 4, 1876, to honor the centennial of America's independence. Others insist that the pole was a marker to guide travelers headed west. Later, according to local history buffs, the tree was chopped down and used as firewood at Sandy Donahue's Saloon. So much for historic preservation. Twice in three years, the new settlement was burned and rebuilt. Fortunately, there was plenty of lumber in the area. The city was incorporated in 1894.

Lumbering is still an important industry and the county is home to more than half of Arizona's domestic sheep. However, tourism is Flagstaff's major enterprise. Northern Arizona University is its largest employer, with a staff of 1,600.

Elevation • 6,905 feet

Location • In Coconino County, on interstates 40 and 17, midway between Arizona's eastern and western borders.

Climate • Warm summers, cool to cold winters. July average high 81.1, low 50.6; January average high 42.2, low 14.6. Rainfall 19.8 inches; snowfall 84.4 inches.

Population • 52,745

Population trend • Gained 15 percent in the past five years.

Property tax • (assessed at ten percent of real value) $10.58 per $100 assessed valuation.

Economy • Although tourism is the main industry, lumbering, light manufacturing and education are important as well. With the presence of Lowell Observatory and a U.S. Geological Survey Landsat office, space science also figures in the economic picture.

Job prospects • The employment situation is "very competitive," according to the local Job Service office. Best prospects are in construction, retail sales, tourism and other service jobs.

Industrial facilities • Four large industrial parks.

Real estate • Three-bedroom home prices range from $90,000 and up, with newer homes around $174,000. A good selection is available in older homes, new subdivisions, townhouses and condos. The market is "very active," according to the local board of realtors.

The media • The daily *Arizona Sun*, and weekly *Nava-Hopi Observer*. Local TV stations, cable feeds from Phoenix and Los Angeles and a cable company.

Medical services • A 128-bed hospital, two convalescent hospitals and several medical clinics.

Transportation • Served by Greyhound, Nava-Hopi Bus Lines and Amtrak. Pulliam Airport has a 7,000-foot runway, with daily scheduled service by America West and feeder airlines.

Education • Northern Arizona University recently was nationally rated as one of the best low tuition fee schools in America. Other facilities include Coconino Community College, eight private schools, several elementary, junior high and high schools.

Local government • Seat of Coconino County since 1891. Incorporated in 1894; mayor, six council members and a city manager.

Places to stay • More than 60 motels, a youth hostel and several RV parks and campgrounds, including camping in the surrounding Coconino National Forest.

Leisure facilities • Three public pools, 20 parks, an ice rink, symphony orchestra, four recreation centers, three golf course and the usual bowling alleys, tennis courts and such. Many NAU facilities are open to the public.

Tourist lures • Flagstaff is Arizona's best located city for sightseeing. It's a short drive to the Grand Canyon, Oak Creek Canyon, the outdoor lures of the San Francisco Peaks and Arizona Snowbowl, plus Sunset Crater, Wupatki, Tuzigoot, Montezuma's Castle and Walnut Canyon national monuments. Local lures include the outstanding Museum of Northern Arizona, several smaller museums, the Lowell Observatory and Riordan State Historic Park.

Contacts • Flagstaff Chamber of Commerce, 101 W. Route 66, Flagstaff, AZ 86004; (520) 774-9541 or (800) 842-7293 and (800) 217-2367; FAX (520) 779-1209.

City of Flagstaff, 211 W. Aspen St., Flagstaff, AZ 86001; (520) 774-5281; FAX (520) 779-7696.

Greater Flagstaff Economic Council, 1300 S. Milton Rd., S-125, Flagstaff, AZ 86001-6354; (520) 779-7658; FAX (520) 556-0940.

JEROME

If you like an idle pace and weatherworn history, you might consider Jerome for retirement. Don't go there looking for work, however. Although it once was a boomtown of copper production, things are pretty quiet these days. It's basically a rustic hillside town frozen in time, popular with history buffs, tourists and a few resident artists.

Historians say Jerome never was pretty. Cantilevered into the slopes of Cleopatra Hill, halfway up Mingus Mountain, it was one of Arizona's largest and wildest mining camps. In 1903, a visiting *New York Sun* reporter called Jerome "the wickedest town in America."

Its terraced streets were lined with saloons and bawdy houses. Sloping yards sprouted tailing dumps and mining gear instead of rose bushes. Homes were so steeply terraced, claim old-timers, that you could look down your neighbor's chimney. Slides were common and the town jail skidded several dozen feet downhill, where it remains to this day. Smelters belched pollution. Nearly a mile underground, men stood in boot-deep water, groveling for copper ore in humid 100-degree heat. Dozens died from falls, blasts and other miscalculations.

The bawdy houses and smelters are gone, along with the miners and most of the littered mining machinery. Jerome survives today as an attraction for visitors fascinated by its wicked past. It has lured a rather youthful population of artists and shopkeepers, as well. Instead of old miners dozing in the sun, one is more likely to see pretty young entrepreneurs or artists who would look more at home in a bikini on Malibu Beach. The weathered business district is terraced on three levels as the highway switchbacks through town. Galleries, curio shops and antique shops occupy many of its old buildings. Red and green scars are still evident in the hillsides, where miners dug for gold, silver and copper.

The first claim was filed on Mingus Mountain in 1876. Prospectors found a little gold and silver and a lot of copper. In 1883 the United Verde Copper Company built a smelter and the boom began; at its peak, Jerome bustled with 15,000 citizens. In less than 80 years, a billion dollars worth of copper, gold, silver, lead and zinc was rooted from 80 miles of tunnels beneath the town. Alternately leveled by fire and rebuilt, tough old Jerome thrived until 1953, when the last copper mine was shut down. The population dwindled to 150, then slowly climbed to its present few hundred as tourists began coming to town.

Elevation • 5,248 feet

Location • In Yavapai County, on the slopes of Mingus Mountain, above the Verde Valley west of Cottonwood.

Climate • Warm summers, cool to chilly winters. July average high 89.2, low 67.1; January average high 49.8, low 32.2. Rainfall 17.95 inches; snowfall 24.9 inches.

Population • about 460

Population trend • Gained 14 percent in the past five years, which amounts to 57 new people.

Property tax • (assessed at ten percent of real value) $13.78 per $100 assessed valuation.

Economy • Tourism.

Job prospects • There aren't many, unless you want to open a boutique or gallery, or work in one. Three of four jobs in town are tied to tourism.

Industrial facilities • None.

Real estate • Three-bedroom home prices start around $50,000, although there aren't many available. Turn-of-the-century fixer-uppers occasionally reach the market and old Victorian style homes can go as high as $200,000.

The media • No local newspaper; TV arrives by relay from Phoenix, Prescott and Flagstaff.

Medical services • The nearest are in Cottonwood.

Transportation • Again, nearest facilities are in Cottonwood.

Education • An elementary and a high school.

Local government ● Incorporated in 1899; mayor and six council members.

Places to stay ● A few motels and bed and breakfast inns, including the stylish new Inn at Jerome.

Leisure facilities ● Three parks and an archives research center.

Tourist lures ● Jerome is the main lure, with several museums, Jerome State Historic Park, an art center in a former brick school complex, several boutiques and restaurants dressed in period décor.

Contacts ● Jerome Chamber of Commerce, P.O. Box K, Jerome, AZ 86331; (520) 634-2900.

Jerome Historical Society, P.O. Box 156, Jerome, AZ 86331; (520) 634-5477.

Town of Jerome, P.O. Box 335, Jerome, AZ 86331; (520) 634-7943.

PAGE

This is the dark horse on our list of suggest Arizona communities. Stuck way up next to the Utah border and tucked into a niche of the Navajo Nation, Page is often overlooked. Yet it offers several pluses—recreational facilities on Lake Powell, a dry climate, low property taxes and a tidy looking town.

Sitting high on a red dirt shelf above Lake Powell and Glen Canyon Dam, Page thrives on tourist business lured by Glen Canyon National Recreation Area. Neither Page nor its high plateau surroundings are particularly attractive, being rather devoid of shrubbery. However, this planned community has a rather clean-swept look. It was created in 1956 as the construction town for Glen Canyon Dam, with features such as underground utilities and a cluster of public schools rimmed by the main residential area.

East of Page is the core of the local economy—the huge coal-fed Navajo Generating Plant, operated by Phoenix' Salt River Project and the Los Angeles Light and Power Company. It's an ongoing target of environmentalists, accused of polluting the skies above the Grand Canyon. Consuming 24,000 tons of coal a day brought by rail from nearby mines, it produces enough electricity for a city of three million.

Elevation ● 4,380 feet

Location ● In Coconino County, between the Navajo Reservation and Glen Canyon National Recreation Area.

Climate ● Very dry; warm to hot summers, chilly to cold winters. July average high 97, low 71; January average high 45, low 24. Rainfall 4.78 inches; snowfall 4.9 inches.

Population • 7,950

Population trend • Gained 20 percent in the past five years.

Property tax • (assessed at ten percent of real value) $9.59 per $100 assessed valuation.

Economy • Tourism and public utilities balance the local economy. An estimated 3.5 million people visit Glen Canyon National Recreation Area each year.

Job prospects • They're good only in tourist services and public utilities. Seventy percent of the jobs are tied to these sources. The local chamber of commerce says overall job prospects are "about average."

Industrial facilities • A 102-acre industrial park.

Real estate • Three-bedroom homes average about $135,000, according to the chamber.

The media • Two weeklies, the *Lake Powell Chronicle* and *Navajo-Hopi Observer*. Television feeds from Phoenix and Salt Lake City, plus a local cable company.

Medical services • A small hospital, two medical clinics and a mental health clinic.

Transportation • Page Airport, with a lighted 5,500-foot runway, is served by Great Lakes Airlines and charter service.

Education • A new campus of Coconino Community College, two elementary, one junior high and one high school.

Local government • Founded as a construction town in 1956, incorporated in 1975; mayor, six council members and a city manager.

Places to stay • About 25 motels and resort hotels, including waterside resorts on Lake Powell; several RV parks, national recreation area and private campgrounds.

Leisure facilities • Three public parks, a new 18-hole and a nine-hole golf course, senior citizen center, recreation center, public pool and tennis courts.

Tourist lures • Glen Canyon National Recreation Area embraces adjacent Lake Powell and Glen Canyon Dam, offering boating, camping, picnicking, fishing and such. The Navajo and Hopi reservations with their great variety of attractions are next door, and both rims of the Grand Canyon are a few hours drive west. Also, Page isn't far from the canyon lands of Utah, just to the north.

Contacts • Page-Lake Powell Chamber of Commerce, P.O. Box 727 (106 S. Lake Powell Blvd.), Page, AZ 86040; (520) 645-2741; FAX (520) 645-3181.

City of Page, P.O. Drawer HH (697 Vista Ave.), Page, AZ 86040; (520) 645-8861; FAX (520) 645-4244.

PAYSON

This mountain retreat in a woodsy setting below the Mogollon Rim might tempt you if you don't mind getting wet and a bit chilly in winter. Although it has historic roots, Payson is a rather ordinary looking town, with typical strip malls and clusters of shopping centers and a few planned subdivisions. Its forested setting and mountainous backdrop of the Mogollon Rim add scenic allure.

Well off Arizona's main traveled routes, it's popular as a summer retreat for Phoenicians fleeing the desert sizzle. As such, it has a considerable number of lodgings for a rather small town. It's enjoying a growth surge, gaining 30 percent in the past five years; many of the new residents are retirees.

Payson first saw life when prospectors found a bit of gold in nearby creek bottoms in 1881. They didn't find much, although the town grew as a ranching center. Author Zane Gray loved the timbered land above Payson and below "The Rim." He built a hunting cabin there, where he wrote many of his books. His cabin was an historic site until recently, when it was destroyed by fire. The local Payson museum has an extensive exhibit on the author. Although most of Payson is modern, a few old buildings along Main Street recall the town's cowboy past.

Elevation • 4,930 feet

Location • In Gila County, 94 miles northeast of Phoenix.

Climate • Warm summers, cool to chilly winters. July average high 92.5, low 58.5; January average high 53.1, low 23.7. Rainfall 20.77 inches; snowfall 25.1 inches.

Population • 11,004

Population trend • Gained 31 percent in the past five years.

Property tax • (assessed at ten percent of real value) $12.61 per $100 assessed valuation.

Economy • Retirement and tourism provide Payson's economic base. More than 60 percent of its population is retired. The community has an active senior center and senior recreation program.

Job prospects • Payson's Economic Development Corporation is working to attract light industry, although job prospects at this writing were below average. Best bets, according to the local Job Service office, are in retail sales, tourism and other service jobs.

Industrial facilities • Two light industrial parks.

Real estate • Housing ranges from older homes in downtown Payson to several woodsy subdivisions and summer cabins. Prices for a three-bedroom home start around $65,000 to $75,000.

The media • Three weeklies, the *Mogollon Advisor, Rim Country News* and *Payson Roundup*. A local TV station, plus cable feeds from Phoenix and a local cable company.

Medical services • A small hospital, medical clinics and three nursing homes.

Transportation • Payson airport has a lighted 5,000-foot runway with charter service available.

Education • A community college plus the usual elementary, junior high and high schools.

Local government • Founded in 1881 and incorporated in 1973; mayor, six council members and a town manager.

Places to stay • About 20 motels and lodges, a dozen RV parks and campgrounds, plus camping in adjacent Tonto National Forest.

Leisure facilities • A senior center, public golf course, two public parks, a small zoo, bowling alleys and tennis courts.

Tourist lures • Tonto National Forest provides the usual hiking, camping, picnicking, fishing and such. The Museum of the Forest has exhibits on Zane Gray and local history, and a new Native American casino on the edge of town offers gaming. Tonto Natural Bridge north of Payson recently has been expanded and improved as a state park.

Contacts • Payson Chamber of Commerce, P.O. Box 1380, Payson, AZ 85541; (520) 474-4515 or (800) 6-PAYSON.

Town of Payson, 303 N. Beeline Highway, Payson, AZ 85541; (520) 474-5242; FAX (520) 474-4610.

Payson Economic Development Corporation, 303 N. Beeline Highway, Payson, AZ 85541; (520) 474-5242; FAX (520) 474-4610.

PINE/STRAWBERRY

Pine and Strawberry are small pine-clad villages a few miles north of Payson, tucked under the Mogollon Rim. Both communities date back to the 1880s although their appearance now is essentially alpine modern.

A post office was established at Pine in 1884 and named for the surrounding pine forests. Strawberry, settled about the same time, got its pleasing name from wild strawberries that grow in the area.

They're both fast-growing although their economy depends heavily on weekend visitors, second-home dwellers from Phoenix and retirees.

Elevation • Pine 5,448 feet; Strawberry 6,047 feet

Location • In Gila County, 13 miles north of Payson and 110 miles northeast of Phoenix.

Climate • Warm summers, cool to chilly winters, July average high 92.5, low 58.5; January average high 53.1, low 23.7, Rainfall 20.77 inches; snowfall 25.1 inches.

Combined population • 3,766

Population trend • Gained about six percent in the past five years and more than doubled since 1980.

Property tax • $13.54 per $100 assessed valuation.

Economy • Primarily tourism and recreation; not much real economic growth.

Job prospects • Very limited; the few available service jobs are rather seasonal, since Pine and Strawberry are primarily summer retreats. They offer better prospects for retirement than for employment.

Industrial facilities • None, although light industry is being sought.

Real estate • Three-bedroom home prices range from $95,000 to $140,000, according to the chamber of commerce.

The media • The weekly *Payson Roundup* is distributed here. TV relays from Phoenix, Tucson and Prescott, plus a cable company.

Medical services • One clinic; other services in Payson.

Transportation • Shuttle bus service to Payson and Phoenix; Payson Airport is 15 miles south.

Education • One elementary school; high school students commute to Payson.

Local government • Pine founded in 1884; both communities unincorporated; services provided by Gila County.

Places to stay • Six motels and four RV parks, plus Forest Service campgrounds in the surrounding mountains.

Leisure facilities • Not much here; see Payson listing above.

Tourist lures • Also see Payson listing.

Contacts • Pine/Strawberry Chamber of Commerce, P.O. Box 333, Pine, AZ 85544; (520) 476-3547.

Gila County Board of Supervisors, 1400 E. Ash St., Globe, AZ 85501; (520) 425-5763.

PRESCOTT

If we were looking for a woodsy place to relocate a family or to retire, we'd be hard-pressed to choose between Prescott and Flagstaff. While Flagstaff is on a major freeway and railway and closer to the Grand Canyon, Prescott is a more attractive town and it's closer to Phoenix.

So, flip a coin.

Friendly natives may gently correct you when you say "Pres-kott." It's "PRESS-kit," with the last syllable bitten off quickly. Even local radio announcers,

• FLAGSTAFF

• PHOENIX

• TUCSON

alleged guardians of proper pronunciation, say it that way.

Once you've learned the language, townsfolk will boast of PRESS-kit's idyllic location, between the dry high desert and the cool pines of PRESS-kit National Forest. It's cooler in summer than Sedona, they'll tell you, and not nearly so crowded. PRESS-kit has several art galleries, they point out, and an active performing arts center.

Two colleges and an aeronautical university provide an academic base. The town has a several museums and the whole of the Bradshaw Mountains for a playground. History? Why, PRESS-kit was where Arizona began! Territorial capital, it was. Hadn't you heard?

When Arizona was sliced free from New Mexico to become its own territory in 1863, the new governor—John N. Goodwin—began casting about for a capital site. The mineral-rich central highland seemed most logical, so a temporary capital was set up first at Fort Whipple, then on Granite Creek to the south. The town of Prescott was laid out in a neat grid and a sturdy log and whipsaw-board governor's mansion was constructed. The fort was moved here to protect the new capital. But in 1867, before something fancier than an oversized log cabin could be built, the capital was shifted to Tucson. Prescott citizens lured it back briefly in 1877 before it settled for good in Phoenix.

No matter, the people said. Who wanted all that political ruckus and traffic, anyhow? The town has done just fine without it, as a trading, ranching and lumbering center.

Prescott today looks more like a vintage New England village than a Southwestern community. The bold, Doric-columned Yavapai County Courthouse occupies a large town square. Early American style homes and occasional Victorians line streets shaded by mature trees. Many business buildings are of sturdy brick. The downtown area appears prosperous despite a commercial exodus to suburban shopping centers. An abundance of motels, restaurants and a few curio shops and antique stores serve the thousands of tourist drawn to this contented, tree-shaded community.

Don't be fooled by Prescott's Eastern look, however. The town is decidedly Western, with several cowboy shops and galleries. Locals claim that their annual Frontier Days is America's oldest rodeo, dating back to 1888.

Elevation ● 5,347 feet

Location ● In Yavapai County, on State Route 89, about midway between Phoenix and Flagstaff.

Climate ● Warm summers, cool to chilly winters. July average high 89, low 58; January average high 50, low 20. Rainfall 18 inches; snowfall 20.6 inches.

Population ● 30,606

Population trend ● Gained 15 percent in the past five years.

Property tax ● $11.60 per $100 assessed valuation.

Prescott served briefly as the Arizona territorial capital and exhibits at the Sharlot Hall Museum recall those days. Mannequin soldiers discuss politics in the log cabin style governor's "mansion."

Economy ● Prescott offers a good economic balance of tourism, education, light manufacturing and retail sales, with lumbering and ranching in the surrounding areas.

Job prospects ● Most in demand are skilled trades and clerical jobs. Four of ten jobs are in the services area, mostly tourism, while retail trade is second and construction is third. Manufacturing is in fourth place, although it's gaining as new light industries are drawn to the area.

Industrial facilities ● Five industrial parks.

Real estate ● Older homes and new planned developments comprise the town's realty mix. Average price of a three-bedroom is $160,000, although many older ones are less.

The media ● The *Daily Prescott Courier* and the weekly *Prescott News*. Local TV stations plus feeds from Phoenix and a cable TV company.

Medical services ● A regional medical center, 358-bed veterans' hospital and domiciliary, six nursing homes, adult day care center.

Transportation ● Served by Greyhound. Ernest A. Love Field has two runways with scheduled air service.

Education ● Embry-Riddle Aeronautical University, Yavapai Community College, Prescott College (private four-year liberal arts), five private schools, six public elementary, two middle and one high school.

Local government • Seat of Yavapai County. Incorporated in 1881; mayor, six council member and a city manager.

Places to stay • About 30 motels, 19 bed and breakfast inns, several national forest campgrounds, six private campgrounds and RV parks.

Leisure facilities • Several public parks, a small zoo, three public pools, two golf courses, several art galleries, a roller skating rink, plus tennis and racquetball courts, bowling alleys and such.

Tourist lures • Surrounding Prescott National Forest offers the usual outdoor pursuits. The town has several museums, including the outstanding Sharlot Hall Museum that includes the original territorial governor's mansion; the Phippen Museum of Western art and the Smoki Museum of Native American lore.

Contacts • Prescott Chamber of Commerce, P.O. Box 1147 (117 W. Goodwin St.), Prescott, AZ 86302; (520) 445-2000.

City of Prescott, P.O. Box 2059 (201 S. Cortez St.), Prescott, AZ 86302; (520) 445-3500.

SEDONA

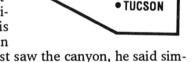

It's no coincidence that three of our favorite Arizona towns—Prescott, Flagstaff and Sedona—are in the state's north central area. The scenery's beautiful, summers are sunny, winters are mild and each place offers a good social, cultural and economic mix.

Sedona is the most affluent of the three and it's certainly in a striking setting, surrounded by the red rock palisades of Oak Creek Canyon. In fact, this may be the most beautiful civic setting in the world. When Frank Lloyd Wright first saw the canyon, he said simply: "Nothing should ever be built here."

Obviously, his advise was ignored. The canyon is dotted with campgrounds and small resorts; Sedona in the lower end is busy with art galleries, gift shops and large resorts. It has been estimated that as many as seven million people a year pass through Oak Creek Canyon and Sedona. Good grief, that's more than the number of visitors to the Grand Canyon!

Sedona is one of the largest and most popular resort areas in Arizona. Its posh spas rival those of Scottsdale, Phoenix and Tucson and they're in more impressive settings. Sedona lures natives as well as outsiders, particularly Phoenicians seeking solace from the summer sun. They return in the fall to admire the saffron leaves of sycamore, aspen and cottonwood along Oak Creek. Sunlight and shadows play

The Coffeepot is one of the most striking red rock formations in the Sedona-Oak Creek Canyon area.

off red sandstone buttes. We find it hard to believe that all who live here don't drop whatever they're doing each evening to admire the sunset.

Despite its tempting beauty, the area didn't attract permanent white settlement until 1876 when one James Thompson began farming here. A Pennsylvania Dutch couple, Carl and Sedona Schnebly, arrived in 1901 and built a boarding house. The following year, they petitioned for a post office, which they offered to operate from their lodge. Carl had two suggestions for the town's name—Schnebly's Station and Oak Creek Crossing. The post office department rejected them, saying they were too long to fit on a cancellation stamp. So Carl's brother Ellsworth told him to name the town for his wife.

A fortunate suggestion, for it's difficult to picture an art colony called Schnebly's Station. Early in this century, Hollywood movie makers were attracted by the area's handsome rock formations. The first film was a silent version of Zane Gray's *Call of the Canyon*. Artists began settling in, drawn by the isolation and beauty. Then resort builders arrived. They put an end to the isolation but more or less protected the setting.

Sedona has grown considerably in recent years, more than doubling its population since 1976. Surprisingly, it wasn't incorporated until 1987. While not a model of urban planning, the town still retains much of its early-day charm. There are no highrises to block those orange-hued rocks and no neon to compete with the canyon's light-and-shadow shows. The community is split between Coconino and Yavapai counties. The original site in Coconino county (which locals call "Uptown Sedona") hasn't changed much in the past 25 years.

Most of the growth is concentrated south on Highway 179 (still in Coconino County) and southwest along 89A on the Yavapai County side. Although these new areas are a bit sprawled, developers have taken a cue from Uptown and resisted neon and highrises. Route 89A through "new" Sedona is lined with spur streets leading to planned residential areas with predictable names like Shadows Estates, Settlers Rest, the Palisades, Western Hills, Rolling Hills and Mystic Hills.

The town is unabashedly tourist-oriented and it is upscale tourism, for the most part. More than two dozen galleries display fine examples of Western and other contemporary art. About 300 artists live here. Performing arts thrive as well. Musicales and plays are presented at the Sedona Arts Center. Each summer, the community sponsors the Jazz on the Rocks Festival and the Sedona Chamber Music Festival.

Elevation ● 4,500 feet

Location ● In lower Oak Creek Canyon, 30 miles south of Flagstaff; divided between Coconino and Yavapai counties.

Climate ● Warm summers and temperate winters with occasional frost. July average high 95.1, low 65.1; January average high 55, low 29.7. Rainfall 17.15 inches; snowfall 8.8 inches.

Population ● 8,910; about 15,500 in the two-county Sedona area.

Population trend ● Gained 15 ten percent in the past five years, mostly on the Yavapai County side.

Property tax ● (assessed at ten percent of real value) $11.74 per $100 assessed valuation.

Economy ● Tourism and affluent retirees fuel Sedona's economic machine.

Job prospects ● More than half the jobs are in retail sales, tourism and related services. There isn't much available in the professions or skilled trades. Most people don't come here to earn money; they come here *with* money.

Industrial facilities ● Tourism is the industry.

Real estate ● Sedona is easy to love but difficult to afford. Average three-bedroom home prices approach $200,000 and those with any sort of view go considerably higher.

The media ● The twice weekly *Sedona-Red Rock News*. Television feeds from Flagstaff, Prescott and Phoenix, plus a cable company.

Medical services ● An outpatient medical clinic with emergency services and a cancer treatment center; hospitals are in Cottonwood and Flagstaff.

Transportation ● Sedona's airport has a 5,100-foot lighted runway, with air charter service.

Education ● Extension courses provided by Yavapai Community College; seven private schools, plus public elementary schools and a high school.

Local government • Incorporated in 1987; government services shared by Coconino and Yavapai counties.

Places to stay • Dozens of motels plus several world-class resorts. Three RV parks and several national forest campgrounds in Oak Creek Canyon.

Leisure facilities • A community center, art center; numerous parks in Oak Creek Canyon; golf and tennis at area resorts.

Tourist lures • Sedona and its setting are the chief lures, of course. The seven million annual visitors take jeep trips into red rock country, hike the canyons, attend music and art festivals and browse the excellent boutiques and galleries. Dozens of miles of hiking trails wind about the red rock ramparts. Scenic drives are popular and the new Red Rock State Park offers hiking, ranger programs and a fine interpretive center.

Contacts • Sedona-Oak Creek Canyon Chamber of Commerce, P.O. Box 478, Sedona, AZ 86339; (520) 282-7722.

City of Sedona, P.O. Box 30002, Sedona, AZ 86336; 282-3113.

VERDE VILLAGE

The planned community of Verde Village was established in 1970, primarily as a retreat for retirees and summer weekenders fleeing Valley of the Sun heat. Three-fourths of its residents are retired. During the 1980s, it was the fastest growing community in the Verde Valley and one of the fastest in Arizona. Things have slowed down a bit since, although it still gained more than 20 percent in the past five years.

Cottonwood and Yavapai County provide virtually all of Verde Village's services. See the Cottonwood listing on page 123 for more details.

Elevation • 3,300 feet

Location • In Yavapai County, adjacent to Cottonwood in the Verde Valley.

Climate • Warm summers, mild to chilly winters. July average high 98.4, low 66; January average high 58.2, low 28.4. Rainfall 12.21 inches; snowfall five inches.

Population • About 8,604

Population trend • Gained 22 percent in the past five years.

Property tax • (assessed at ten percent of real value) $12.36 per $100 assessed valuation

Contact • Verde Valley Chamber of Commerce, 1010 Main St., Cottonwood, AZ 86326; (520) 634-7593.

WILLIAMS

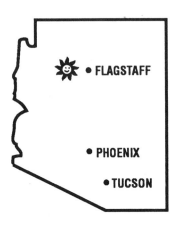

Think of Williams as a small, sleepy Flagstaff. Like its larger brother, it's rimmed by national forests, with four season and easy access to northwestern Arizona's natural attractions. Unlike Flagstaff, it chugs along at an idle pace, with very little growth and few prospects for job-seekers. Retirees might find its woodsy setting attractive, although winters are cold. This is your place if you're the outdoor type seeking small-town living. You can golf in summer and hit the slopes at the Williams Ski Area in winter.

Williams is the closest town to the South Rim of the Grand Canyon, and its chamber likes to boast about that. In fact, it calls itself the Williams-Grand Canyon Chamber of Commerce. A vintage steam train chugs visitors between the town and that grand gorge.

The small business district is caught in a pleasant 1930s time warp. Other than several new motels, it has changed little from the days when it was an important pause on the Santa Fe Railway and old Route 66. Cattle ranching began in the area in the late 1870s, and the railroad arrived in the 1880s to haul logs for the local timber industry.

The town and its main street are named for randy old mountain man and guide Bill Williams. He prowled these parts for a quarter of a century until the Utes got him in 1849. To honor his spirit, townsfolk dress up as mountain men and shady ladies and stage frontier celebrations over Memorial Day and Labor day weekends.

Elevation ● 6,770 feet

Location ● In Coconino County, 30 miles west of Flagstaff on I-40; 60 miles south of the Grand Canyon.

Climate ● Temperate summers, mild to cold winters. July average high 83.1, low 54.8; January average high 44.3, low 21.3. Rainfall 21.21 inches; snowfall 75.8 inches.

Population ● about 2,690

Population trend ● Gained about six percent in the past five years.

Property tax ● (assessed at ten percent of real value) $9.63 per $100 assessed valuation.

Economy ● The town's slow-paced economy is dependent primarily on tourism, with a bit of lumbering, mining and ranching.

Job prospects ● They're very scarce; tourist jobs here are seasonal.

Industrial facilities ● One 40-acre industrial park.

Real estate • There's little in the way of new construction. Homes are mostly old and mostly in the $50,000 to $60,000 range.

The media • One weekly, the *Williams News*. Television via relay from Flagstaff and Phoenix, plus cable.

Medical services • An emergency medical center; nearest hospital is in Flagstaff.

Transportation • Greyhound and Nava-Hopi Bus Lines. The historic Grand Canyon Railway runs between Williams and the canyon. Williams Municipal Airport has a 6,000-foot runway; no scheduled air service; charters available.

Education • One elementary and one high school.

Local government • Incorporated in 1901; mayor, six council members and a city manager.

Places to stay • About 25 motels and the attractive new Fray Marcos Hotel; several RV and trailer parks, plus campgrounds in the surrounding Kaibab National Forest.

Leisure facilities • Community center, five public parks, a golf course, riding stables, bowling alley, tennis courts and the Williams Ski Area.

Tourist lures • The Grand Canyon, obviously, is the biggest lure, closely followed by the Grand Canyon Railway that takes vintage rail buffs there. A deer farm and petting zoo is just outside of town, and the surrounding national forest lures the outdoor set.

Contacts • Williams-Grand Canyon Chamber of Commerce, 200 W. Railroad Ave., Williams, AZ 86046; (520) 635- 4061.

City of Williams, 200 W. Railroad Ave., Williams, AZ 86046; (520) 635-1494.

Chapter ten
METROPOLITAN MIDDLE
PHOENIX AND THE VALLEY OF THE SUN

The Valley of the Sun, a great desert basin rimmed by ruggedly handsome peaks, is the economic, political and social heart of Arizona. Nearly 72 percent of the state's population lives in Maricopa County, which includes the Valley of the Sun and desert regions southwest of there. Most of the valley's 20 communities have merged together like thin pancake batter, creating an urban megalopolis 30 miles across. It's beginning to resemble a desert version of the Los Angeles basin.

Despite its urban sprawl, the area still retains some of the flavor of frontier Arizona. It's a delightfully curious mix of Old West and New Wave. You can pull on your Levi's and eat cowboy steaks or wrap yourself in society's most sophisticated trappings and nibble daintily on *foi gras.*

THE WAY IT WAS ● In a state rich with Spanish, Mexican and cowboy lore, the settlement of the Phoenix basin was rather routine. Even its founder had a boring name—John Smith. Native Americans farmed the area for several centuries, diverting water from the Salt River. Judging from archaeological sites, their population may have reached 100,000. Then they mysteriously vanished around 1400 A.D., abandoning their irrigation canals.

Later Pima Indians noted the deserted ditches and called their builders "Hohokam," which means "gone away" or "used up."

This Sonoran Desert basin dozed in the sun until pioneer John Smith started a hay camp in 1864. Former Confederate soldier Jack Swilling arrived three years later and formed a company of unemployed miners to dig out the abandoned Hohokam canals. The group soon had a fine wheat and barley crop growing. One of the settlers, an educated Englishman named Darrel Duppa, named the settlement "Phoenix." He predicted that a great city would rise from the site of the former Indian camp, as the fabled Phoenix bird rises from its own ashes every 500 years.

This Phoenix didn't take that long.

The area grew quickly, particularly after the Roosevelt Dam was completed on the Salt River in 1911, encouraging agricultural expansion. Then the valley got a share of water from the Central Arizona Project as new diversion dams were completed on the Colorado River. The Phoenix bird really took off, like the roadrunner with Wile E. Coyote on its tail. It has never looked back.

World War II brought the military, seeking year-around weather for flight and combat training. At war's end, all of that sunshine tempted many GIs to return.

THE WAY IT IS • The valley has become a major urban center with attendant congestion and even an occasional tinge of smog. In less than 50 years, this busy region has made the transition from barley fields and cow ponies to planned subdivisions and helicopter traffic spotters. During much of the Eighties, Phoenix was America' fastest growing large city.

Phoenix is the urban core of a glop of 20 fused-together communities. Some of these peripheral towns have grown even faster than their leader. During the boom years of the Eighties, communities such as Mesa, Glendale, Tempe and Scottsdale doubled and tripled their populations. New planned communities such as Fountain Hills have emerged in recent years.

Growth slowed during an economic slump early in the Nineties. Las Vegas has since taken the title as America's fastest growing large city, and Nevada has become the fastest growing state. However, the Phoenix bird and its neighbors are off and running again. The Valley of the Sun population is approaching two and a half million, making it one of the largest metropolitan areas in the country.

In listing the cities of Arizona's metropolitan core, we include some communities that are outside the Valley of the Sun. A few are beyond the valley's outer fringes to the west and northeast, and others are south, along the Interstate 10 corridor between Phoenix and Tucson. Actually, no one has specifically defined the Valley of the Sun's boundaries, although it generally encompasses the desert basin encompassed by the hills that surround the city. "Valley of the Sun" is an invention of local boosters, not cartographers.

PHOENIX

It's great that the Phoenix bird rose to build a new city over Hohokam canals. But did the old bird have to get this big? From 1980 until 1987, it ranked first in population gain among major U.S. cities, swelling by 30 percent. It's now the seventh largest city in America. As it grows, in annexes new territory. In late 1995, it surpassed Los Angeles, not in population but in total land area.

Phoenix is not only growing; it's rebuilding and improving. A $1.1 billion downtown renewal project is nearing completion, bringing a new convention center, art center, professional baseball stadium, science and history museums, performing arts theater, aquatic center and public parks and plazas.

The Phoenix bird is thus providing a total environment for urban living. Even with a few growing pains, it's one of the cleanest, safest and most appealing large cities in America. It was rated second in the nation for visitor services, accommodations and dining by the New York-based Zagat Guide survey. It has more *Mobil Travel Guide* five-star resorts than any other city in the country. The American Automobile Association also gives the area high marks, awarding its prestigious five-diamond rating to a pair of resorts and four diamonds to a dozen more.

Even with all of these amenities, it's one of the least expensive major cities in America. A survey several years ago indicated that it was the third cheapest in the country for lodging and meals. The Carl Bertrelsmann Foundation rated Phoenix as the "Best-run City in the World" in 1993. It's also a major league city, home to the National Basketball Association's Phoenix Suns, the National Football League's Arizona Cardinals and the new baseball expansion team, the Arizona Diamondbacks.

Amazingly, in one of the largest cities in America, in an urban core of high rises and busy sidewalks, you can still find a place to park.

Elevation • 1,117 feet

Location • In Maricopa County; the geographic and economic heart of the Valley of the Sun.

Climate • Warm to hot summers; balmy winters with some chilly evenings. July average high 104.4, low 78.3; January average high 64.6, low 38. Rainfall 6.74 inches; rare traces of snow.

Population • 1,082,610

Population trend • Gained five percent in the past five years, after growing by more than 30 percent in the decade of the Eighties.

Property tax • (assessed at ten percent of real value) Varies with the area; averages $18.19 per $100 assessed valuation.

Economy • It's versatile, vibrant and growing. Tourism and manufacturing produce most of the income, employing more than 300,000 people, accounting for nearly half the jobs. Phoenix is the nation's third largest producer of electronics. The services sector and retirement also provide significant portions of the economic base.

Job prospects • Obviously, they're varied. Tourism and other services employ the most people—28.1 percent. Next is manufacturing with more than 18 percent, followed by retailing at 17.7 percent. Thousands of seasonal tourist jobs open up in winter. Since Phoenix is the state capital, the government is a major employer. The city's unemployment rate is generally well below the national average.

Industrial facilities • They're extensive, with numerous industrial parks, many with air or rail service.

Real estate • Housing is likewise varied, with homes ranging from $70,000 to $80,000 in older southwest Phoenix. Prices start around $100,000 for a three-bedroom home in the newer developing areas. The city's overall housing cost is higher than most of the rest of the state, yet much lower than many other American urban areas. Phoenix home prices are about half what they are in Los Angeles and the San Francisco Bay Area.

The media • The merged *Arizona Republic* and *Phoenix Gazette*, plus 50 smaller newspapers and other periodicals in the metropolitan area. Eight local TV stations and a full-service cable company.

Medical services • Twenty hospitals, two psychiatric hospitals and numerous clinics and extended care facilities.

Transportation • Served by Greyhound and Amtrak. Sky Harbor International Airport is the ninth largest in the world for operations, and it's the home base for America West Airlines. More than 20 carriers offer more than 400 daily departures. Eleven other airports are in the area.

Education • Arizona State University is in nearby Tempe; Phoenix has 79 technical and business colleges, four religious colleges and five community colleges, plus numerous public elementary, middle and high schools.

Local government • Incorporated in 1881; became the state capital in 1889. The city government is operated by a mayor, an eight-member council and a city manager.

Places to stay • Nearly 200 resorts, motels and hotels; dozens of mobile home and RV parks.

Leisure facilities • An extensive assortment of spare time lures—public swimming pools, golf courses, tennis courts, art galleries and 38 public parks, including seven huge wilderness parks in the surrounding mountains. Phoenix is among the world's leaders in total acreage of public park lands.

Tourist lures • Only the Grand Canyon draws more visitors to Arizona than Phoenix. Tourist attractions include the excellent Heard Indian Museum, new science, technology and history museums and several other archives. Other lures include the Arizona State Capitol Museum, Desert Botanical Garden, Heritage Square with historic homes, and the highly regarded Phoenix Zoo. Of course, many visitors come just for the sun—to luxuriate in luxury resorts.

Contacts • Community and Economic Development Office, City of Phoenix, 200 W. Washington St., 20th Floor, Phoenix, AZ 85003-1161; (602) 262-5040.

Phoenix & Valley of the Sun Convention and Visitors Bureau, 400 E. Van Buren St., Suite 600, Phoenix, AZ 85073; (602) 262-7176.

Phoenix Economic Growth Group, 400 N. Fifth St., Room 1625, Phoenix, AZ 85004; (602) FOR-PHNX or (602) 253-9747.

Phoenix Chamber of Commerce, 201 N. Central, Suite 2700, Phoenix, AZ 85073; (602) 495-2183.

APACHE JUNCTION

This town on the outer eastern edge of the Valley of the Sun came of age in the last decade as a Snowbird and retirement retreat. Apache Junction has nearly a hundred RV and mobile home parks and it's also a bedroom community for the greater Phoenix-Scottsdale area.

Scattered over ruggedly scenic desert below the legendary Superstition Mountains, the town sits at the junction of the Apache Trail (State Highway 88) and U.S. 60. It's the gateway to the Salt River Canyon recreation area, the Superstitions and Tonto National Forest.

The "Trail" was carved through the rough Salt River Canyon early in this century as a construction road for the Theodore Roosevelt Dam. Completed in 1911, the dam is the cornerstone of the Salt River Project, providing water to the Valley of the Sun. In the 1920s, Highway 60 was cut through the Pinal Mountains to the south, linking Phoenix with the copper mines of the Globe-Miami area.

Apache Junction was born in 1922 when entrepreneur George Cleveland Curtis put up a tent and started peddling sandwiches and water to travelers at the intersection of the two routes.

Elevation • 1,715 feet

Location • In Pinal County near the foothills of the Superstition Mountains, at the junction of highways 60, 88 and 89.

Climate • Hot, dry summers; warm, mild winters. July average high 104.3, low 74.2; January average high 64.9, low 35.6. Rainfall 7.52 inches; rare traces of snow.

The Superstition Mountains form a dramatic backdrop for the community of Apache Junction.

Population ● 19,525

Population trend ● Gained about seven percent in the past five years.

Property tax ● (assessed at ten percent of real value) $17.18 per $100 assessed valuation.

Economy ● It's based almost entirely on the three R's of Arizona growth—recreation, retirement and real estate. Its popularity as a retirement area and a bedroom community to the Valley of the Sun has led to a moderate boom in home construction.

Job prospects ● They aren't very good, although it's a nice place to live if you're willing to commute to work in Phoenix—or if you don't have to work. Retail trades, services and public administration comprise half the work force.

Industrial facilities ● No industrial parks since the town is primarily residential.

Real estate ● Several planned communities, including senior villages, have been built in recent years. An average three-bedroom detached home is from $65,000 and up.

The media ● One weekly, the *Apache Junction Independent*. TV provided by Phoenix, plus relays from Tucson and cable channels.

Medical services ● A medical clinic, and a hospital eight miles west.

Transportation ● Served by Greyhound; nearest airport is Phoenix Sky Harbor.

Education ● Apache Junction extension of Central Arizona College (two-year), plus four elementary, one junior high and one high school.

Local government • Incorporated in 1978; mayor, six council members and a city manager.

Places to stay • A few motels and nearly a hundred mobile home and RV parks.

Leisure facilities • Four public parks and a public pool.

Tourist lures • The Superstition Mountains, home to the legendary Lost Dutchman Mine, are in the town's back yard. Lost Dutchman State Park offers camping, picnicking and hiking. Reservoirs of the Salt River Canyon and old Western style towns such as Tortilla Flat and Gold Field also draw visitors.

Contacts • Apache Junction Chamber of Commerce, P.O. Box 1747, Apache Junction, AZ 85217; (602) 982-3141.

Department of Development Services, City of Apache Junction, 1001 N. Idaho Rd., Apache Junction, AZ 85217; (602) 671-5083; FAX (602) 671-5102.

ARIZONA CITY

Invented in 1960 as a planned community midway between Phoenix and Tucson, Arizona City offers a recreational lake, golf course and parks. It sits amidst rich agricultural fields.

Although the population is small, its percentage of increase is nearly 40 percent in the past five years—one of the highest rates in the state.

Elevation • 1,505 feet

Location • In Pinal County near the Interstate-10 and I-8 junction; about eight miles south of Casa Grande.

Climate • Warm to hot summers; warm winters with cool evenings. July average high 105, low 75.1; January average high 67, low 35.7. Rainfall 8.45 inches; rare traces of snow.

Population • Approximately 3,000

Population trend • Gained 39 percent in the past five years.

Property tax • (assessed at ten percent of real value) $20.83 per $100 assessed valuation.

Economy • It's based largely on light industry and retail, with some retirees.

Job prospects • Average to good. The town is working to attract smokeless industries and has had some success. Agriculture is still active in the area.

Industrial facilities • Two small industrial parks.

Real estate • Virtually all homes are in planned developments, since this is a new city. Prices for a three-bedroom home range from $70,000 to $80,000.

The media • The weekly *Arizona City Independent*, and the *Daily Dispatch* from nearby Casa Grande; TV via cable.

Medical services • One medical center.

Transportation • Also see Casa Grande.

Education • Central Arizona College near Casa Grande; an elementary and high school in Arizona City.

Local government • Unincorporated; government services provided by Pinal County.

Places to stay • Six motels and two RV parks in the surrounding area.

Leisure facilities • An 18-hole golf course, small recreational lake, public park, community center and tennis courts.

Tourist lures • Not many. Nearby Picacho Peak State Park, site of the westernmost battle of the Civil War, offers camping, picnicking and hiking. Casa Grande National Monument is also is nearby.

Contact • Arizona City Chamber of Commerce, P.O. Box 5, Arizona City, AZ 85223; (520) 466-5141.

AVONDALE

This is the largest of several small communities on the western rim of the Valley of the Sun, known locally as West Valley. It's also the fastest growing town in the area, gaining more than 40 percent population in the past five years. If you don't care for the fused together metro-glop of greater Phoenix, you might like to settle out here.

One can still find open desert between the borders of Avondale, Goodyear, Buckeye and Litchfield Park. Go a short distance farther west and you'll find only miles and miles of mostly uninhabited desert—all the way to the California border.

The demographics of these communities are similar. Percentage wise, they're growing much faster than the ballooning suburbs of Phoenix, although they're starting from a much smaller numeric base. This growth is spurred in part by the recent arrival of a Lufthansa pilot training center and Lockheed Martin facility adjacent to the nearby Phoenix-Goodyear Airport. The towns offer a balanced economy of manufacturing, retailing and a bit of agriculture. (See also listings for Buckeye, Goodyear and Litchfield Park below.)

Avondale was developed by the Goodyear Tire and Rubber Company, which came here initially to grow cotton for tire treads, then it started an aviation facility. A post office was opened in 1911 and the town was incorporated in 1945.

Elevation • Approximately 1,000 feet

Location • In Maricopa County, on the western edge of the Valley of the Sun just off I-10; about 20 miles from downtown Phoenix.

Climate • Warm to hot summers; balmy winters with cool evenings. July average high 106.8, low 75.3; January average high 66.9, low 35.8. Rainfall 7.56 inches; rare traces of snow.

Population • About 23,950

Population trend • Gained nearly eight percent a year during the past five years.

Property tax • (assessed at ten percent of real value) $15.02 per $100 assessed valuation.

Economy • Nearby Phoenix-Goodyear Airport, Luke Air Force Base, farming, light industry and retailing provide a balanced economic base.

Job prospects • There's considerable employment diversity among these fringe towns and job prospects range from average to good.

Industrial facilities • Several industrial parks are in the area.

Real estate • Avondale's growth has spurred the local construction industry. A variety of housing is available, from older homes starting around $70,000 to master planned communities and "ranchettes" that range well beyond $100,000.

The media • The weekly *West Valley View* covers the local scene; dailies come from Phoenix. TV also is from Phoenix and a cable company serves the area.

Medical services • A 192-bed hospital is 12 miles away; Avondale has a 120-bed nursing center.

Transportation • Served by Greyhound. The Phoenix-Goodyear Airport, operated by the city of Phoenix, is nearby, with an 8,500-foot runway. Sky Harbor International Airport is about 20 miles east.

Education • Estrella Mountain Community College, plus the usual elementary and middle schools and two high schools.

Local government • Incorporated in 1946; mayor, seven-member council and a city manager.

Places to stay • Four motels, a resort and several RV parks in the area.

Leisure facilities • Six public parks, five golf courses, an auto race track, community center and senior center, plus tennis, racquetball and handball courts.

Tourist lures • It's a family town, not a tourist town. Locals like the solitude of the surrounding desert, not yet devoured by asphalt. It's a short drive to the many tourist and cultural offerings of the Valley of the Sun.

Contacts • Tri City West Chamber of Commerce, 501 W. Van Buren, Suite K, Avondale, AZ 85223; (602) 932-2260; FAX 932-9057.

Economic Development Department, City of Avondale, 525 N. Central, Avondale, AZ 85323; (602) 932-2400.

BUCKEYE

Beginning life as a farming town in 1888, Buckeye got its nice name from the Buckeye Canal, one of the first modern irrigation ditches in the state.

This quiet hamlet west of Phoenix is one of the slowest growing communities in the valley and it still maintains a small town atmosphere. However, industrial developments around nearby Avondale, Goodyear and Litchfield Park should spur more activity in this decade.

Elevation • 890 feet

Location • In Maricopa County, on the far western edge of the Valley of the Sun just south of Interstate 10; about 30 miles from Phoenix.

Climate • Warm to hot summers; balmy winters with cool evenings. July average high 107.3, low 74.3; January average high 67.1, low 34.3. Rainfall 7.08 inches; rare traces of snow.

Population • About 5,130

Population trend • Gaining only about one percent a year in the past five years, although recent expansions at nearby Phoenix-Goodyear Airport may spur future growth.

Property tax • (assessed at ten percent of real value) $15.52 per $100 assessed valuation.

Economy • Agriculture and light manufacturing.

Job prospects • Average to below average job availability in retail sales and at a few small factories. Farming still provides 11 percent of the local payroll, while services lead with nearly 20 percent and 14 percent is in retailing.

Industrial facilities • Several small industrial parks are close to Interstate-10.

Real estate • A few modern subdivisions are a-building, and a few older homes are on the market. Prices range from $50,000 to $80,000 for modest three-bedroom dwellings.

The media • Three weeklies, the *Buckeye Valley News, Westsider* and *West Valley View*. Dailies come from Phoenix, along with most TV channels. The area also has a cable company.

Medical services • A 24-hour emergency medical center; eight hospitals within 36 miles.

Transportation • Served by Greyhound. Buckeye Municipal Airport has a 4,300-foot runway and it's being expanded. Sky Harbor International is about 35 miles away.

Education • One private elementary school, plus a public elementary and high school.

Local government • Incorporated in 1931; mayor, six-member council and town manager.

Places to stay • Six motels, seven mobile home parks and an RV park.

Leisure facilities • Three public parks, a community center, an 18-hole golf course 14 miles east, and tennis, racquetball and handball courts.

Tourist lures • None; folks head for Phoenix for those.

Contacts • Buckeye Valley Chamber of Commerce, P.O. Box 717 (904 Monroe Ave.), Buckeye, AZ 85326; (602) 386-2727.

Town of Buckeye, P.O. Box 175, Buckeye, AZ 85326; (602) 256-2488.

Western Gateway Team, 800 S. Litchfield Rd., Goodyear, AZ 85338; (602) 932-9138.

CAREFREE & CAVE CREEK

Sitting on the far northeastern fringes of the Valley of the Sun, these hamlets are twins in location only. As the cute name suggests, Carefree is a modern planned community. It appeals primarily to retired folks and commuters to Phoenix and Scottsdale. Cave Creek is on the rustic side, a Western style town that began as a mining camp in the 1870s.

Both communities are in attractive rocky desert surrounded by rockier hills. They rate high on our list of desirable Arizona villages, particularly for retired folks. However, temporary winter facilities are rather limited for Snowbirds.

The two hamlets balance one another nicely. One can luxuriate in luxury resorts such as the Boulders and shop at stylish boutiques in Carefree, and then get a cowboy steak at a restaurant-saloon in Cave Creek.

Interstate 17, a few miles west, offers a quick 25-minute trip to downtown Phoenix. For serious shopping and dining, upscale Scottsdale is just a few miles south of Carefree.

Elevation • Carefree 2,500 feet; Cave Creek 2,200 feet

Location • In Maricopa County, 25 miles northeast of Phoenix.

Climate • Warm to hot summers; mild winters with some chilly evenings. July average high 102, low 75.4; January average high 62, low 38.8. Rainfall 12.35 inches; rare traces of snow.

Population • Carefree 1,975; Cave Creek 2,855

Population trend • Carefree gained 18 percent in the past five years; Cave Creek had a slight population loss.

Property tax • $10.26 per $100 of assessed valuation.

Economy • It's pretty much based on tourism and desert living. The towns aren't working to attract industry.

Job prospects • They're quite limited since the focus here is retirement and commuting to Phoenix and Scottsdale.

Industrial facilities • None.

Real estate • Housing is expensive in this highly desirable area, ranging from $160,000 and up.

The media • One weekly, the *Foothills Sentinel* and a monthly, the *Carefree Enterprise*. Daily newspapers and TV service from Phoenix, plus a cable company.

Medical services • Small clinics only; extensive facilities available in Scottsdale and Phoenix.

Transportation • Nearest commercial transit is in Scottsdale and Phoenix; Sky Harbor International Airport is about 25 miles away. Carefree has a general aviation facility with a 4,100-foot runway.

Education • Two elementary schools, junior high and high school.

Local government • Cave Creek was incorporated in 1986 and Carefree in 1984. Council-manager government in Cave Creek; mayor, six council members and a town administrator in Carefree.

Places to stay • Two resorts and six bed & breakfast inns.

Leisure facilities • Two community centers, an adult center, two public parks and three golf courses, plus many more in the Paradise Valley and Scottsdale area.

Tourist lures • Folks come here mostly for the striking rocky desert scenery, the boutiques of Carefree and the frontier ambiance of Cave Creek. The surrounding desert rises into the wilds of Tonto National Forest, with hiking trails, Indian ruins and ample solitude.

Contacts • Carefree/Cave Creek Chamber of Commerce, P.O. Box 734 (748 Easy St.), Carefree, AZ 85377; (602) 488-3381.

Town of Carefree, P.O. Box 740, Carefree, AZ 85377; 488-3686.

Town of Cave Creek, 37622 N. Cave Creek Rd., Cave Creek, AZ 85331; (602) 488-1400.

CASA GRANDE

A thriving working class town, Casa Grande was named for a large Hohokam Indian adobe about 20 miles away. It was established in 1879 as a way station on a railroad being built to link Phoenix and Tucson. Incorporated in 1915, it's the largest community in Pinal County.

The surrounding area is essentially irrigated desert. The countryside isn't particularly attractive, although the area is tidy, the climate's nice and homes are affordable. The town is becoming popular with retirees, and it offers two senior centers and several mobile home parks. A few Snowbirds light here as well, drawn by the relatively inexpensive facilities.

Elevation • 1,398 feet

Location • In Pinal County off I-10, about midway between Phoenix and Tucson.

Climate • Warm to hot summers; dry, balmy winters with cool evenings. July average high 106.2, low 76; January average high 66, low 35. Rainfall 8.12 inches; rare dustings of snow.

Population • 20,880

Population trend • Gained nine percent in the past five years.

Property tax • $16.80 per $100 assessed valuation.

Economy • Originally agricultural based, it's shifting toward light industry and the services sector.

Job prospects • They're "average," according to the local Job Service office. The best possibilities are in retail sales, tourist-related work and business skills such as word processing and sales.

Industrial facilities • Eight industrial parks, some with rail access.

Real estate • There's a modest amount of new home construction in the area, plus some older houses on the market, with prices of a three-bedroom ranging from $55,000 to $80,000.

The media • One daily newspaper, the *Casa Grande Dispatch.* TV relays from Phoenix, plus a local cable company.

Medical services • A 100-bed hospital and long-term care facility.

Transportation • Served by Greyhound. Casa Grande Airport has two 5,200-foot runways; served by feeder and charter lines.

Education • Signal Peak campus of Central Arizona Community College is east of Casa Grande; one private elementary school plus eight public elementary and one high school.

Local government • Incorporated in 1915; mayor, six council members and a city manager.

Places to stay • Since Casa Grande is on the heavily traveled Phoenix-Tucson corridor, it has 14 motels and 15 RV parks.

Leisure facilities • Ten public parks, four golf courses within ten miles, two senior centers, two public pools, plus the usual tennis courts, bowling alleys and such.

Tourist lures • This is a good base of operations for exploring north and south because of its midway location between Arizona's two metropolitan centers. Casa Grande Ruins National Monument and the fine Gila River Indian Arts and Craft Center are nearby.

Contacts • Greater Casa Grande Chamber of Commerce, 575 N. Marshall St., Casa Grande, AZ 85222; (520) 836-2125.

City of Casa Grande, P.O. Box 15011 (300 E. Fourth St.), Casa Grande, AZ 85230; (520) 421-8600.

Greater Casa Grande Valley Economic Development Foundation, 201 E. Third St., Casa Grande, AZ 85222; (520) 836-6868.

CHANDLER

This is another of the Valley of the Sun's authentic boomtowns, zooming from 29,673 in 1980 to nearly 90,000 in 1990 and 128,035 in 1995. The Chandler growth rate has been more than triple that of the rest of Maricopa County. All of this adds up to an abundance of new housing, good job prospects and a generally upscale economy.

• FLAGSTAFF

PHOENIX

• TUCSON

Chandler doesn't have the cultural and tourist offerings of other valley communities, but no matter. Everything is within a few minutes' drive. Tempe's Arizona State University, for instance, is just across the freeway.

The town began in the early 1890s when Canadian-born veterinarian Alexander John Chandler staked out a 1,800-acre ranch. A ambitious entrepreneur, he brought in irrigation water and then subdivided and sold off parcels for small farms. He went on to establish a resort, bank and other properties to become his namesake town's leading citizen. There's not much agriculture left today, however. The primary crop is subdivisions.

Elevation • 1,210 feet

Location • In Maricopa County, southeast of Phoenix.

Climate • Warm to hot summers; balmy winters. July average high 103.8, low 76.4; January average high 65, low 37.3. Rainfall 8.42 inches; rare traces of snow.

Population • 128,035

Population trend • Gained 41 percent in the past five years.

Property tax • (assessed at ten percent of real value) $13.85 per $100 assessed valuation.

Economy • Active and diversified, with a mix of construction, high tech industries, retail trade and service jobs.

Job prospects • Space age firms like Intel Corporation, Microchip Technology and Space Data Corporation offer good potential, along with construction and retailing. Also, it's a short drive to the even larger Phoenix job market.

Industrial facilities • Fifteen industrial parks, many with rail and air service.

Real estate • Prices for three-bedroom detached homes range from $80,000 to well beyond $100,000.

The media • The daily *Chandler Tribune* and weekly *Chandler Independent*. Phoenix provides local television, and Chandler has a cable company.

Medical services • A 120-bed hospital and several small medical clinics.

Transportation • Served by Greyhound. Two local airports have lighted runways; Phoenix Sky Harbor International is 15 miles away.

Education • Two private elementary schools, a private high school and numerous public elementary, junior high and high schools.

Local government • Incorporated in 1920; mayor, six council members and a city manager.

Places to stay • Three hotels and four motels, plus dozens more in adjacent cities.

Leisure facilities • Three golf courses, three public pools, various parks and playing fields, plus tennis and racquetball courts.

Tourist lures • Most are elsewhere, although Chandler has a nicely done historical museum.

Contacts • Chandler Chamber of Commerce, 218 N. Arizona Ave., Chandler, AZ 85224; (602) 963-4571; FAX (602) 963-0188.

City of Chandler, Department of Development & Community Services, 125 E. Commonwealth St., Chandler, AZ 85225; 786-2734.

FLORENCE

Sitting off to the eastern side of the Phoenix-Tucson corridor, Florence is a pleasant surprise. It's one of Arizona's oldest towns, dating from 1866 when one Levi Ruggles laid out a townsite near a ford in the Gila River. This is a handsome place today, with fine 19th century homes in the Florence Townsite National Historic District. Many of these are listed on the National Register of Historic Places.

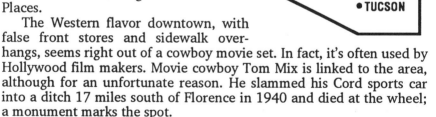

The Western flavor downtown, with false front stores and sidewalk overhangs, seems right out of a cowboy movie set. In fact, it's often used by Hollywood film makers. Movie cowboy Tom Mix is linked to the area, although for an unfortunate reason. He slammed his Cord sports car into a ditch 17 miles south of Florence in 1940 and died at the wheel; a monument marks the spot.

Florence is the seat of Pinal County and its 1891 courthouse is an architectural gem—a yellow brick structure with gingerbread trim and a hexagonal clock tower. The town also is home to the Arizona State Prison, built in 1909 to replace the aging Yuma Territorial Prison.

Elevation • 1,493 feet

Location • In Pinal County, midway between Phoenix and Tucson on U.S. Highway 79.

Climate • Warm to hot summers; balmy winters with cool evenings. July average high 106.1, low 74; January average high 66.8, low 36.1. Rainfall 9.5 inches; occasional traces of snow.

Birds of a feather (pigeons in this case) flock about the elaborate clocktower of the Pina County Courthouse in Florence.

Population • 11,440

Population trend • Gained 52 percent in the past five years.

Property tax • (assessed at ten percent of real value) $14.89 per $100 assessed valuation.

Economy • It's heavily focused on public administration, because of its county seat status and the adjacent state prison; these facilities account for more than half of the local payroll.

Job prospects • Construction, services and retail trades offer potential, with the current growth trend. Largest employers are the county government with 1,500 and Arizona State Prison with 1,700.

Industrial facilities • No industrial parks.

Real estate • Three-bedroom home prices range from $60,000 to $85,000.

The media • One weekly, the *Florence Reminder*; daily news coverage is provided by the *Casa Grande Dispatch*. TV relays from Phoenix and Tucson, plus cable.

Medical services • A 91-bed hospital, a nursing home and a residential care home.

Transportation • Nearest airport is in Coolidge, ten miles away; no scheduled air or bus service.

Education • One each—elementary, junior high and high schools.

Local government • Seat of Pinal County since 1875. Incorporated in 1908; mayor, six council members and a town manager.

Places to stay • A motel and two RV parks.

Leisure facilities • Two nine-hole golf courses, two public parks, a recreation center, a public pool and tennis courts.

Tourist lures • The historic downtown district draws visitors, along with the courthouse and McFarland State Historic Park, which honors the former U.S. Senate majority leader, Arizona governor and chief justice of the Arizona supreme court. Casa Grande Ruins National Monument is nearby; in fact, it's closer to Florence than to the town of Casa Grande.

Contacts • Florence Chamber of Commerce, P.O. Box 929 (219 Bailey St.), Florence, AZ 85232; (520) 868-9433.

Pinal County Development Board, P.O. Box 967 (135 N. Pinal St.), Florence, AZ 85232; (520) 868-4331.

Town of Florence, P.O. Box 490 (133 N. Main St.), Florence, AZ 85232; (520) 868-5889.

FOUNTAIN HILLS

An upscale planned community started in 1970, Fountain Hills is carefully laid over a rugged desert panorama. It was created by Lake Havasu City's McCulloch Properties of London Bridge fame, and designed by Charles Wood Jr., who also fashioned the original Disneyland layout.

Fountain Hills is much more stylish than either of these. However, since McCulloch likes to have a gimmick, this community boasts the world's tallest fountain as its focal point. It spurts skyward from a nicely landscaped lake, and the town is built around it.

Although retired people are drawn to Fountain Hills, it has a rather low median age of 37. Many residents are professionals who commute to work in the Valley of the Sun.

Elevation • 1,520 to 3,000 feet

Location • In Maricopa County, 30 miles northeast of Phoenix and a few miles east of Scottsdale.

Climate • Warm to hot summers; balmy winters with some cool evenings. July average high 105.1, low 74.2; January average high 66.7, low 36.4. Rainfall 8.06 inches; occasional traces of snow.

Population • 15,500

Population trend • Gained 40 percent in the past five years.

Property tax • $14.19 per $100 assessed valuation.

Economy • It's essentially an upper middle class bedroom town, with small businesses and services as its economic core.

Job prospects • An unemployment rate of less than three percent is misleading since Fountain Hills doesn't have much of a job base. It's populated mostly with commuters and retirees.

Industrial facilities • None.

Real estate • Housing is predictably expensive in this upscale town. Three-bedroom detached homes start around $140,000 and newer models top $280,000.

The media • The weekly *Times of Fountain Hills* and monthly *Sentinel*. Daily newspapers and TV from Phoenix, plus a cable company.

Medical services • Two family health centers and a walk-in clinic; other facilities in Scottsdale, plus a Mayo Clinic four miles west of Fountain Hills.

Transportation • Mesa and Scottsdale airports are 13 miles away and Phoenix Sky Harbor is 24 miles.

Education • A private K-12 school and the usual public elementary, middle and high schools.

Local government • Incorporated in 1989; governed by the Town of Fountain Hills Council.

Places to stay • A few local motels, plus numerous hotels, motels and RV parks in adjacent communities.

Leisure facilities • Two public parks, three golf courses, an equestrian center, community center and several public tennis courts.

Tourist lures • Some come to see that tall fountain, while the surrounding desert draws hikers and seekers of solitude. McDowell Mountain Regional Park is just north of town; Saguaro Lake and Canyon Lake of the Salt River Project are northeast.

Contact • Fountain Hills Chamber of Commerce, P.O. Box 17598 (16838 E. Palisades Ave., #2), Fountain Hills, AZ 85269; (602) 837-1654; FAX (602) 837-3077.

GILBERT

To call Gilbert a dynamic growth city is an understatement. It leaped from 5,717 in 1980 to about 30,000 in 1990 and 54,935 in 1995. Current population estimates put it at 70,000. It was Arizona's fastest growing city in the last decade.

Booming Gilbert is geared more to employment and family raising than to retirement. It has one of the lowest unemployment rates in the states. There's nothing particularly scenic about the rather level farmland and desert terrain hereabout. What Gilbert offers is room to grow, and another 20,000 homes are expected by the millennium.

The town isn't all new. It dates back to an 1890 homestead filed by William A. Gilbert and it was incorporated in 1920. However, it dozed for decades in the desert heat until it caught the Valley of the Sun growth bug in the 1980s.

Elevation ● 1,273 feet

Location ● In Maricopa County's southeast corner, next door to Chandler and about 20 miles from downtown Phoenix.

Climate ● warm to hot summers; balmy winters with cool evenings. July average high 104.3, low 80; January average high 64.9, low 35.6. Rainfall 7.66 inches; occasional traces of snow.

Population ● Approximately 72,000

Population trend ● Gained 147 percent in the past six years.

Property tax ● (assessed at ten percent of real value) $14.12 per $100 assessed value.

Economy ● A pro-growth attitude, broad employment base with several high tech industries and expanded shopping centers add fuel to Gilbert's economic engine.

Job prospects ● It offers one of Arizona's best job markets, with an unemployment rate hovering around three percent and a constantly expanding job base. The labor force increased by nearly 50 percent in the Eighties and it continues to grow. Retail trade and services account for 40 percent of local jobs while factories provide about 20 percent.

Industrial facilities ● More than a dozen industrial parks, many with rail and air service.

Real estate ● Older three-bedroom homes start around $90,000 and new subdivisions range up to $500,000.

The media ● The daily *Gilbert Tribune*, plus the dailies from Phoenix. TV also comes from Phoenix and from a local cable company.

Medical services ● Two hospitals in adjacent Chandler and four in Mesa.

Transportation ● Served by Greyhound. Chandler and Mesa municipal airports are nearby; Phoenix Sky Harbor is 19 miles northwest.

Education ● Chandler/Gilbert Community College is a mile south, Mesa Community College is three miles northwest and Arizona State University is within a short commute. Gilbert has the full range of public schools.

Local government ● Incorporated in 1920; mayor, six council members and a town manager.

Places to stay ● Numerous motels and RV parks in Chandler and Mesa.

Leisure facilities ● Twenty-four golf courses in surrounding areas including three in Gilbert, public parks and pool, recreation center, racquet ball and tennis courts.

Tourist lures ● While not a tourist town, Gilbert is not far from the Superstition Mountains and Salt River Canyon; the many lures of Phoenix-Scottsdale are within a short drive.

Contacts ● Gilbert Chamber of Commerce, P.O. Box 527 (202 N. Gilbert St.), Gilbert, AZ 85234; (602) 892-0056.

Economic Development Department, Town of Gilbert, 1025 S. Gilbert Rd., Gilbert, AZ 85296; (602) 503-6000.

GLENDALE

Another of the mushroomburbs of the Valley of the Sun, Glendale is a mix of residential areas, shopping centers and manufacturing. Nearby Luke Air Force Base, the nation's largest fighter training facility, provides civilian employment; it was annexed by Glendale in 1995. Electronics, precision metal working and casting and aerospace activities also add to the job base.

Like Chandler and Gilbert, Glendale's main asset is room to grow. It began rather modestly as a farming settlement by the Illinois Church of the Brethren in 1892 and it progressed rather slowly until it caught the growth bug of recent decades.

Despite its explosive growth and the attendant newness, downtown Glendale is historically charming, with lots of antique shops, tearooms and such. A jolly little trolley takes visitors about the Catlin Court Historic District, where old homes have been converted into specialty boutiques.

Elevation ● 1,100 feet

Location ● In Maricopa County, northwestern area of the Valley of the Sun.

Climate ● Warm to hot summers; mild winters. July average high 104.4, low 78.3; January average high 64.6, low 38. Rainfall 6.74 inches; rare traces of snow.

Population ● 177,055

Population trend ● Increased by 20 percent in the past five years; nearly doubled in population from 1980 to 1995.

Property tax ● (assessed at ten percent of real value) $13.75 per $100 assessed valuation.

Economy ● It's rolling right along, and it spans the spectrum from metal fabricating to light manufacturing and services. One of the world's largest shopping malls, with 1.3 million square feet of retail space, opened in 1994, adding 2,000 workers to the Glendale payroll.

Job prospects ● They're generally excellent and they cover a broad range, including manufacturing, aerospace, communications, precision metal working, chemicals, electronics, warehousing, services and retail sales. The Honeywell Corporation is Glendale's largest employer.

Industrial facilities • Numerous industrial parks and factories.

Real estate • A three-bedroom home ranges from $80,000 to $100,000 and beyond.

The media • Two weeklies, *The Glendale Star* and *The Prospector*, plus the monthly *Arrow*. Daily newspapers and TV from Phoenix; local cable service.

Medical services • Three hospitals, six nursing homes and several medical clinics; other facilities in surrounding communities.

Transportation • Served by Greyhound. Glendale Airport has a 5,350-foot lighted runway; Phoenix Sky Harbor is about 30 miles away.

Education • The American Graduate School of International Management; a new College of Osteopathic Medicine operated by Midwestern University; the west campus of Arizona State University; several technical schools and the usual public schools.

Local government • Incorporated in 1910; mayor, six-member council and city manager.

Places to stay • Four motels and business-oriented hotels, nine RV parks, plus other facilities in surrounding communities.

Leisure facilities • Forty-six public parks, three golf courses, a tennis center, six public swimming pools, three bowling centers and two roller skating rinks.

Tourist lures • Glendale isn't a tourist town, although the Valley of the Sun's many attractions are nearby.

Contacts • Glendale Chamber of Commerce, P.O. Box 249 (7105 N. 59th Ave.), Glendale, AZ 85311; (800) ID-SUNNY or (602) 280-1321.

City of Glendale, 5850 W. Glendale Ave., Glendale, AZ 85301; (602) 930-2800.

GOODYEAR

If the name sounds familiar, it's because this little town was established by the Goodyear Tire and Rubber Company in 1916—not to make tires but to raise cotton for tire cords. Originally, it was going to be called Egypt. Goodyear soon had thousands of acres under cultivation, and the firm later located its aircraft division here, along with Lockheed Martin in later years. Although it has remained small for decades, Goodyear has had a recent growth surge.

This is another of those small communities on the western edge of the Valley of the Sun that appeals to people who want to see more desert than asphalt. It isn't ruggedly handsome desert like that around Scottsdale and Fountain Hills, but at least it's open space, and some desert mountains are nearby.

Elevation • Approximately 1,000 feet

Location • In Maricopa County, on the western fringe of the Valley of the Sun, known locally as the Southwest Valley; 17 miles from Phoenix.

Climate • Warm to hot summers; mild winters. July average high 106.8, low 75.3; January average high 66.9, low 35.8. Rainfall 7.56 inches; occasional trace of snow.

Population • About 10,000

Population trend • Gaining 14 percent a year.

Property tax • (assessed at ten percent of real value) $12.88 per $100 assessed valuation.

Economy • The economic base is centered around the Phoenix-Goodyear Airport. The Airline Training Center Arizona, operated by Lufthansa, trains commercial airline pilots and the Lockheed Martin facility is adjacent, occupying a million-square- foot campus.

Job prospects • With large employers such as Lockheed Martin, Rubbermaid and Poore Brothers, area job prospects are varied and generally plentiful.

Industrial facilities • More than 2,000 acres of industrial property, some with parks, in an area known as the Western Maricopa Enterprise Zone.

Real estate • Four master-planned communities are in the area, with prices for a three-bedroom home ranging from $70,000 to $250,000.

The media • Two weeklies, the *Westsider Chronicle* and *West Valley View*. Daily news and TV programming comes from Phoenix and a local cable company.

Medical services • A 24-hour emergency clinic and medical plaza; a 192-bed hospital is 12 miles away.

Transportation • Bisected by I-10 and served by Greyhound. Phoenix-Goodyear Municipal Airport has an 8,500-foot lighted runway. Sky Harbor is about 25 miles east.

Education • Estrella Mountain Community College, plus the usual public schools.

Local government • Incorporated in 1946; mayor, six-member council and city manager.

Places to stay • A few motels, small hotel and a large resort.

Leisure facilities • Five golf courses, several public parks, a community center, pool and tennis courts; Estrella Mountain Regional Park is nearby.

Tourist lures ● Phoenix International Raceway is nearby and the lures of Phoenix-Scottsdale are less than an hour's drive.

Contacts ● City of Goodyear, 119 N. Litchfield Rd., Goodyear, AZ 85338; (800) 872-1749 or (602) 932-3910; FAX (602) 932-3028.

Tri City West Chamber of Commerce, 501 W. Van Buren, Suite K, Avondale, AZ 85223; (602) 932-2260; FAX (602) 932-9057.

Western Gateway Team, 800 S. Litchfield Rd., Goodyear, AZ 85338; (602) 932-9138.

LITCHFIELD PARK

This town west of Phoenix was established by the Goodyear Tire and Rubber Company in 1918 and originally named Litchton, then changed to Litchfield Park in 1926. It was named for the firm's vice president Paul W. Litchfield. It was he who had conceived the idea of raising cotton in adjacent Goodyear for tire cords. Litchfield Park was designed as a model company town and much of that careful community design is still evident.

Growth has been slow in recent years, although it's beginning to pick up because of new facilities at nearby Phoenix-Goodyear Airport and westward spread of the ever-expanding Phoenix economy.

Elevation ● About 1,000 feet.

Location ● In Maricopa County, just north of Goodyear, on the western edge of the Valley of the Sun.

Climate ● Warm to hot summers; mild winters. July average high 106.8, low 75.3; January average high 66.9, low 35.8. Rainfall 7.56 inches; occasional trace of snow.

Population ● 3,465

Population trend ● Gained less than four percent in the past five years.

Property tax ● $14.93 per $100 assessed valuation.

Economy ● The economic base is diversified to include light industry, retail trade and services. The nearby Litchfield Naval Air Facility and Phoenix-Goodyear Airport are important economic elements.

Job prospects ● The unemployment rate is rather low and nearby industries such as Rubbermaid, McKesson and a large grocery distribution center provide job possibilities.

Industrial facilities ● Six industrial parks are nearby.

Real estate ● A few subdivisions are being built, with three-bedroom homes priced between $65,000 and $85,000. Some older homes may be found for around $50,0000 although these are becoming scarce.

The media • Two weeklies, the *Westsider Chronicle* and *West Valley View*. Daily news and TV programming comes from Phoenix and a local cable company.

Medical services • A 192-bed hospital is 12 miles east of town.

Transportation • Served by Greyhound. Phoenix-Goodyear Municipal Airport has an 8,500-foot lighted runway. Sky Harbor is about 20 miles east.

Education • Extension courses from Maricopa Community College in nearby Goodyear; the usual public schools in the area.

Local government • Founded in 1918; incorporated in 1987; mayor, six-member council and city manager.

Places to stay • The large Wigwam Resort; motels and RV parks in nearby communities.

Leisure facilities • Four public parks, three golf courses and a public swimming pool.

Tourist lures • None; Litchfield Park is less than hour from Phoenix-Scottsdale lures.

Contacts • City of Litchfield Park, 214 W. Wigwam Blvd., Litchfield Park, AZ 85340; (602) 935-5033; FAX (602) 935-5427.

Tri City West Chamber of Commerce, 501 W. Van Buren, Suite K, Avondale, AZ 85223; (602) 932-2260; FAX (602) 932-9057.

Western Gateway Team, 800 S. Litchfield Rd., Goodyear, AZ 85338; (602) 932-9138.

MESA

Among cities with more than 100,000 population, Mesa was second in the country in growth during the Eighties. Its people count zoomed from 152,404 in 1980 to 288,091 in 1990, an increase of nearly 80 percent. Growth slowed in this decade as available land began to fill up, and it became hemmed in by expanding neighbor cities. However, it's Arizona's third largest city, after Phoenix and Tucson.

Mesa was settled by a group of Mormons who set up camp on a bluff above the Salt River in 1877. They weren't very original in picking a name for their settlement; *mesa* simply means bluff or flat top hill in Spanish. Like the pioneers of neighboring Phoenix, they cleaned out old Hohokam canals along the river and soon had themselves a thriving little farming town.

Those early Mormons wouldn't recognize their creation today, of course. Suburban scatter has buried all except a few farm fields on the city's outer reaches. Despite its sprawling growth, downtown Mesa is quite attractive, with Spanish colonnade sidewalks, brick crosswalks and streets lined with palm and orange trees.

Elevation • 1,225 feet

Location • In Maricopa County, 14 miles east of Phoenix.

Climate • Warm to hot summers; mild winters. July average high 104.3, low 74.1; January average high 64.9, low 35.6. Rainfall 7.52 inches; occasional trace of snow.

Population • 350,000

Population trend • Gained 14 percent in the past five years.

Property tax • $11.11 per $100 assessed valuation.

Economy • Despite slowed growth, Mesa's economy is broad-based and solid. Seven of *Fortune Magazine's* top five hundred companies are located here. Production ranges from propulsion equipment and helicopters to food processing and electronics.

Job prospects • With a thriving economy and a low jobless rate, this is a good place to find work. Among its chief employers are Mc-Donnell Douglas Helicopters, Rosarita Foods, General Motors Proving Grounds and Motorola.

Industrial facilities • Twenty or more industrial parks, plus several large manufacturing complexes.

Real estate • A variety of homes is available, from conventional subdivisions to planned communities to condos and townhouses. Home prices for a three-bedroom detached unit start around $80,000 and range well beyond $100,000.

The media • The daily *Mesa Tribune* and the weekly *Mesa Independent*. Phoenix and a local cable company furnish the television.

Medical services • Four hospitals, 18 extended care and convalescent homes and several medical clinics.

Transportation • Served by Greyhound. Falcon Field has a lighted 4,300-foot runway; Phoenix Sky Harbor is 12 miles west of Mesa.

Education • Mesa Community College, the east campus of Arizona State University and the usual public schools.

Local government • Incorporated in 1883; mayor, six-member council and city manager.

Places to stay • About 60 hotels and motels, plus many RV and mobile home parks with more than 30,000 total spaces.

Leisure facilities • Numerous public parks, 25 golf courses in the area, ten public pools, plus tennis, handball and racquetball courts.

Tourist lures • Mesa has five archives, including the excellent Mesa Southwest Museum downtown, and the Champlin Fighter Museum and Confederate Air Force Museum at Falcon Field. The Chicago Cubs do their spring training here in February and March.

Contacts • Mesa Chamber of Commerce, P.O. Box 5820 (120 N. Center St.), Mesa, AZ 85211-5820; (800) 283-6372 or (602) 827-4700; FAX (602) 827-0727.

City of Mesa Economic Development, 100 N. Center, Mesa, AZ 85201; (800) 290-6372 or (602) 644-2398.

Planning Department, City of Mesa, 55 N. Center St., Mesa, AZ 85201; (602) 644-2185.

PARADISE VALLEY

If you like awesome rocky desert scenery and you can afford the prices, this can indeed become your paradise. There's little work available; folks come here either to retire or to commute to high-paying jobs. Situated in a high desert basin between Scottsdale and Carefree, Paradise Valley is the Beverly Hills of the Valley of the Sun. It's a contented scatter of expensive homes, estates tucked into rough-hewn foothills and an occasional resort.

It was established in the late 1880s as a farming community by settlers who diverted water from a tributary of the Salt River. By the post-World War II years, most of the farms had been bought up as homesites by the more prosperous folks of growing Phoenix.

Elevation • 1,421 feet

Location • In Maricopa County, north of the Phoenix Mountains, between Scottsdale and Carefree-Cave Creek.

Climate • Warm to hot summers; mild winters. July average high 104.1, low 80.9; January average high 64.5, low 42.6. Rainfall 8.40 inches; snowfall very rare.

Population • 12,930

Population trend • Gained ten percent in the past five years.

Property tax • (assessed at ten percent of real value) $14.00 per $100 assessed valuation.

Economy • Residents bring their own economy in the form of fat bank accounts. Most folks work elsewhere or they can afford not to work at all. The town has a small business and commercial district.

Job prospects • Not much to offer; unemployment is low become most residents are retired or they commute to jobs outside.

Industrial facilities • None.

Real estate • Homes rival those of Sedona as the most expensive in Arizona, starting around $150,000 and going into the millions for walled estates and mini-ranches. As the old saying goes, "If you have to ask the price—"

The media • Two weeklies, the *Paradise Valley Voice* and *Paradise Valley Independent*. Phoenix stations and cable companies provide TV.

Medical services • Three hospitals in the area; two emergency centers and five extended care facilities.

Transportation • Mostly BMWs and Mercedes. Scheduled air service from Scottsdale Municipal Airport (feeder lines) and Phoenix Sky Harbor, about 15 miles away.

Education • A mix of private and public schools.

Local government • The Town of Paradise Valley, which doesn't encompass all of the valley, was incorporated in 1961, with a mayor, six-member council and town manager.

Places to stay • The valley offers some of Arizona's most elegant resorts, plus a few smaller hotels and upscale motels.

Leisure facilities • Eight golf course, two swimming pools, plus various tennis and racquetball courts at the resorts.

Tourist lures • Visitors come here mostly to envy the posh estates, or to stay at the resorts. Nearby North Mountain Park and Squaw Peak offer picnicking and hiking.

Contact • Greater Paradise Valley Chamber of Commerce, 3135 E. Cactus Rd., Paradise Valley, AZ 85032; (602) 482-3344; FAX (602) 482-2261.

PEORIA

Once a quiet farming town on the northwest edge of the Valley of the Sun, Peoria has been caught up in the greater Phoenix growth bug. Its population leaped from 12,171 in 1980 to 50,000 in 1990 and to nearly 70,000 in 1995.

The town was established in 1886; settlers named it for their hometown of Peoria, Illinois, of which it bears absolutely no resemblance. Despite its rapid growth, it retains some of its small town characteristics and open desert and farms still surround much of the community. Most of the industrial areas are focused along a roadway that loops around the town from the U.S. 60 freeway.

Elevation • About 1,100 feet

Location • In Maricopa County, about 20 miles northwest of Phoenix.

Climate • Warm to hot summers; mild winters. July average high 106.3, low 74.7; January average high 66.5, low 35. Rainfall 7.65 inches; rare traces of snow.

Population • 69,970

Population trend • gained 39 percent in the past five years.

Property tax • (assessed at ten percent of real value) $13.92 per $100 assessed valuation.

Economy • City officials are very pro-growth. The Peoria Economic Development Group is working to draw both business and industry.

Job prospects • With its industrial, medical and retail growth, Peoria offers above average employment opportunities. The services industry is the largest employer at 28 percent, followed by retailing with 19 percent. Construction and manufacturing provide about one in four jobs.

Industrial facilities • Two industrial parks with rail access.

Real estate • A good selection of homes is available, with prices for a three-bedroom unit ranging from $80,000 to $100,000.

The media • Two weeklies, the *Peoria Times* and *The Westsider.* Daily news and TV from Phoenix and a local cable company.

Medical services • Five hospitals and five extended care facilities within a five-mile radius.

Transportation • Served by Greyhound. Glendale Municipal Airport is adjacent; Phoenix Sky Harbor is about 25 miles away.

Education • Rio Salado Community College offers extension classes; the usual public schools.

Local government • Incorporated in 1954; mayor, six-member council and a city manager.

Places to stay • A motel and two RV parks; other motels and RV parks nearby.

Leisure facilities • Ten public parks, a community center, two golf courses, a public pool and tennis courts.

Tourist lures • As evidenced by its single motel, tourists don't flock here. Lake Pleasant Regional Park is 15 miles north, providing fishing, boating and swimming.

Contacts • Peoria Chamber of Commerce, P.O. Box 70 (8355 Peoria Ave.), Peoria, AZ 85380; (602) 979-3601.

City of Peoria, 8401 W. Monroe St., Peoria, AZ 85345; (602) 412-7300.

Peoria Economic Development Corporation, 10601 N. 83rd Dr., Peoria, AZ 85435; (602) 486-2011.

SCOTTSDALE

When we first visited this mountainous desert region 25 years ago, Scottsdale was a quiet cowboy style hamlet. As we explored its Western wear stores, art galleries and curio shops, words like "quaint" and "charming" came to mind. Those shops still exist, although they're surrounded by a burgeoning suburbia. Scottsdale has become the Valley of the Sun's most fashionable large community.

About 20 years ago, Phoenix began spilling northward, threatening to engulf Scottsdale. In self defense, the little town went on an annexation binge and promptly covered the pretty desert landscape with its own suburban scatter. Yet it remains one of the Valley of the Sun's most inviting towns, with some of the area's most opulent resorts. Scottsdale's growth, although rapid, has been more controlled than most other cities. It retains the same Southwest and Santa Fe style architecture that visitors remember when the town was much smaller. Since it's on the outer edge of the Phoenix megalopolis, a brief drive north takes you into a desert that is still free of subdivisions and service stations.

The craggy Camelback Mountain, so named because it resembles a kneeling camel, offers a dramatic backdrop to the city. Most of the posh resorts are tucked into its foothills, while others are in the rock-rimmed Paradise Valley to the north.

All of this upscale sprawl had rather humble beginnings. In 1894, Rhode Island Banker Albert G. Utley came here, subdivided 40 acres of desert and sold off lots. Utleydale or Utleyburg didn't sound right, so he named the new town for former Army chaplain Winfield Scott, an early resident who did much to encourage settlement. Through the years, it became famous as a charming little Western town, way out in the desert beyond Phoenix. Horses had the right-of-way and hitchin' rails stood before false-front stores. Scottsdale prided itself in being one of America's most Western towns. Much of that flavor is now buried in suburban sprawl, although Old Town Scottsdale still retains that yesterday look.

Elevation • 1,260 feet

Location • In Maricopa County, just northeast of Phoenix.

Climate • Warm to hot summers; mild winters. July average high 104.8, low 77.5; January average high 64.8, low 37.6. Rainfall 7.05 inches; rare traces of snow.

Population • 163,700

Population trend • Gained 25 percent in the past five years.

Property tax • (assessed at ten percent of real value) $11.41 per $100 of assessed valuation.

Economy • It's a mix of tourism, upscale shopping and financial services. Some of the valley's finest retail malls and boutiques are here and—for some odd reason—so are many of its largest new car dealers.

Job prospects • Other than the tourist industry, most of Scottsdale's employment base is clerical and white collar. About 65 percent of the jobs are in retailing, finances and services.

Industrial facilities • Several light industrial complexes.

Real estate • Scottsdale embraces some of the valley's most expensive homes, right up there with Fountain Valley and Paradise Valley. Plan on starting in the high $100,000's.

The media • One local daily, the *Scottsdale Progress*. Daily newspapers and telly feeds come from next-door Phoenix.

Medical services • Four hospitals, two clinics, three emergency medical centers and a psychiatric hospital.

Transportation • Scottsdale Municipal Airport, with an 8,250-foot runway, has commuter hops to Sky Harbor, just ten miles away. And yes, that does seem odd. Presumably, they don't serve in-flight meals.

Education • Scottsdale Community College, plus several private schools and the usual public schools.

Local government • Founded in 1888; mayor, six-member council and city manager.

Places to stay • More than 40 resorts and lodges, including some of the most elegant in Arizona; limited RV facilities.

Leisure facilities • About 30 golf courses in the area—some public and some at resorts, plus numerous parks, three public pools, more than a hundred art galleries and many tennis, racquetball and handball courts—on and off the resort properties.

Tourist lures • The drive from Scottsdale through Paradise Valley to Carefree/Cave Creek provides some of the finest desert vistas in the American West. Mountain parks in the area offer picnicking and hiking. Old Town Scottsdale is popular for its fine shops, galleries and restaurants and a small historical museum.

Contacts • Scottsdale Chamber of Commerce, 7343 Scottsdale Mall, Scottsdale, AZ 85251; (602) 945-8481.

City of Scottsdale, P.O. Box 1000 (3939 Civic Center Rd.), Scottsdale, AZ 85251; (602) 945-8481.

SUN CITY & SUN CITY WEST

The world's largest senior community, Sun City covers a patch of low, landscaped desert northwest of Phoenix. It was founded by the Del E. Webb company in 1960, reached its planned capacity of 45,000 in the 1980s and has grown very little since. Newer Sun City West, two and a half miles away, is taking up the slack, going from zero to nearly 26,000 residence since it started in 1978.

Sun City residents enjoy a comfortable, self-contained lifestyle, with their golf courses, swimming pools, recreation centers, crafts classes and social clubs. Sun City is home to the Sundome Center for the Performing Arts, America's largest single-level auditorium.

SIDE NOTE: Although Webb is famous as a creator of retirement communities, historians find him more interesting for another reason. He was the contractor for Bugsy Siegel's Fabulous Flamingo in Las Vegas in 1946. The project ran way over budget and fell months behind schedule, and Bugsy was accused of skimming funds. Although none of this was Webb's fault, he became mighty nervous during construction delays, so Siegel reportedly told him: "Don't worry, Del, we only kill each other." A few months after the Fabulous Flamingo opened, Bugsy's comment became his prophesy; he was gunned down in his girlfriend Virginia Hill's mansion in Bel Air.

Elevation • About 1,000 feet

Location • In Maricopa County, 20 miles northwest of Phoenix.

Climate • Warm to hot summers; mild winters. July average high 106.3, low 65.2; January average high 66.5, low 35. Rainfall 7.65 inches; rare traces of snow.

Population • Sun City 45,000; Sun City West 26,000.

Population trend • Sun City gained 18 percent and Sun City West 59 percent in the past five years.

Property tax • (assessed at ten percent of real value) $13.66 per $100 of assessed valuation in Sun City, $13.48 in Sun City West.

Economy • It's based almost entirely on retirement income, which supports a small services and retailing industry.

Job prospects • Very few; most folks come here to *quit* working.

Industrial facilities • None.

Real estate • All homes are in planned developments, with prices starting around $90,000 and climbing beyond $200,000. Detached homes, cluster homes and duplexes are available. To live here, at least one family member must be 55 or older, and none can be younger than 18.

The media • The daily *News Sun* and three weeklies, the *Sun City Independent, Westsider* and *Sun City Western News*. TV from Phoenix and cable companies.

Medical services • One hospital in Sun City and three others nearby; several extended care facilities in the area.

Transportation • Served by Greyhound. Glendale and Phoenix-Goodyear airports are nearby. Phoenix Sky Harbor is 40 minutes southeast, served by Super Shuttle and Airport Express.

Education • Rio Salado Community College offers adult classes here. Public schools are in adjacent towns.

Local government • Both Sun City and Sun City West are unincorporated; administrative services are provided by homeowners associations and by Maricopa County.

Places to stay • Four motels and three RV parks within a few miles of the two retirement communities.

Leisure facilities • Seven recreation centers in Sun City and four in Sun City West; eight area golf courses, the Sundome Center for the Performing Arts; plus extensive senior-oriented recreational activities, with swimming pools, golf, tennis and health clubs.

Tourist lures • Very little within the communities. An attractive desert park with the mundane name of White Tank Mountain provides hiking and picnicking, ten miles west. Lake Pleasant Regional Park is 15 miles west of the retirement communities, offering boating, hiking, swimming, riding and picnicking.

Contacts • Northwest Valley Chamber of Commerce, P.O. Box 1519 (12425 W. Bell Rd., Suite 305), Surprise, AZ 85374; (602) 583-0692.

Sun City • Del E. Webb Development Company, 13323 W. Meeker Blvd., Sun City, AZ 85375, (602) 975-2270.

Sun City West • 13323 W. Meeker Blvd., Sun City, AZ 85375; (800) 341-6121 or (602) 546-5126.

TEMPE

Arizona State University dominates both the cultural and economic life of this fast-growing suburb. More than 70 percent of Tempe's residents are college-educated, and the large campus functions as the area's cultural center.

Tempe began life in 1872 when Charles Trumbull Hayden opened a general store and flour mill on the banks of the Salt River. He called the place Hayden's Ferry. Well-traveled Englishman Darrel Duppa, who had named Phoenix, commented in 1878 that this area resembled the Vale of Tempe in Thessaly, Greece, and the name took hold.

Many of the town's early buildings, including Hayden's home, have been preserved in the Old Town section near the ASU campus. The look of Tempe is a pleasant mix of contemporary and Western rustic, with palm-lined streets and shaded sidewalks. Tempe can be regarded as the sports capital of Arizona, since the NFL's Arizona Cardinals play at ASU's stadium, along with the Sun Devils of the Pac Ten. Further, the Anaheim Angels conduct their spring training in Tempe.

The new Rio Salado Project, currently under construction, will broaden Tempe's sports and recreational base. A 5.5 mile long section of the dry Salt River bed is being converted into parklands, playing fields, lakes, picnic sites, hiking trails and an equestrian center

Elevation • 1,105 feet

Location • In Maricopa County, just southeast of Phoenix.

Climate • Warm to hot summers; mild winters. July average high 104.3, low 73.4; January average high 65.5, low 35.4. Rainfall 7.63 inches; rare traces of snow.

Population • 155,610

Population trend • Gained about nine percent in the past five years.

Property tax • $12.90 to $14.28 per $100 of assessed valuation.

Economy • Manufacturing forms Tempe's broad economic base, with retailing, services and—obviously—the huge campus of Arizona State University making major contributions. More than 20 percent of the Valley of the Sun's high tech jobs are in Tempe.

Job prospects • They're usually rather good. One job in three is in the services sector. Manufacturing accounts for 22.2 percent of the paychecks, followed by retail trades with 16.7 percent. ASU is the community's largest single employer.

Industrial facilities • They're extensive; Tempe has more than 70 industrial parks, offering space for heavy and light industry and warehousing.

Real estate • Median price for a three-bedroom detached home is $91,500.

The media • The daily *Tempe News Tribune* and the weekly *New Times.* TV and cable from Phoenix.

Medical services • One hospital, two extended care units and several medical clinics.

Transportation • Served by Greyhound. Sky Harbor International Airport is next door, actually closer to Tempe than to any other Valley of the Sun city.

Education • ASU is a commanding presence, as the country's fifth largest university campus, with 46,000 students. Tempe also has three private Christian schools plus eight private elementary and high schools, and the usual public schools. Several campuses of the Maricopa Community College District are nearby.

Local government • Incorporated in 1894; mayor, six-member council and city manager.

Places to stay • More than 30 hotels and motels, plus several mobile home and RV parks.

Leisure facilities • Forty-three public parks, four public pools, five golf courses, plus tennis and racquetball courts, various playing fields and a community center.

Tourist lures • Arizona State University campus is attractive and worth a visit, offering several galleries and museums. Tempe also has three museums, including the excellent new Arizona Historical Society Museum.

Contacts • Tempe Chamber of Commerce, P.O. Box 28500 (909 E. Apache Blvd.), Tempe, AZ 85285; (602) 967-7891.

City of Tempe, 31 E. Fifth St., Tempe, AZ 85281; (602) 967-2001.

WICKENBURG

This may be the cutest little cowboy town in Arizona. Wickenburg *works* at being Western, with balconied store fronts, boardwalks and a friendly down-home attitude. "Tie up, come in and swap stories," invites a sign outside Ben's Saddlery. The town calls itself the dude ranch capital of the world, and real cowboys still ride herd in the surrounding high desert. The small downtown area is cutely Western. Century-old false-front stores tempt visitors with cowboy cloth-

ing, Indian crafts and curios. It also has a few antique stores and several galleries sell paintings, sculptures and bronzes; most have Western themes.

Gold, not cattle, put the town on the map. In 1863, an Austrian named Henry Wickenburg hitched his hopes to an ornery burro and began prospecting in the nearby hills. He struck it rich with the Vulture Mine. Some say he picked up a rock to throw at a vulture—or at his stubborn mule—and the rock was veined with gold. Either version of the story sounds like campfire talk. However, one truth is undeniable: Gold mines in the area yielded $30 million between 1863 and 1900. Miners needed water to wash their diggin's, so they settled along the banks of the Hassayampa River and Wickenburg was born.

Ore from 80 mines poured into town, along with the usual ration of drifters, rascals and fallen angels. At its prime, Wickenburg was the third largest city in Arizona, and one of the wildest. Folks were too busy seeking gold to build a jail, so they simply chained the bad guys to a large mesquite tree. During visiting hours, prisoners' relatives would come out and have a picnic. The tree still stands, at Tegner Street and Wickenburg Way.

As the mines played out, cattlemen began running their herds in the brushy desert. Easterners, reading newspaper reports and dime novels about the Wild West, came out to see what all the excitement was about. Dude ranching, born in Montana, quickly spread to Arizona. Wickenburg and Tucson were early dude ranch centers, and they still are. Nowadays, of course, folks call them guest ranches.

Elevation • 2,100 feet

Location • In Maricopa County, 58 miles northwest of Phoenix on U.S. Highway 93/60.

Climate • Warm to hot summers; mild winters. July average high 103.6, low 69.7; January average high 63.3, low 30. Rainfall 10.77; rare traces of snow.

Population • About 5,500

Population trend • Grew about five percent in the past five years.

Property tax • $10.10 per $100 of assessed valuation.

Economy • Tourism has replaced gold and cattle as the town's reason for being. Indeed, 80 percent of Wickenburg's jobs are directly tied to visitor services. The town attracts a few retirees and Snowbirds, and a little gold still trickles down from the hills.

Job prospects • Despite a low unemployment rate, Wickenburg's job potential is average or below. Growth, which generates jobs, is rather slow and the locals seem to like it that way.

Industrial facilities • A small industrial park.

Real estate • A few modern subdivisions are a-building and the average three-bedroom home starts around $95,000.

The media • The weekly *Wickenburg Sun*; Phoenix provides the dailies and the TV, although there's a local cable company.

Medical services • One hospital and two extended care facilities.

Transportation • Served by Greyhound and Reno-Las Vegas Bus Line. A lighted, 5,000-foot runway at Wickenburg airport; no scheduled service; charter only.

Education • Two private Christian schools and the usual public schools.

Local government • Incorporated in 1909; mayor, six-member council and town manager.

Places to stay • About ten motels, five guest ranches, and a dozen mobile home and RV parks.

Leisure facilities • A community center, youth center, five public parks, two golf courses, a public pool and several tennis courts.

Tourist lures • Wickenburg has several historic buildings in the downtown and one of the finest small archives in the West—the Desert Caballeros Western Museum. Several ghost towns sleep in the nearby hills, while saguaro cactus and Joshua trees thrive in the surrounding desert. Hassayampa River Reserve protects a riparian woodland.

Contacts • Wickenburg Chamber of Commerce, 216 N. Frontier St., Wickenburg, AZ 85390; (520) 684-5479.

Town of Wickenburg, 155 N. Tegner St., Suite A, Wickenburg, AZ 85390; (520) 684-5451.

YOUNGTOWN

The grandaddy of senior villages, Youngtown was started in 1954 by the Youngtown Land and Development Company. Although it's the world's first planned retirement town, it has remained small and compact while next door Sun City and Sun City West have mushroomed. It's an attractive, neatly groomed town with an active retail core and typical planned-community amenities such as a clubhouse, lake, four parks, a cactus garden and a health club.

Location • In Maricopa County, 15 miles northwest of Phoenix.

Elevation • Approximately 1,000 feet.

Climate • Warm to hot summers; mild winters. July average high 106.3, low 74.7; January average high 66.5, low 35. Rainfall 7.65 inches; rare dustings of snow.

Population • 2,675

Population trend • Little change; the population has remained stable in recent years.

Property tax • $13.40 per $100 of assessed valuation.

Economy • It's retirement based, with its income derived from pensions, savings and investments.

Job prospects • Mostly, the residents work at retirement. More than half the town's few jobs are in the service, financial and retail sectors.

Industrial facilities • None.

Real estate • Home prices start around $80,000 to $90,000 for a two or three-bedroom unit.

The media • Served by the weekly *Sun City Independent* and dailies from Phoenix, which also provides TV service; a local cable company is available as well.

Medical services • One extended care facility; hospitals in surrounding communities.

Transportation • Served by Greyhound. Glendale and Phoenix-Goodyear airports are nearby; Sky Harbor is 28 miles away.

Education • Rio Salado Community College offers adult education classes in nearby Sun City. Public schools are in adjacent towns.

Local government • Incorporated in 1960; mayor and six-member council.

Places to stay • One hotel and two motels.

Leisure facilities • Clubhouse, lake, four parks and a desert botanical garden.

Tourist lures • Lake Pleasant Regional Park is 15 miles west, with boating, hiking, swimming, riding and picnicking.

Contacts • Town of Youngtown, 12030 Clubhouse Square, Youngtown, AZ 85363; (602) 933-8286.

Northwest Valley Chamber of Commerce, P.O. Box 1519 (12425 W. Bell Rd., Suite 305), Surprise, AZ 85374; (602) 583-0692.

Chapter eleven

TUCSON & BEYOND
THE SOUTHEAST AND FAR EAST

We begin our final community chapter with a quick lesson in what's left of Arizona's geography. Although eastern Arizona represents a large chunk of the state, much of it is rather thinly populated. High prairie and mountains cover a good part of the area, with chilly winters that might discourage potential retirees. Tucson and Sierra Vista in the southeast are major exceptions.

As you head southeast from the Valley of the Sun, the land slopes gradually upward. If you follow I-10 from Phoenix, you'll gain more than a thousand feet by the time you reach Tucson, although this is still desert terrain. Heading east from Tucson, you'll encounter scattered mountain clusters, floating like alpine islands on a high prairie. If you then go northeast, you hit more prairie and mountains. An evergreen belt between Clifton and Springerville in east central Arizona resembles the Pacific Northwest, although it's not nearly as wet. West of there, in the White Mountains, are more evergreen forests. To the north, you'll encounter high prairie around Holbrook and Winslow. Continuing north, you reach the huge Navajo-Hopi Reservation, occupying all of the state's northeastern corner.

The rumpled regions of eastern Arizona offer much for the wanderer, hiker, hunter and fisherperson. However, except for bustling Tucson and a town or two in the southeast, the region's potential for job-hunters or retirees is limited.

We like many of the towns in this area—sturdy, no-nonsense places like Willcox, Clifton, Safford, Holbrook and Globe. Most are cast in pleasant time warps with turn-of-the-century neighborhoods and brick business districts, although some have started growing a bit.

THE WAY IT WAS • Arizona's historic roots began in the southeast when Spanish padres and explorers came in search of souls and gold. Franciscan Father Marcos de Niza entered this region in 1539, then 30-year-old conquistador Francisco Vásquez de Coronado followed a year later in his legendary quest for the fabled cities of Cibola. He probably traveled up the San Pedro River Valley just east of Sierra Vista.

In 1700, Father Eusebio Francisco Kino established Mission San Xavier at the native village of Bac, near today's Tucson. South of there, the military garrison of Tubac was founded in 1752 to put down a Pima rebellion, and a presidio was erected at Tucson in 1775.

Americans began settling the southeast after the 1848 Treaty of Guadalupe Hidalgo ceded much of Arizona to the United States. However Tucson remained part of Mexico until the Gadsden Purchase of 1854, which gave the state its present southern border.

The area's original residents, of course, could care less if this land "belonged" to Mexico or the United States. It was *their* land and they fought valiantly to keep from losing it to the intruders. Apache warriors Cochise and Geronimo gained international fame for their stubborn resistance—a fame somewhat distorted by later novelists and movie producers. Not until Geronimo's final surrender in 1886 was southeastern Arizona considered "safe" for settlement.

Some of the settlers proved to be considerably less civilized than those they displaced. During the late 1800s, wild mining camps and cowboy towns produced copper, beef and violence. The most publicized single event in Western history occurred in a Tombstone alley in 1881. Virgil, Wyatt and Morgan Earp and their friend Doc Holliday advanced on five rowdies, challenged them to fight and then opened fire at point-blank range. The gunfight at the O.K. Corral lasted only 30 seconds and claimed three lives. It has since consumed thousands of pages of pulp fiction and endless reels of movie film. One of the reasons for its enduring fame was that gunfighter-lawman Wyatt Earp later became a dime novelist.

THE WAY IT IS • The eastern third of Arizona offers interesting contrasts. While Tucson is the state's second largest city, the southeast corner has few residents and the far east is one of the least populated areas of the state. The northeast is dominated by Native American reservations. Outside of Tucson, the region's only large communities are Green Valley and Sierra Vista; both are in the southeast.

With its mountains, national monuments and historic sites, the southeast has emerged in recent years as a popular tourist destination.

Some newcomers have chosen to stay, attracted by the benign climate and inexpensive housing of places like Green Valley, Sierra Vista and Bisbee. In the mountains north and east of here, a few retirees are discovering such hamlets as Pinetop, Lakeside, Springerville and Show Low. Springerville and Safford are commercial centers, offering modest potential for job seekers.

Our community list begins with Tucson, one of our favorite cities anywhere. Although it's a major urban center, it is rather different than Phoenix. Tucson is history, old money and tradition. Phoenix is new wave, fast paced, new money and very pro-growth. Although Tucson is growing as well, life is a bit slower here. It's more focused on the past and present than on some glossy future.

The two are quite similar geographically; both occupy desert basins surrounded by rugged mountains. Tucson is 1,300 feet higher, so it's a bit cooler despite its more southerly location. The biggest difference is—well—bigness itself. Phoenix is nearly twice as large and its husky suburban cities make the metropolitan area even larger. By contrast, Tucson is an urban island with few communities on its periphery.

TUCSON

Sitting in a cactus garden and surrounded by five mountain ranges, Tucson is one of America's most versatile cities. In winter, you can work on your suntan at poolside, then drive to the Mount Lemmon ski area and strap on the sticks. The city offers a generous mix of cultural activities, visitor attractions and shopping, with an excellent academic overlay provided by the University of Arizona.

Although Tucson was in Mexican territory after the signing of the Treaty of Guadalupe Hidalgo, it was in American hands. Members of the Mormon Battalion had occupied it during the Mexican War two years earlier and they weren't about to give it up. Then the 1854 Gadsden Purchase formalized its status as an American possession.

However, Tucson's history reaches well beyond that period. When Father Kino visited in 1687, he found Tohono O'odham Indians living in a village they called *Stjukshon* (Stook-shon). It means "blue water at the base of a black mountain," referring to springs in the now-dry Santa Cruz River and Sentinel Peak. The Spanish altered it to *Tucson*, which initially was pronounced "TUK-son." Kino returned in 1700 to build Mission San Xavier in the Indian village of Bac.

The town of Tucson was started in 1775 by a wandering Irishman who was scouting for the Spanish crown. Settlers began moving into the area and the original inhabitants naturally objected. They went on the warpath and a walled presidio was built to protect the intruders. This was the first walled city in America—although it was still part of Spain.

After the Gadsden Purchase, Tucson continued growing as a ranching and provisioning center. A Butterfield Stage stop was opened in 1857 and the town's cantinas became notorious hangouts for drifters, outlaws and randy cowpokes. Folks said the outpost was so primitive that stage passengers who spent the night had to sleep in a "Tucson bed"—using their stomach for a mattress and their back for a blanket.

The pueblo suffered the indignity of capture by rebel Texas troops during the Civil War. They were evicted by a pro-Union California battalion following the Battle of Picacho Pass in 1862—the war's westernmost conflict. Tucson lured the territorial capital from Prescott in 1867, only to have it taken away ten years later. By the turn of the century, this was a busy if still somewhat remote town of 10,000. World War II brought thousands of servicemen to Davis-Monthan Army Air Corps Base. Many of them liked the idea of January suntans and returned.

Tucson boomed after the war and—like its larger neighbor to the north—galloped off in all directions. Today, this vast carpet of commerce covers 500 square miles—more than metropolitan L.A. However, much of this land is taken up in large desert preserves, such as 17,000-acre Tucson Mountain Park.

Today's Tucson wears its Spanish heritage rather handsomely. Red-tile and flat-roofed pueblo architecture predominates. The town has more good Mexican restaurants than you can shake a tortilla at. Mexican arts and crafts add color to curio shops. Many signs are bilingual, since 26 percent of Pima County's citizens are Hispanic.

Tucson's growth during the Eighties was slower than Phoenix and its growth still lags behind the Valley of the Sun. However, it's hardly sitting still. From 1980 until 1995, its population zoomed from 330,537 to 447,075, an increase of 35 percent.

Elevation • 2,390 feet

Location • In Pima County, 110 miles southeast of Phoenix and 90 miles north of Mexico.

Climate • Warm to hot summers; mild winters with some chilly evenings. July average high 100.1, low 73.3; January average high 66, low 36.7. Rainfall 10.73 inches; occasional traces of snow.

Population • 447,075

Population trend • Gained about ten percent in the past five years.

Property tax • $14.36 per $100 assessed valuation.

Economy • Manufacturing, tourism, the federal government (mostly at Davis-Monthan Air Force Base) and high tech industries provide the bricks for Tucson's economic foundation. The largest single employer is the University of Arizona.

Job prospects • Major employment areas are in tourism and other services, accounting for a fourth of the jobs. Retail sales, manufacturing and transportation offer potential as well. Best job possibilities are in the machinist trades, aircraft maintenance, electronics and communications, according to the local Job Service office.

Industrial facilities • They range from heavy fabricating plants to space age electronics firms. Several industrial parks offer complete facilities, including rail and air.

Real estate • Tucson's housing is varied, ranging from older homes in the downtown area to elegant gated communities in the foothills. Much of the architecture, both old and new, is Spanish and pueblo style. Prices for a three-bedroom home range from $70,000 to well beyond $100,000.

The media • Two dailies, the *Tucson Star and Tucson Citizen*, plus several suburban weeklies and shoppers; nine TV stations and cable.

Medical services • Fifteen hospitals, including fine facilities at the University of Arizona's medical school; also several clinics and extended care units.

Transportation • Reached by Greyhound and Amtrak. Tucson International Airport is served by more than a dozen airlines.

Education • The University of Arizona is the community's academic and cultural focal point. Other schools include Tucson branches of the business and management-focused University of Phoenix, Pima Community College, ten business and vocational schools, more than a hundred private and parochial schools and the usual public schools.

Local government • The seat of Pima County, incorporated in 1877; mayor, six-member council and city manager.

Places to stay • More than 150 hotels, motels and resorts, including some of most elegant in the state; also several dude ranches in the surrounding desert. Dozens of RV and mobile home parks.

Leisure facilities • More than 40 public and private golf courses, 128 city and county parks including huge Tucson Mountain Park, about 20 museums and galleries, 23 municipal pools, plus tennis, racquetball and handball courts and sports fields.

Tourist lures • Mission San Xavier del Bac, the much-heralded Arizona-Sonora Desert Museum, Saguaro National Park, Old Tucson western movie town, Mount Lemmon ski area, regional mountain parks and numerous other attractions. Several museums and galleries are on the campus of the University of Arizona.

Contacts • Tucson Metropolitan Chamber of Commerce, P.O. Box 991 (465 W. St. Mary's Rd.), Tucson, AZ 85702; (520) 792-2250.

Greater Tucson Economic Council, 33 Stone, Suite 800, Tucson, AZ 85701; (520) 622-6413; FAX (520) 622-6413.

Metropolitan Tucson Convention & Visitors Bureau, 130 S. Scott Ave., Tucson, AZ 85701; (520) 624-1817 or (800) 638-8350.

City of Tucson, 255 W. Alameda, Tucson, AZ 85726; (520) 791-4204.

BISBEE

This sturdy old mining town is canti-levered into the steep flanks of Mule Pass Gulch. Like Jerome, Bisbee is the sort of place where your upper neighbor can look down your chimney. The post office department complains that it's too steep for mail delivery.

Headframes and tailing dumps mark the slopes; corrugated buildings shelter smelters and stamp mills. Hillsides have been ripped away to expose orange, rust and gray-green wounds. You *know* this is mining country. Coming into Bisbee, you see something even more dramatic—the great terraced cavity of the Lavender Pit Mine. It's so close it appears ready to swallow the town.

Why do we recommend Bisbee as a place to settle? It's rich in history, it has a classic 19th century downtown area, handsome old homes and a temperate year-around climate. Further, it's a short hop to Mexico and Tucson. The surrounding terrain is varied, since Bisbee is on a topographic bridge between the Sonoran Desert and eastern high country. The town has a minus, however: The job market id very weak.

Although it emerged as a mining center, Bisbee didn't burst into glory overnight. It grew steadily and sturdily as big corporations gouged deep into the earth for copper, gold, silver, lead and zinc. Army Scout Jack Dunn filed a claim in the area in 1877, then he brought in one George Warren as a partner. Warren cheated Dunn out of his share, found some investors, and eventually sold to a conglomerate headed by Judge DeWitt Bisbee of San Francisco. The group formed the Copper Queen Mine Company and eventually merged with the large Phelps Dodge Corporation.

Reveling in this wealth, the town grew as a sort of vertical San Francisco, with plush Victorian homes, fine restaurants and—of course—bordellos. Brewery Gulch was Bisbee's version of San Francisco's Barbary Coast, with more than 50 drinking, gambling and whoring establishments. At its peak, Bisbee was the world's largest copper mining town, with 20,000 residents. Phelps Dodge operated the underground Queen Mine and the Lavender open pit mine until 1975 when diminishing returns and falling copper prices closed those operations.

Logic says Bisbee should have withered and died, but retirees and tourists began coming, drawn by the mild climate and sturdy charm of the old town. Boutiques, galleries and antique shops were opened in the red brick and tufa stone buildings. Bed & breakfast inns proliferated. The Queen Mine, unable to process copper economically, is processing visitors by offering underground tours. The town even attracts a few movie companies, since the hillside buildings can become—with a little creative camera work—a bit of Old Spain, Greece or Mexico.

Elevation • 5,490 feet

Location • In Cochise County, just above the Mexican border.

Climate • Warm summers; cool winters with chilly evenings. July average high 89.3, low 64.5; January average high 56.9, low 33.7. Rainfall 16.21 inches; snowfall 4.54 inches.

Population • About 7,000

Population trend • Relatively stable; slight population loss in the past five years.

Property tax • $14.19 per $100 assessed valuation.

Economy • Tourism and light manufacturing have stabilized the town since the big mines shut down.

Job prospects • They aren't strong since growth is rather stagnant. Best prospects are in retail and wholesale trades, tourist and other service jobs. The local Job Service office rates employment prospects as "below average."

Industrial facilities • Several small industrial parks are available, including one at the airport. Nearby Naco has a "twin plant" operation on both sides of the border. However, it employs Mexican "guest workers" in all but management posts.

Real estate • Three-bedroom detached homes range from $55,000 upwards. Restored or restorable Victorians go for much more.

The media • The daily *Bisbee Review* and two weeklies, the *Bisbee Observer* and *Bisbee Gazette*. TV service from Tucson, plus cable.

Medical services • A hospital with combined acute care and long term care capabilities.

Transportation • Bridgeport Transport runs buses to Tucson. Bisbee Municipal Airport has a 5,990-foot lighted runway; no scheduled air service.

Education • Cochise Community College is 17 miles east; Bisbee has an elementary, junior high and high school.

Local government • Incorporated in 1905; mayor, six council members and a city manager.

Places to stay • Several motels and two historic hotels, 13 bed & breakfast inns; four campgrounds and RV parks.

Leisure facilities • Seven public parks, a golf course, galleries and boutiques, tennis courts and a ball park.

Tourist lures • Three museums and more than 20 art galleries and antique shops in Bisbee's historic downtown area. Public underground tours at the Queen Mine and viewing areas at the Lavender open pit mine.

Contacts • Bisbee Chamber of Commerce, P.O. Drawer BA (Seven Naco Rd.), Bisbee, AZ 85603; (520) 432-5421.

City of Bisbee, 118 Arizona St., Bisbee, AZ 85603; 432-5446.

CATALINA

Although it's a rather ordinary looking community, Catalina occupies an impressive setting—tucked into the foothills of the Santa Catalina Mountains above Tucson. It's primarily a retirement area; the planned senior villages of SaddleBrooke and Sun City Vistoso are four miles away.

The town was established in the 1950s by land developers. It has experienced considerable growth in the past two decades, more than doubling its 1970 population.

Location • In Pima County, about 20 miles north of Tucson on Highway 77.

Elevation • 3,100 feet

Climate • Warm summers; mild winters with cool evenings. July average high 93.2, low 67.3; January average high 57.7, low 34.3. Rainfall 16 inches; occasional traces of snow.

Population • 5,529

Population trend • Gained about 13 percent in the past five years; many of the newcomers are retirees.

Property tax • (assessed at ten percent of real value) $17.98 per $100 assessed valuation.

Economy • There isn't much of an economic base; Catalina is mostly retirement oriented, with a few small businesses.

Job prospects • Not very good. Its unemployment rate is higher than the state average. Most working folks commute to nearby Tucson.

Industrial facilities • None

Real estate • Housing is cheaper than in Tucson, which is one of the area's big draws. Prices for detached homes begin around $65,000 in Catalina. In the nearby retirement communities of SaddleBrooke and Sun City Vistoso, they start around $80,000.

The media • The semi-monthly *Catalina Oracle*. Daily newspapers and TV relays from Tucson, plus a local cable company.

Medical services • One county clinic; the nearest hospitals are in Tucson.

Transportation • No commercial transport or airport; Tucson International is about 25 miles south.

Education • A public elementary and middle school; the nearest high school is nine miles away.

Local government • Village council with nine elected representatives.

Places to stay • Three resorts within a ten-mile radius.

Leisure facilities • A public swimming pool and park.

Tourist lures • Nearby Catalina State Park offers hiking, camping, picnicking and such. Hiking trails extend into the Santa Catalina Mountains of Coronado National Forest.

Contact • Greater Catalina/Golder Ranch Village Council, P.O. Box 8674 CRB, Catalina (Tucson), AZ 85738; (520) 791-2265.

CLIFTON/MORENCI

One of Arizona's early mining towns, Clifton was platted in 1873. There are two theories concerning its name, depending on your historian: It's a derivation of "Clifftown" for the surrounding bluffs, or it was named after the Clifton copper mine; Henry Clifton was an early investor in the area. Morenci (*mor-EN-cee*), established in 1884, was named for the Michigan home town of an early mine official.

The Phelps Dodge Corporation came to the area in 1882 and—through the generations—it bought mining companies and claims until it was the sole operator. It eventually bought the town of Morenci, and then dismantled it because it sat on rich copper deposits. But no matter; company officials built a prim new community in 1969, with a shopping center, theater, bowling alley, swimming pool, motel, restaurants, video store—all of humanity's basic needs. Phelps Dodge now owns 22,000 acres and employs more than half of the area's population, 2,400 people.

Elevation • 3,466 feet

Location • Greenlee County in southeastern Arizona.

Climate • Warm summers; chilly winters with cool evenings. July average high 101.4, low 71.3; January average high 61.2, low 31.1. Rainfall 12.06 inches; occasional traces of snow.

Population • Clifton 3,000; Morenci 2,424

Population trend • Stable; gaining about one percent a year.

Property tax • (assessed at ten percent of real value) $7.17 per $100 assessed valuation.

Economy • Based primarily on copper mining, ranching, agriculture and a little tourism.

Job prospects • A few available in mining, with the large Phelps Dodge operation; otherwise the job outlook is quite limited.

Real estate • Not much on the market; homes begin around $60,000.

Media • The weekly *Copper Era, Courier* and *The Wild West*; television via cable.

Medical services • One outpatient clinic.

Industrial facilities • No industrial parks.

Transportation • No commercial transit; general aviation at Greenlee County Airport.

Education • An elementary, junior high and high school.

Local government • Clifton incorporated 1873; Morenci in 1882. Mayor, six-member council and city manager in Clifton; Morenci is essentially a company town.

Places to stay • Three motels, two bed & breakfast inns and a boarding house.

Leisure facilities • Golfing, baseball and soccer fields, tennis courts, public swimming pools and a bowling alley.

Tourist Lures • Phelps Dodge mine tour at Morenci; hiking, rockhounding and hunting in the surrounding mountains.

Contacts • Greenlee County Chamber of Commerce, P.O. Box 1237 (66 N. Coronado Blvd.), Clifton, AZ 85533; (520) 865-3313.

Town of Clifton, P.O. Box 1415, Clifton, AZ 85533; (520) 865-4146; FAX (520) 865-4472.

GREEN VALLEY

A semi-arid no-man's land in the high desert of the Santa Cruz River Valley south of Tucson has emerged as a carefully planned community, primarily of senior citizens. Established in 1964, Green Valley has become one of Arizona's largest retirement communities. Some folks from Tucson unkindly refer to it as "Wrinkle City."

More than just a senior village, it offers shopping centers and other amenities that make air-conditioned desert living quite pleasant. Its location is appealing as well, between Tucson and the twin towns of Nogales, Arizona and Mexico. The Mexican Nogales offers the best shopping of all Arizona border towns.

Elevation • 2,900 feet

Location • In Pima County, 25 miles south of Tucson on Interstate 19.

Climate • Warm to hot summers; mild winters with some cool evenings. July average high 101.3, low 68.4; January average high 67.1, low 31. Rainfall 10.86 inches; snowfall rare.

Population • 25,600

Population trend • Gained 24 percent in the past seven years.

Property tax • $11.88 per $100 assessed valuation.

Economy • Most of it is based on retirement income, since 85 percent of its residents are pensioned. A few workers commute north to Tucson.

Job prospects ● The town doesn't offer much more than service, retail and clerical jobs. The Green Valley Chamber of Commerce describes employment prospects as "below average."

Industrial facilities ● None

Real estate ● Most homes are set into attractive parklike complexes, rimmed by common areas or golf courses. Prices for a three-bedroom home start around $110,000. The market is mostly in attractive subdivision homes, townhouses and condos, according to the Green Valley Association of Realtors.

The media ● The twice-weekly *Green Valley News & Sun.* Tucson provides daily newspaper and TV service, and there's a local cable company.

Medical services ● A 24-hour emergency clinic, two extended care facilities and a mental health clinic.

Transportation ● Buses of Citizen Auto Stage run between Tucson and Nogales, stopping in Green Valley. Tucson International Airport is 23 miles north.

Education ● One elementary school; high school students go to Sahuarita, three miles north.

Local government ● Unincorporated; services provided by Pima County and various homeowners' associations.

Places to stay ● Two motels.

Leisure facilities ● Typical senior village amenities—seven golf courses, several swimming pools, tennis and shuffleboard courts, putting greens and a driving range.

Tourist lures ● The Titan Missile Museum is next door, and historic Tubac and Tumacacori National Monument are 30 miles south. Madera Canyon, 12 miles southeast, is particularly noted for bird-watching; it also offers picnicking, hiking and camping.

Contact ● Green Valley Chamber of Commerce, P.O. Box 566 (270 W. Continental, Room 100), Green Valley, AZ 85622; (520) 625-7575.

HOLBROOK

The seat of sparsely populated Navajo County, Holbrook is an ordinary looking community alongside the Little Colorado River with an old fashioned, clean-swept downtown. It's noted mostly as a gateway to Petrified Forest National Park and the huge Navajo-Hopi Reservation. It has a few motels and restaurants and a lot of rock shops selling gems, thunder eggs and things petrified. With population lazing somewhere between slow growth and no growth, Holbrook doesn't offer much opportunity for the job seeker, although its

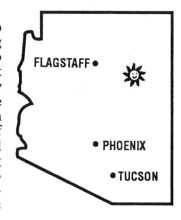
FLAGSTAFF ●
● PHOENIX
● TUCSON

small town atmosphere, low home prices and relatively temperate climate may appeal to retirees.

Holbrook was founded in 1882 as a railroad terminal and provisioning post for area ranches, and named for H.R. Holbrook, chief engineer of the Atlantic & Pacific Railroad. The town's original name was much more colorful—Horsehead Crossing. It was the commercial center for the Aztec Ranch, one of the largest spreads in America. It ran 60,000 head of cattle over a million acres of open range, and it was nicknamed the Hashknife outfit because of its spade-shaped brand. Bad management and falling beef prices shut down the huge operation at the turn of the century.

The town managed to hang on, supported by other area ranches and, more currently, by tourists bound for Petrified Forest and other travelers along Interstate 40.

Elevation • 5,080 feet

Location • On I-40 and Highway 66 in Navajo County, 90 miles east of Flagstaff.

Climate • Warm summers; cool winters with cold evenings. July average high 94.3, low 60.4; January average high 47.4, low 18.5. Rainfall about 20 inches; some traces of snow.

Population • 5,070

Population trend • Gained about eight percent in the past five years.

Property tax • $11.31 per $100 assessed valuation.

Economy • There isn't a strong economic base here, except for the nearby Cholla Power Plant.

Job prospects • Other than summer tourist jobs, employment prospects aren't strong.

Industrial facilities • City-run business park with airport and freeway access.

Real estate • Average home price is $45,000 to $65,000.

The media • Bi-weekly *Holbrook Tribune* and cable TV.

Medical services • One medical clinic.

Transportation • Holbrook Municipal Airport has a 6,700-foot lighted runway with general aviation facilities; no scheduled air service.

Education • Two private schools, branch campus of Northland Pioneer College; two public elementary, one junior high and one high school.

Local government • Incorporated in 1917; mayor, six-member council and city manager.

Places to stay • Because of adjacent Petrified Forest National Park, it has more than 25 motels, two RV parks and camping at nearby Cholla Lake.

Leisure facilities • Five city parks, a county recreation complex with ball courts, a playground and picnic area.

Tourist lures • Courthouse Museum is near downtown, Petrified Forest National Park is 20 miles east and the huge Navajo-Hopi Reservation is to the north, offering Canyon de Chelley and Navajo national monuments and historic Hopi pueblos.

Contacts • Holbrook Chamber of Commerce, 100 E. Arizona St., Holbrook, AZ 86025; (800) 524-2459 or (520) 524-6558; FAX (520) 524-1719.

Economic Development Department, City of Holbrook, P.O. Box 70 (465 First Ave.), Holbrook, AZ 86025, (520) 524-2413; FAX (520) 524-2159.

ORO VALLEY

Cradled by handsome peaks, Oro Valley has replaced Gilbert as the fastest growing community in Arizona. It more than tripled its size in the Eighties and it continues to move along at a brisk pace, more than doubling its population in the past five years. The town offers an attractive mix of modern subdivisions, golf courses and the cactus gardens of the surrounding Sonoran Desert. All of this is within half an hour of Tucson.

Oro Valley was settled as a farming area after World War II, was incorporated in 1974 and caught the growth bug as Tucson and the rest of Arizona began booming in the Eighties.

Elevation • 2,450 feet

Location • In Pima County, six miles from the northern edge of Tucson.

Climate • Warm to hot summers; mild winters with cool evenings. July average high 100.3, low 70.6; January average high 66.6, low 32.4. Rainfall 15.68 inches; half an inch of snowfall.

Population • Approximately 21,000

Population trend • Gaining nearly 16 percent a year during the Nineties.

Property tax • (assessed at ten percent of real value) $14.71 per $100 assessed valuation.

Economy • This is primarily a commuter and retirement community, so most of the economy is based on retail trade and the services sector.

Job prospects • Other than retailing, they're limited in Oro Valley itself; many workers commute to Tucson.

Industrial facilities • None.

Real estate • Most homes are in modern subdivisions; median price of a three-bedroom detached home is $167,000.

The media • The daily *Oro Valley Territorial*, weekly *Oro Valley Explorer*; TV from Tucson, plus cable.

Medical services • Clinics only; many hospitals in Tucson.

Transportation • No airport or commercial transportation.

Education • The usual public schools.

Local government • Incorporated in 1974; mayor, four-member council and town manager.

Places to stay • Sheraton El Conquistador Resort Hotel; abundant facilities in nearby Tucson.

Leisure facilities • Golf courses, public parks, swimming pool and tennis and racquetball courts.

Tourist lures • The Santa Catalina Mountains offer hiking, picnicking and other outdoor pursuits; Catalina State Park is just east.

Contact • Town of Oro Valley, 11000 N. La Cañada Dr., Oro Valley, AZ 85737; (520) 297-2591.

PINETOP-LAKESIDE

We recommend these two towns only as retirement places, primarily because of their attractive forested settings. Both Pinetop and Lakeside are perched rather dramatically on the edge of the Mogollon Rim, just above the wooded White Mountain Apache Indian Reservation.

It gets cold here in winter since it's well over a mile high, although residents don't suffer Minnesota style blizzards. They do get occasional white Christmases. With a limited employment base, Pinetop and Lakeside offer little potential for relocating families.

The two communities were founded by Mormons in the early 1880s. Lakeside was named because of its proximity to several small lakes. While there's no shortage of pine trees hereabouts, Pinetop actually as named for a saloon keeper who served the soldiers at Fort Apache. The two burgs were incorporated as a single town in 1984.

Elevation • 7,200 feet

Location • In Navajo County in east central Arizona, just above the White Mountain Apache Reservation.

Climate • Mild summers and rather cold winters. July average high 85.8, low 55.5; January average high 44.2, low 17.7. Rainfall 22.31 inches; snowfall 38.2 inches.

Population • 2,615

Population trend • Gained seven percent in the past five years.

Property tax • $11.11 in Pinetop; $10.86 in Lakeside.

Economy • It's mostly tourism and recreation oriented, with a handful of jobs in light industry.

Job prospects • In a word—"scarce." Most folks come here to get away from work, not to find it.

Industrial facilities • A 90-acre light industrial park.

Real estate • Woodsy chalet style homes are typical of the area and they're not terribly expensive. A modest three-bedroom home ranges between $80,000 and $100,000.

The media • Two biweeklies, the *White Mountain Independent* and the *Apache Scout.*

Medical services • A small hospital in nearby Show Low.

Transportation • White Mountain Passenger Lines provides bus service. The nearest airport is in Show Low.

Education • Northland Pioneer College has a campus in Show Low; the usual public schools in Pinetop-Lakeside.

Local government • Incorporated in 1984; mayor, six council members and a town manager.

Places to stay • Numerous motels and rustic cabins, plus the large summer and winter Sunrise Resort on the Apache reservation.

Leisure facilities • Three golf courses, a health center, two pools, a 70-acre recreation area, tennis and racquetball courts.

Tourist lures • Thousands come to escape the desert heat and sniff the pine-scented air of the surrounding Apache-Sitgreaves National Forest. Adjacent White Mountain Reservation offers hunting, camping, hiking and a Native American casino with full gaming. The Apaches' Sunrise Resort is one of the leading ski areas in the state and it also has an active summer program.

Contacts • Pinetop-Lakeside Chamber of Commerce, P.O. Box 266 (592 White Mountain Blvd.), Lakeside, AZ 85929; (520) 367-4290.

Town of Pinetop-Lakeside, P.O. Box 10 (1360 Niels Hansen Lane), Lakeside, AZ 85929; (520) 368-8696.

White Mountain Regional Development Corporation, P.O. Box 3440, Show Low, AZ 895901; (520) 537-3777.

White Mountain Apache Enterprises, P.O. Box 220, Whiteriver, AZ 85941; (520) 338-4385 or (520) 338-4386.

SAFFORD

A well-tended old farm town, Safford is on the verge of a mini-boom with the development of a large copper mine nearby. It's an appealing little community that might attract folks looking for a rural lifestyle. A modestly active economy offers some job prospects, a few housing developments are underway and prices are affordable.

Established as a farming community in 1872, Safford is the commercial and retail hub of the attractive Gila Valley in southeastern Arizona. Mount Graham, one of Arizona's tallest peaks at 10,713 feet, provides an imposing backdrop and its Coronado National Forest offers an abundance of outdoor lures. Sheltered from rainfall and sitting below 3,000 feet, Safford has a dry climate more akin to a desert than a farming valley. Hot summers provide the proper environment for cotton, one of the area's major crops. The seat of Graham County, Safford is a well-tended town with a middle America look. Sturdy brick and masonry buildings define the downtown area, while carefully kept old homes stand along tree-shaded streets.

A state-of-the-art Discovery Park and science center is being built on the edge of town, and adjacent Thatcher is home to Eastern Arizona College, which has a fine little anthropology museum.

Elevation • 2,900 feet

Location • In Graham County in southeastern Arizona.

Climate • Warm to hot summers and balmy winters with chilly evenings. July average high 99.7, low 70.2; January average high 61.1, low 29.1. Rainfall 8.3 inches; snowfall 1.3 inches.

Population • 8,855

Population trend • Increased by about 20 percent in the past five years.

Property tax • (assessed at ten percent of real value) $12.77 per $100 assessed valuation

Economy • Agriculture is the area's leading industry, with 35,000 acres of the Gila Valley under irrigation. The new Phelps Dodge copper mine should kick-start an otherwise sluggish economy. Other important economic elements are services, light manufacturing, retailing and public employment, primarily at Eastern Arizona College.

Job prospects • There are needs in medical, professional and technical areas, according to the local chamber of commerce. The unskilled and semi-skilled job markets are rather limited until the mine starts hiring.

Industrial facilities • An industrial park near the airport and a few small parks elsewhere. Local industries include several label-making factories, a solar pump plant and two cotton gins.

Real estate • Three-bedroom homes range from $60,000; a few housing developments are underway with new homes starting in the high $70's.

The media • The weekly *Eastern Arizona Courier*; television via cable.

Medical services • A small hospital and few doctors' clinics.

Transportation • Served by Greyhound. Safford Regional Airport meets the area's general aviation needs; charter service is available.

Education • Eastern Arizona College (two year) in next-door Thatcher, four private grade schools, a private high school and the usual public schools.

Local government • The seat of Graham County; mayor, five-member council and a city manager.

Places to stay • Seven motels, two bed & breakfast inns, eight mobile home and RV parks, two guest ranches and numerous camp-sites in adjacent national forests.

Leisure facilities • Community parks, an 18-hole golf course, two health clubs, swimming pools and mineral spas, tennis and basketball courts and ball fields.

Tourist lures • The 200-acre Discovery Park opened in 1995 and continues expand to expand. There are two small museums downtown and a museum of anthropology on the Eastern Arizona College cam-pus. Mount Graham offers outdoor pursuits and it's home to an inter-national observatory. Nearby Roper Lake State Park offers camping, swimming and fishing.

Contacts • Graham County Chamber of Commerce, 1111 Thatcher Blvd., Safford, AZ 85546; (520) 428-2511.

City of Safford, 717 Main St., Safford, AZ 85546; (520) 348-3100.

SHOW LOW

This is where the Pinetop-Lakeside folks come to shop. Show Low is the commercial center of this high mountain region. Somewhat lower than Pinetop-Lakeside, it's a bit milder in winter.

Once was the hub of a ranching area, Show Low got its unusual name from a low-ball poker expression. If you "show low"—have the lowest cards—you win. It seems that C.E. Cooley and Marion Clark had built up a 100,000-acre cattle spread in the 1870s. After six years, they de-cided to break up the partnership, and drew cards to see who would buy who out. Cooley drew the deuce of clubs; Clark moved on. Show Low's main drag is called Deuce of Clubs in honor of that curious event.

Despite is colorful roots, the town today has no historic flavor. The business district is basically three miles of strip malls along Deuce of Clubs. Most of the area's visual appeal comes from its location be-tween wooded hills and high grasslands.

Elevation • 6,300 feet

Location • In the White Mountain foothills of Navajo County in east central Arizona.

Climate • Warm summers; cool winters with cold evenings. July average high 85.8, low 55.5; January average high 44.2, low 17.7. Rainfall 23 inches; snowfall 35 inches.

Population • 5,830

Population trend • Gained 16 percent in the past five years.

Arizona's southeastern area contains several natural attractions, including Chiracahua National Monument east of Sierra Vista, with its fantastic rhyolite formations.

Property tax • (assessed at ten percent of real value) $9.80 per $100 assessed valuation

Economy • It's a bit more diverse than Pinetop-Lakeside, with a mix of tourism and related services, retail trade, logging and forest products manufacturing.

Job prospects • Limited; there isn't much beyond lumbering and tourist related services.

Industrial facilities • A small industrial park with airport access.

Real estate • It's a mix of older downtown homes, a few subdivisions on the fringes and chalet style homes among the trees. Prices start around $80,000 for a three-bedroom house.

The media • Two biweeklies, the *White Mountain Independent* and the *Apache Scout*.

Medical services • A small hospital and several clinics.

Transportation • White Mountain Passenger Lines offers bus service. The Show Low Airport has a 6,000-foot lighted runway, with commuter flights to Phoenix.

Education • Show Low campus of Northland Pioneer Community College; four elementary, one junior high and one high school.

Local government • Incorporated in 1953; mayor, six council members and a city manager.

Places to stay • About 15 motels, nine campgrounds and five RV parks.

Leisure facilities • A golf course, public parks, soccer fields, tennis and racquetball courts.

Tourist lures • A repeat of Pinetop-Lakeside: People are drawn by the piney woods and the recreational lures of the White Mountain Apache Reservation.

Contacts • Show Low Chamber of Commerce, P.O. Box 1083 (951 W. Deuce of Clubs), Show Low, AZ 85901; (888) 746-9569 or (520) 537-2326.

White Mountain Regional Development Corporation, P.O. Box 3440, Show Low, AZ 85901; (800) 818-2520; FAX (520) 537-3830.

City of Show Low, 200 W. Cooley Rd., Show Low, AZ 85901; (520) 537-5724.

White Mountain Apache Enterprises, P.O. Box 220, Whiteriver, AZ 85941; (520) 338-4385 or (520) 338-4386.

White Mountain Regional Development Corporation, P.O. Box 3440, Show Low, AZ 895901; (520) 537-3777.

SIERRA VISTA

Started in 1956 as a retirement and vacation retreat, Sierra Vista has mush-roomed to become the largest city in eastern Arizona. More than one in three Cochise County residents lives here. Rivaling neighboring Tucson in land area, it looks more like a well-planned suburb than a town. It's an expansive spread of shopping centers, subdivisions, service stations and stop lights. Growth has slowed recently to about in recent years to about three percent a year.

Despite the suburban sprawl, it can have appeal to relocating families and retirees, although job prospects aren't as strong as they were a few years ago. Surrounding mountains provide an impressive backdrop and it's close to Chiricahua National Monument, Coronado National Memorial and the legendary gunslinger town of Tombstone. National climate experts rate this area as one of the most temperate in the nation. With an average maximum high of 75 and low of 50, it's practically a room temperature community. Housing is quite inexpensive, with detached homes available for as little as $55,000. The area is decidedly pro-growth and it has extensive retirement facilities. For those who want to get above the desert heat, Sierra Vista is a good bet.

Elevation • 4,623 feet

Location • In Cochise County, 70 miles southeast of Tucson.

Climate • Warm summers; mild winters with cool evenings. July average high 88.6, low 66.4; January average high 58.4, low 43.2. Rainfall 14.64 inches; snowfall seven inches.

Population • 37,815

Population trend • Gained 14 percent in the past five years.

Property tax • (assessed at ten percent of real value) $14.07 per $100 of assessed valuation.

Economy • Once retirement oriented, Sierra Vista's economy is diversifying into light manufacturing, the services sector and expanding retail trade.

Job prospects • With slower growth, employment possibilities are below average, according to the local Job Service office. Best bets are in retail sales and public administration. The largest employer is next-door Fort Huachuca, with more than 11,700 military and civilian personnel drawing government paychecks, although future cutbacks could reduce this.

Industrial facilities • Two industrial parks; Sierra Vista is a "Foreign Trade Zone Grantee."

Real estate • Three-bedroom home prices begin around $55,000 and range well beyond $100,000. The market is "moderately active," according to the Sierra Vista Association of Realtors. The market mix includes older homes, new subdivisions, townhouses and condos.

The media • The daily *Sierra Vista Herald* and the weekly *Huachuca Scout*. Television feeds from Tucson, Nogales and Phoenix, plus cable service.

Medical services • Three hospitals, two extended care facilities and several clinics.

Transportation • Served by Bridgewater Transport, with connections to Greyhound in Tucson. Sierra Vista Municipal Airport has three runways, with feeder service and charters.

Education • Cochise Community College; five public elementary, one junior high and one high school.

Local government • Incorporated in 1956; mayor, six- member council and city manager.

Places to stay • About a dozen motels; several RV and mobile home parks, mostly in next-door Huachuca City.

Leisure facilities • A community center, nine public parks, four swimming pools, two golf courses and tennis and racquetball courts.

Tourist lures • Sierra Vista is near Coronado National Memorial, Chiricahua National Monument, Fort Bowie National Historic Site, historic Tombstone and Ramsey Canyon Nature Preserve. A fine military museum is located in Fort Huachuca, one of the oldest still-active Army posts in the American West.

Contacts • Sierra Vista Chamber of Commerce, 21 E. Wilcox Dr., Sierra Vista, AZ 85635; (800) 288-3861 or (520) 458-6940.

Sierra Vista Economic Development Foundation, P.O. Box 2380, Sierra Vista, AZ 85636; (520) 458-6948.

City of Sierra Vista, 2400 E. Tacoma St., Sierra Vista, AZ 85635; (520) 458-3315.

SPRINGERVILLE & EAGAR

Although not generally regarded as retirement communities, Springerville and Eagar offer possibilities for pensioners who don't mind nippy winters. However, they have little job potential.

Springerville may appeal to those seeking the quiet life and perhaps a fine old home on a tree-lined street. Eagar is essentially a Springerville suburb, although it has a larger population and its own city government. Housing is inexpensive in both, the tax rate is low and the surrounding hills offer outdoor recreation and a couple of historic pueblo sites. It's a short drive to Sunrise Ski Area and other lures of the White Mountain Apache Reservation and Apache-Sitgreaves National Forest.

Eager was named for 1871 settler John T. Eager, not for an ambitious beaver. The spelling has since been changed to "Eagar" for reasons that are lost to historians; maybe there were too many beaver jokes. About the time Eager's Eagar was getting started, Henry Springer opened a trading post four miles north. It was granted a post office in 1879 and it has outpaced Eagar commercially to become the trading center of a large cattle ranching region. The twin towns are in Round Valley, a grassy basin on the northeastern edge of the White Mountains.

Elevation ● 6,965 feet

Location ● In Apache County on U.S. Highways 60 and 191 in east central Arizona, near the New Mexico border.

Climate ● Warm summers; cool winters with cold nights. July average high 83.3 low 51.6; January average high 46.7, low 14.6. Rainfall about 23 inches; snowfall 36 inches.

Population ● Springerville 2,000; Eagar 4,515.

Population trend ● Ten percent gain in the past five years.

Property tax ● $6.63 per $100 of assessed valuation.

Economy ● It's a mix of tourism, lumbering and agriculture and it's not particularly active.

Job prospects ● The area unemployment rate tends to run higher than the rest of the state. Limited opportunities are available in tourism, lumbering and retailing.

Industrial facilities ● A few small industrial areas.

Real estate ● Most homes on the market are used although there is some new construction. Prices for a three-bedroom fixer-upper can be as low as $40,000; newer homes start around $70,000 and a few "ranchettes" on wooded acreages go considerably higher.

The media • The biweekly *Apache Observer*; daily news comes from Phoenix and Albuquerque. TV relays bring in Phoenix, Tucson and cable channels.

Medical services • A small hospital, convalescent hospital and a ten-unit assisted living apartment.

Transportation • Springerville Babbitt Field has two lighted runways; charter service only.

Education • Northland Pioneer College, plus public schools.

Local government • Both incorporated in 1948 and both with mayors, six-member councils and town managers.

Places to stay • About six motels in Springerville and Eagar; nine RV parks in the area and several campgrounds in the national forest.

Leisure facilities • "Enosphere" at Northland Pioneer College is a multi-use dome hosting cultural and sports activities; other campus recreational facilities also are available to the public. Springerville has a public pool, two parks and tennis and racquetball courts. Eager also has a pool and tennis and racquetball courts, plus three parks and a large multi-purpose facility at its high school.

Tourist lures • The White Mountains offer the usual outdoor appeal, and it's a short drive to the Sunrise summer and winter resort on the White Mountain Apache reservation. Despite their small size and rural demeanor, Springerville and Eagar have several museums, focusing on local history, art and Native American archeology. Nearby are two Indian ruins—Raven Site and Casa Malpais Pueblo.

Contacts • Round Valley Chamber of Commerce, P.O. Box 31 (148 E. Main St.) Springerville, AZ 85938-0031; (520) 333-2123.

Town of Springerville, P.O. Box 390, Springerville, AZ 85938; (520) 333-2656.

Town of Eagar, P.O. Box 1300 (174 S. Main St.), Eagar, AZ 85925; (520) 333-4128.

Apache County Economic Security Corporation, P.O. Box 767, St. Johns, AZ 85936; (520) 333-5469 in Springerville and Eagar.

TOMBSTONE

If you'd like to rub shoulders with history and you're attracted by mild climate and inexpensive housing, this may be the place. Don't expect any fancy subdivisions or golf courses. Tombstone is as funky as it sounds, with false front buildings, boardwalks and cowboy-style tourist trappings.

This rough-hewn frontier village has been called "the town too tough to die." Of course it can't die; Hollywood would never permit that. A few years ago, two more movies were added to the long list

of movies portraying the legendary gunfight at the O.K. Corral.

The town's roots can be traced to Ed Schieffelin, a prospector who decided to check out the rocky hills southeast of present-day Tucson in 1877. He was warned that the Apaches were on the warpath.

"All you'll find out there is your tombstone," a friend advised.

Ed found a big silver strike instead, and called it—appropriately— the Lucky Cuss. Word spread and other argonauts poured in. A town was platted two years later, in Goose Flat, two miles from Schieffelin's hillside mine. It soon became one of the largest, wildest and wickedest mining camps in the Southwest. It attracted such characters as Doc Holliday, Johnny Ringo, Bat Masterson and—of course—the Earp brothers. Wyatt was co-owner of the Oriental Saloon, where gunslinger Luke Short was a faro dealer.

By 1881, Tombstone boasted 10,000 citizens and it became the seat of Cochise County. In that same year, the Earps shot it out with the Clantons and McLaurys near the O.K. Corral. Actually, it was more of a blood feud than a police action. The Earps had accused the Clantons and McLaurys of cattle thievery and sheltering stage robbers at their ranches. The cowboys boasted openly that they would kill the Earps for besmirching their reputations.

"They tried to pick a fuss out of me," Wyatt testified at the hearing following the corral shootout.

After the excitement from the West's most publicized gun battle faded, Tombstone began fading as well. Most of the downtown area burned in 1882. A few years later, water began seeping into its mines. Falling silver prices and labor problems closed the last of the mines early in this century. The county seat was moved to Bisbee in 1931 and the town too tough to die was on the verge of doing it. The population dropped to 150.

Then tourists began trickling in, lured by stories of the Earp brothers and the shootout. The town's old Western look, unchanged because nobody could afford to modernize, became an asset. However, that asset has been overdone. Tourists buy frozen yogurt and John Wayne posters and visit museums that are mostly fronts for souvenir shops. Still, there's an air of legitimacy about all of this. Tombstone is a national historic landmark and the courthouse is a state historic park. Visitors clunk along boardwalks shaded by overhangs from false front stores. They catch rides in horse-drawn surreys and watch reenactments of the shootout. These occur several times a day and according to local historians, they're probably more accurate than anything portrayed by Hollywood.

Elevation ● 4,540 feet

Location ● In Cochise County, 17 miles northeast of Sierra Vista.

Climate ● Warm summers; mild winters with cool evenings. July average high 93.7, low 65.4; January average high 61.4, low 33.6. Rainfall 12.77 inches; snowfall seven inches.

Bad guys bite the dust in this reenactment of the shoot-out at the O.K. Corral, a 30-second gun battle that put Tombstone in the history books.

Population • 1,315

Population trend • Gained seven percent in the past five years. Some new subdivisions are rising between Tombstone and Sierra Vista.

Property tax • (assessed at ten percent of real value) $15.03 per $100 of assessed valuation.

Economy • Other than selling cowboy souvenirs and snow cones? Not much else. The economy is almost all tourist-based.

Job prospects • There aren't any to speak of, other than working in tourist shops. Even the O.K. Corral shootout players are unpaid amateurs. However, employment centers of Sierra Vista and Bisbee are a short drive away.

Industrial facilities • None.

Real estate • Home prices outside the historic district start as low as $50,000; restored or restorable historic homes are rare and are considerably higher.

The media • The legendary *Tombstone Epitaph* is still published although it's now a tourist paper; the news is more than a century old. There is a contemporary weekly called the *Tombstone Tumbleweed*.

Medical services • Emergency facilities in Tombstone; nearest hospital is in Sierra Vista, 17 miles southwest.

Transportation • Tombstone has an unpaved landing field; the nearest air service is in Sierra Vista.

Education • Community college in Sierra Vista; the usual public schools in Tombstone.

Local government • Incorporated in 1881; mayor, four-member council and city clerk.

Places to stay • About a dozen motels and bed & breakfast inns; three RV parks.

Leisure facilities • Three public parks, a swimming pool and two tennis courts.

Tourist lures • Tombstone's rustic look and reputation are the only lures it needs. It has five historic museums and quasi-gift shop museums, many century-old buildings and of course, the O.K. Corral. The original Boot Hill cemetery on the edge of town is now a tourist attraction; visitors enter through a gift shop.

Contacts • Tombstone Chamber of Commerce, P.O. Box 995 (Allan and Fourth streets), Tombstone, AZ 85638; (520) 457-3929.

City of Tombstone, P.O. Box 339, Tombstone, AZ 85638; (520) 457-3562.

TUBAC

Most historians say Arizona was born in Tubac. Established as a Spanish presidio in 1752, it's the state's oldest non-Indian settlement. The year before, Pima Chief Oacpicagigua led a revolt against missionaries and settlers. The army was called to quell the uprising, then the troops stayed to build a fort.

Tubac commander Juan Bautista de Anza left here in 1776 on his historic overland trek to establish the pueblos of San Jose and San Francisco in California. After Mexico won its independence from Spain in 1821, troops were withdrawn from Tubac. The settlement—harassed by Apache raids— was abandoned. The Gadsden Purchase brought the community under America's protection and it was resettled. In 1860, it was Arizona's largest town. Then the Civil War pulled American troops away, and hostile Apaches again forced its abandonment. Resettlement came after the Apaches finally were subdued late in the 19th century.

Today, slightly weathered little Tubac is a serious art colony, with many galleries housed in a mix of old and new adobe and brick buildings. This is where "art and history meet," proclaims a sign at the edge of town. A dozen or more boutiques, import and curio shops also line its quiet streets, selling Indian and Southwest crafts and assorted giftwares.

Statistically, Tubac is growing rapidly, gaining more than 16 percent a year in the Eighties, then slowing during the Nineties. However, it had only 230 citizens in 1980 so it's hardly threatening to become a metropolis. Two thirds of its new residents are retired.

Elevation • Approximately 3,000 feet

Location • In Santa Cruz County, 40 miles south of Tucson on Interstate-19.

Climate • Warm to hot summers; mild winters with cool evenings. July average high 97.1, low 65.5; January average high 65.9, low 31.2. Rainfall about 10 inches; rare traces of snow.

Population • 1,146

Population trend • Gained 27 percent in the past five years.

Property tax • (assessed at ten percent of real value) $13.88 per $100 of assessed valuation.

Economy • It's based mostly on tourism and retirement.

Job prospects • They're very limited; a few jobs may be available in retailing and tourist services.

Industrial facilities • None.

Real estate • There isn't much on the market; homes start around $60,000.

The media • Nearest newspaper is the *Green Valley News & Sun* published 20 miles away. TV feeds from Tucson and Nogales.

Medical services • A small clinic; hospital in Nogales, 23 miles south.

Transportation • Served by Greyhound and Citizens Bus Lines; no airport.

Education • Two elementary schools and a junior high; upper grades are bussed elsewhere

Local government • Unincorporated; services provided by Santa Cruz County.

Places to stay • A country club near Tubac, a few small motels in the area and the Rio Rico resort, ten miles south.

Leisure facilities • Tubac Center for the Arts, several galleries, boutiques and a community center.

Tourist lures • Visitors are drawn mostly by the galleries, boutiques and Southwest style cafés. Tubac State Historic Park is located here and Tumacacori National Monument is a few miles south.

Contact • Tubac Chamber of Commerce, P.O. Box 1866, Tubac, AZ 85646; (520) 398-2704.

WINSLOW

"I'm standing on a corner in Winslow, Arizona;

Such a fine sight to see..."

The author of that 1970s' song made popular by the Eagles, "Take It Easy," wasn't referring to Winslow itself, but to a pretty girl driving by in a flatbed Ford. However, this quite old prairie town in northeastern Arizona is attractive in a homey sort of way. It may offer potential for both job-seekers and retirees, assuming they don't mind rather cold winters.

Winslow is an old-fashioned community with a sturdy brick business district rimmed by tree-lined residential areas. Nearby are considerably older villages—the Homol'ovi ruins of the Anasazi. The town was established in 1882 as a railway division point, and named for

General Edward F. Winslow, president of the St. Louis and San Francisco Railroad. Despite its remote location, it thrived as a cattle and freight center.

Folks who enjoy sightseeing may like the fact that Winslow is within a one or two-hour drive of several attractions, including Petrified Forest National Park, the Painted Desert and Meteor Crater. Flagstaff is 60 miles west.

Elevation ● 4,850 feet

Location ● On the western edge of Navajo County on I-40, just south of the Navajo Nation.

Climate ● Warm summers, cool to cold winters. July average high 93.6, low 62.9; January average high 45.6, low 19.6. Rainfall 7.33 inches; snowfall 11.2 inches.

Population ● 10,780

Population trend ● Gained about two percent in the past five years.

Property tax ● (assessed at ten percent of real value) $12.69 per $100 assessed valuation.

Economy ● Moderately active, with a balance of retail trade, services, rail shipping and area ranching.

Job prospects ● Average to above average; major employers are the Santa Fe Railway and a nearby Arizona State Prison. Some light manufacturing, lumbering and seasonal tourism work is available.

Industrial facilities ● A few small industrial parks.

Real estate ● Housing is quite inexpensive; three-bedroom home prices start around $40,000.

The media ● The weekly *Winslow Mail* and *The Reminder*.

Medical services ● A 42-bed hospital; Native American outpatient clinic; convalescent home and three medical clinics.

Transportation ● Served by Greyhound and Amtrak; Winslow Airport offers general aviation services.

Education ● Winslow campus of Northland Pioneer College, plus the usual public schools.

Local government ● Town founded in 1882 and incorporated in 1900; mayor, six-member council and city administrator.

Places to stay ● Seventeen motels and two RV parks.

Leisure facilities ● Golf course, public indoor and outdoor pools and community parks. McHood Park, five miles southeast, offers fishing, boating, swimming and picnicking.

Tourist lures ● Homol'ovi Ruins State Park north of town, plus nearby attractions of Petrified Forest National Park, Painted Desert, Meteor Crater and the Hopi and Navajo reservations.

Contacts ● Winslow Chamber of Commerce, P.O. Box 460 (300 W. North Rd.), Winslow, AZ 86047; (520) 289-2434 or 289-2435.

City of Winslow, 21 Williamson Ave., Winslow, AZ 86047; (520) 289-2422.

PART THREE
THE ATTRACTIONS

Once you've settled in your special corner of Arizona, you'll want to explore the rest of the state. But where to begin? You already know that it's an amazingly diverse place, with snow-clad pinnacles as well as cactus gardens.

In the chapters that follow, we've divided the state into six major tourist areas, and added a special section on exploring next-door Mexico. Much of the information was distilled from our comprehensive statewide guidebook, Arizona Discovery Guide. If you'd like more details than we list in these chapters, you might want to pick up a copy at a local book store. Or it can be ordered directly from the publisher; specifics are at the end of this book. We also recommend other books on Arizona's attractions, history and the Indian nations in Chapter nineteen.

Chapter twelve

THE NORTHWEST

GRAND CANYON AND VICINITY

We begin our exploration with the state's most famous attraction—that magnificent 227-mile-long chasm across its northwest corner. Indeed, despite its fame as a sunbelt retirement haven, Arizona is officially known as the "Grand Canyon state." This is its most visited landmark, drawing four million people a year.

This high country corner of Arizona contains other lures as well. Find time to explore the remote and intriguing Arizona Strip on the northern side of the canyon, and Glen Canyon National Recreation area adjacent to Page. South of the Grand Canyon, you can hike down to the isolated Indian village of Supai, deep in a scenic chasm and reached only by foot or horseback. Or you can catch a vintage steam train that runs between the Grand Canyon and the woodsy town of Williams.

Grand Canyon National Park • One of the world's most famous attractions, the Grand Canyon is not a single ravine but a vast network of hundreds of chasms carved deeply into the Kaibab section of the Colorado Plateau. Most people visit the South Rim, which has extensive facilities including lodges, restaurants, museums, gift shops, campgrounds and even an airport. The less visited yet equally spectacular North Rim is our favorite. It's uncrowded, drawing only a tenth as many visitors as the opposite side, and it offers complete—if scaled down—visitor facilities.

The Grand Canyon's grandeur is best appreciated from below the rim; this view is from Horseshoe Mesa, reached by a South Rim trail.

The best way to experience the canyon is to hike into its wild depths from either rim, or run the roller-coaster rapids of the Colorado River. You can book overnight accommodations at Phantom Ranch at the bottom of the canyon, or reserve spots at several campgrounds. This must be done well in advance; Phantom Ranch lodgings should be booked a *year* or more ahead. Whitewater rafting through the canyon is popular and you can send for a list of outfitters (see below).

The South Rim remains open the year around, while the North Rim—which is much higher—closes after the first serious snowfall, usually in late October.

For information • Superintendent, Grand Canyon National Park, P.O. Box 129, Grand Canyon, AZ 86023. Call (520) 638-7888 or (520) 638-7770 for South Rim information and (520) 638-7864 for North Rim information.

Backcountry Reservations office, P.O. Box 129, Grand Canyon, AZ 86023. (Backcountry camping and hiking reservations can be made only by mail or in person.)

Grand Canyon National Park Lodges (South Rim, Phantom Ranch and Trailer Village RV park reservations), P.O. Box 699, Grand Canyon, AZ 86023; (520) 638-2401 or (520) 638-2631.

TW Recreational Services, Inc. (North Rim reservations), P.O. Box 400, Cedar City, UT 84720; (801) 586-7686.

For a list of river runners: River Sub-District, Grand Canyon National Park, P.O. Box 129, Grand Canyon, AZ 86023; (520) 638-7843.

Williams

Below the South Rim, the plateau slopes southwesterly through Kaibab National Forest, turning into a high prairie of Joshua trees and bunchgrass. If you follow U.S. Highway 180 and then State Route 64 south, you'll climb into more forest and hit the little town of Williams at Interstate 40. This wooded community is home to a steam train that will take you right back to the Grand Canyon.

For area information • Williams-Grand Canyon Chamber of Commerce, 200 Railroad Ave., Williams, AZ 86046; (520) 635-4061.

Grand Canyon Railway • *Grand Canyon Boulevard and Railroad Avenue, Williams; (800) THE TRAIN or (520) 635-4000; mailing address: 123 N. San Francisco, Suite 210, Flagstaff, AZ 86001; (520) 773-1976.* ☐ This firm has resumed the historic train run from Williams to the South Rim that began in 1901. It uses vintage steam trains in the summer and 1950 era diesel locomotives the rest of the year.

Hualapai/Havasupai Reservations

Northeast of Williams, much of the Grand Canyon is rimmed by the Hualapai and Havasupai Indian reservations. An eight-mile hike (or horseback ride) through pretty Havasu Canyon will take you to one of America's most remote villages.

Havasu Canyon and the village of Supai • *For camping permits or overnight lodging and horseback trips, contact: Havasupai Tourist Enterprise, Supai, AZ 86436; (520) 448-2121.* ☐ To reach the trailhead for the Supai hike, follow historic Highway 66 west from Williams and then go north on Indian Route 18 through the Hualapai Reservation to Hualapai Hilltop. From there, you can hike or ride down to Supai village, reached only by trail through Havasu Canyon, which is a tributary chasm of the Grand Canyon. Below the village are several camping areas and two beautiful waterfalls. Back at the top, a new Native American casino perches near the edge of the canyon.

THE ARIZONA STRIP AND GLEN CANYON

If you visit the Grand Canyon's North Rim, you'll pass through the Arizona Strip. Isolated from the rest of the state by the great chasm, this high plateau covering 12,000 square miles is home to only a handful of people. Many are descendants of early Mormon pioneers who came down from Utah in the mid-1800s. Towns in the area such as **Colorado City** and **Fredonia** are still predominately Mormon. Following State Route 389 southeast from Colorado City, you'll encounter one of Arizona's many national monuments. Not surprisingly, this one has Mormon roots:

Pipe Spring National Monument • *HC-65, Box 5, Fredonia, AZ 86022; (520) 643-7105. Visitor center/museum open daily 8 to 4:30; ranch buildings open until 5.* ☐ This small preserve contains the great fortified ranch headquarters of an early Mormon cattle spread. You can tour furnished rooms in the fortress-like ranch house and climb a low, steep bluff for a nice panorama of the Arizona Strip's grasslands. A Native American gaming casino, not connected with Pipe Spring, is just above the national monument.

From here, the highway continues into **Fredonia**, where it merges with U.S. 89-A and swings southward. You can follow it and State Route 67 through Kaibab National Forest to the Grand Canyon's North Rim. Or continue east on 89-A to **Marble Canyon**, a steep walled ravine where the Colorado River begins slicing into this high plateau. Most river-runners put in at **Lee's Ferry,** just northeast of the hamlet of Marble Canyon. A part of Glen Canyon National Recreation Area, it has a campground and several historic exhibits.

Page

If you continue following 89-A east and then take U.S. 89 north, you'll enter Page. Adjacent is the Glen Canyon National Recreation Area, encompassing a mighty dam and a flooded canyon behind it.

For area information ● Page-Lake Powell Chamber of Commerce, P.O. Box 727 (106 S. Lake Powell Blvd.), Page, AZ 86040; (520) 645-2741.

Glen Canyon National Recreation Area ● *P.O. Box 1507, Page, AZ 86040; (520) 645-2511.* ◻ Within this area are Glen Canyon Dam, Lake Powell and a million acres of eroded desert sandstone. Glen Canyon, whose serpentine side ravines and fantastic formations rivaled those of the Grand Canyon, was inundated by the dam. You can see the tops of this geological wonderland by taking boat cruises in and out of the finger-like fjords of Lake Powell. They depart from Wahweap Marina near Page; call (520) 645-2433 or (800) 528-6154.

While you're in the neighborhood, take a guided or self-guiding tour of Glen Canyon Dam and stop at the Carl Hayden Visitor Center and Museum. It's open daily 7 a.m. to 7 p.m. in summer and 8 to 5 the rest of the year.

FLAGSTAFF AND SURROUNDS

During most of this northwestern Arizona exploration, you've been in huge Coconino County, which covers 18,629 square miles. If you head east on I-40, you'll encounter the county seat of Flagstaff. It's the gateway to some of Arizona's most varied attractions. Within a short drive are seven national parks and monuments (including some of America's finest Indian ruins), Arizona's largest ski area and highest peak, and the red rock beauty of Oak Creek Canyon.

For area information ● Flagstaff Chamber of Commerce, 101 W. Route 66, Flagstaff, AZ 86004; (520) 774-9541 or (800) 842-7293 and (800) 217-2367.

ATTRACTIONS IN AND NEAR FLAGSTAFF

Arizona Snowbowl and Humphreys Peak • *P.O. Box 40, Flagstaff, AZ 86002; (520) 779-1951 for the Snowbowl.* ☐ Although primarily a ski area, the Snowbowl also is popular with summer visitors. You can take a sky tram to the dizzying heights of the San Francisco Peaks and hike into the Kachina Wilderness Area. A trail leads from the Snowbowl to the top of Humphreys Peak, tallest in Arizona at 12,633. It's not a technical climb; it's just a long, hard trudge.

Lowell Observatory • *1400 W. Mars Hill Rd., Flagstaff, AZ 86001; (520) 774-2096. Daily 9 to 5; tours at 10, 11, 1 and 3. (Shorter hours in the off-season.) Night sky shows Monday, Tuesday, Wednesday and Saturday at 8, 8:45 and 9:30.* ☐ Privately-endowed Lowell Observatory sits atop a pine-covered mesa less than a mile from downtown Flagstaff. Visitors can view celestial exhibits and join lecture tours or wander about the grounds on their own.

Museum of Northern Arizona • *Route 4, Box 720 (Fort Valley Road, three miles north), Flagstaff, AZ 86001; (520) 774-5213. Daily 9 to 5.* ☐ Housed in a handsome fieldstone and timber complex, this museum is "dedicated to the anthropology, biology, geology and fine arts of the Colorado Plateau." Remodeled and modernized a few years ago, it's one of the state's finest archives.

Riordan State Historic Park • *Riordan Ranch Road downtown (P.O. Box 217), Flagstaff, AZ 86002; (520) 779-4395. Daily 8 to 5 in summer; hours may be shorter the rest of the year.* ☐ Now surrounded by downtown Flagstaff, this state park contains the pioneer Riordan brothers' elaborate and unusual double-home, joined in the middle by a gaming room and restored to its original rustic splendor.

Sunset Crater Volcano National Monument • *Twelve miles north of Flagstaff on U.S. 80, and then east; mailing address: 2717 N. Steves Blvd., Suite 3, Flagstaff, AZ 86004; (520) 556-7042. Visitor center open daily 8 to 5.* ☐ The focal point of this park is an almost perfect volcanic cindercone with a burnt orange cast, particularly evident at sunset. (And thus, the name.) It's surrounded by the wild geological turmoil of eruptions that date back more than 700 years.

Wupatki National Monument • *Fourteen miles north of Sunset Crater; mailing address: 2717 N. Steves Blvd., Suite 3, Flagstaff, AZ 86004; (520) 527-7040. Visitor Center open daily 8 to 5.* ☐ Wupatki is home to several ancient Indian ruins scattered about a high volcanic prairie. The largest and most elaborate is Wupatki Pueblo, a short walk from the visitor center. It's a four-story, 100-room condo built of sandstone blocks instead of the usual adobe.

Flagstaff to Winslow

Eastbound from Flagstaff on Interstate 40, you'll discover several other attractions. One of them comes from the mysterious past; another from out of space.

For area information • Winslow Chamber of Commerce, P.O. Box 460 (300 W. North Rd.), Winslow, AZ 86047; (520) 289-2434.

Walnut Canyon National Monument • *Seven miles east on I-40, then three miles south; (520) 526-3367. Visitor center and ruins open daily 8 to 5.* ☐ Steep-sided Walnut Canyon shelters an elaborate Sinagua cliff dwelling built about 800 years ago. Recessed into overhangs between the rim and canyon floor, the ruins can be reached by a 251-step trail from the visitor center. Save some energy for the return trip!

Meteor Crater • *Forty miles east of Flagstaff to Meteor Crater exit, then six miles south. Address: Meteor Crater Enterprises, 603 N. Beaver, Suite C, Flagstaff, AZ 86001; (520) 774-8350. Daily 6 to 6 in summer, shorter hours the rest of the year.* ☐ Imagine this: a monster chunk of nickel and iron weighing millions of tons streaks earthward at 43,000 miles an hour. It slams into the ground with a force that buries fragments hundreds of feet deep. What you'll see is the massive hole that it left, plus an excellent museum with displays concerning meteorites, the universe and America's space program.

Homol'ovi Ruins State Park • *Just north of Winslow on State Highway 87. Address: HC63 Box 5, Winslow, AZ 86047; (520) 289-4106.* ☐ In contrast to partially restored Wupatki and Walnut Canyon ruins, Homol'ovi Ruins State Park shelters several unrestored sites. These are remnants of 13th to 16th century Anasazi villages as they looked before the archaeologists and anthropologists arrived. A fine new visitor center was opened recently.

Little Painted Desert County Park • *Just off State Route 87, about 13 miles north of Winslow; gates open 8 a.m. to 9 p.m.* ☐ This is a surprising jewel of a park—a mini badlands of softly contoured, pastel hued sandstone. From a parking area, you can drive or walk along rim roads in either direction for varied vistas of this fluted amphitheater of erosion. A trail from the north rim road takes you into the sensuously rounded landscape.

SEDONA AND THE VERDE VALLEY

If you head south of Flagstaff on U.S. 89-A, you'll enter a mosaic of natural beauty, upscale tourism and pre-history. You will discover the red ramparts of Oak Creek Canyon; the galleries, boutiques and elegant resorts of Sedona; the ancient Indian ruins of the Verde Valley and the rustic copper mining town of Jerome.

For area information • Camp Verde Chamber of Commerce, P.O. Box 1665, Camp Verde, AZ 86322; (520) 567-9294.

Jerome Chamber of Commerce, P.O. Box K, Jerome, AZ 86331; (520) 634-2900.

Sedona-Oak Creek Canyon Chamber of Commerce, P.O. Box 478, Sedona, AZ 86339; (520) 282-7722.

Verde Valley Chamber of Commerce, 1010 S. Main St., Cottonwood, AZ 86326; (520) 864-7593.

The road into **Oak Creek Canyon** is one of the prettiest drives in America. It twists down through thick ponderosa forests to the valley floor, where it follows sparkling Oak Creek. At the lower end, the canyon emerges into a stunning panorama of red rock pinnacles, buttes and fairy castles.

You'll shortly encounter **Sedona**, surrounded by this splendid red rock display. Take time to explore its upscale shops and galleries, particularly in Tlaquepaque, a Spanish colonial style complex just southeast of town on State Route 179.

Inquire at the Coconino National Forest office or the chamber of commerce about scenic drives and hikes in the area. Several operators offer jeep trips into the red rock formations and balloon flights above them.

Stop to admire the **Chapel of the Holy Cross**; it's tucked among red rock formations on Chapel Road off Highway 179, two miles south of town. With a huge cross forming its façade, it rivals the rocks themselves as one of the area's most appealing attractions.

Sedona to Jerome

Back on Highway 89-A, head south into the Verde Valley and you'll encounter one of Arizona's newest state parks. Beyond the park are four more intriguing attractions. Two are remnants of the dim past and two are of more recent vintage.

Red Rock State Park ● *South of Sedona, to the left off Highway 89-A. Address: HC Box 886, Sedona, AZ 86336; (520) 282-6907. Park open daily 8 to 6; visitor center 9 to 5.* ◻ A former millionaire's vacation retreat, this area backdropped by red rock ramparts was opened as a state park in 1991. It's a state-of-the-environment park, with a strong focus on the ecosystems of Oak Creek and nearby rock formations. Its Center for Environmental Education teaches visitors about the flora, fauna and history of the area.

Tuzigoot National Monument ● *Between Cottonwood and Clarkdale on Tuzigoot Road. Address: P.O. Box 68, Clarkdale, AZ 86324; (520) 634-5564. Daily 8 to 7 in summer, 8 to 5 the rest of the year.* ◻ These extensive Sinagua ruins crown a low ridge north of Clarkdale. They were built around the 13th century, abandoned and then restored as a WPA project during the Depression.

Montezuma's Castle National Monument ● *Southeast of Clarkdale, just east of I-17. Address: P.O. Box 219, Camp Verde, AZ 86322; (520) 567-3322. Daily 8 to 7 in summer, 8 to 5 the rest of the year.* ◻ It's not a castle and it was never visited by the Aztec chief Montezuma. It's a small yet dramatic ruin perched high in a cliff face. Nearby and equally interesting (and equally misnamed) is **Montezuma Well,** a limestone sinkhole rimmed by several pueblo ruins.

Montezuma's Castle occupies a dramatic niche in a cliff face above the Verde Valley.

Fort Verde State Historic Park • *In the town of Camp Verde, just south of Montezuma's Castle. Address: P.O. Box 397, Camp Verde, AZ 86322; (520) 567-3275. Daily 8 to 4:30.* ◻ The park preserves remnants of a frontier army post built in the 1870s to protect settlers from the people they had rudely displaced. A museum spotlights the Native American and white history of the Verde Valley.

Jerome

If you follow 89-A southwest through the Verde Valley, you'll climb into the flanks of Mingus Mountain and enter the scruffy remnants of one of Arizona's most interesting old mining towns. Jerome isn't a ghost town but a lively tourist village with museums, 19th century homes, art galleries, curio shops and antique stores. From the late 1870s to the 1950s, billions of dollars in copper, gold and silver were gouged from Mingus Mountain's steep slopes. Several attractions here are worth stops:

Jerome State Historic Park • *P.O. Box D, Jerome, AZ 86331; (520) 634-5381. Daily 8 to 5.* ◻ The park embraces the estate of James S. "Rawhide Jimmy" Douglas, owner of the Little Daisy Mine and one of Jerome's wealthiest copper barons. The mansion offers a mix of period furnishings, historic photos, videos and mining exhibits.

Jerome Historical Society Mine Museum • 200 Main Street, Jerome, AZ 86331; (520) 634-5477. Daily 9 to 4:30; gift shop open until 5. ☐ Although not professionally done, the museum is nicely arrayed with a series of tableaux about Jerome and its boom days.

Gold King Mine Museum • *P.O. Box 125, (just above town), Jerome AZ 86331. Open daily 9 to 5:30.* ☐ This scruffy clutter of early day mining equipment and 19th century memorabilia walks a fine line between a museum and a junkyard. And therein lies its character.

Prescott

Continuing southeast from Jerome on Highway 89-A, you'll climb over the shoulders of Mingus Mountain, drop down into a grassy valley and begin climbing again—into the wooded Bradshaw Mountains of Prescott National Forest. Cradles among these trees is Prescott, one of our favorite Arizona towns. It has a New England look and a Western attitude, and it offers several museums and galleries.

For area information • Prescott Chamber of Commerce, P.O. Box 1147 (117 W. Goodwin St.), Prescott, AZ 86302; (800) 266-7534 or (520) 445-2000.

THE ATTRACTIONS

Phippen Museum of Western Art • *4701 N. Highway 89 (seven miles north), Prescott, AZ 86302; (520) 778-1385. Wednesday-Monday 10 to 4, Sunday 1 to 4, closed Tuesday.* ☐ This fine museum, named in honor of noted local artist George Phippen, exhibits paintings, bronzes, ceramics and other works of past and present Western artists.

Sharlot Hall Museum • *415 W. Gurley St., Prescott, AZ 86302; (520) 445-3122. Monday-Saturday 10 to 5 and Sunday 1 to 5 from April through October; shorter hours the rest of the year.* ☐ Covering more than a city block, the Sharlot Hall complex contains a dozen furnished historic buildings, either original or reconstructed. The centerpiece is the governor's "mansion," a log cabin that served as the official residence when Prescott was the territorial capital in the late 1800s.

Smoki Museum • *100 N. Arizona St. (P.O. Box 123), Prescott, AZ 86302; (520) 445-1230. Tuesday-Saturday 10 to 4 and Sunday 1 to 4, closed Wednesday.* ☐ Pronounced "Smoke-Eye," this museum houses a significant collection of artifacts of Southwest Indians and other American tribes, including stone tools, baskets and pottery excavated from local sites.

Yavapai County Courthouse and Plaza • *Gurley and Montezuma streets.* ☐ The Greco-Roman style courthouse and surrounding tree-shaded plaza give Prescott a typical New England look. However, the town is definitely Western, as evidenced by the nearby cowboy galleries and shops.

Across from the courthouse along Montezuma Street is "Whiskey Row," once the town's bawdy district and now a solid rank of old style store fronts. Most of the saloons are gone, replaced by gift shops and boutiques. The **Bead Museum** at 140 S. Montezuma is worth a peek; it contains thousands of beads and beadwork; open Monday-Saturday 9:30 to 4:30.

NEARBY ATTRACTIONS

Two lures are within a short drive of Prescott—one southeast and one southwest. Either direction will take you quickly from pines to cactus. If you head southeast on State Route 69, you will soon hit Interstate 40, bound for Phoenix. At Cordes Junction, you'll encounter a most curious complex:

Arcosanti • *HC 74, Box 4136, Mayer, AZ 86333; (520) 632-7135. Daily 9 to 5; tours on the hour 10 to 4 with a four-person minimum. Adjacent bakery-café; accommodations available.* ◻ Arcosanti is the creation of Italian architect and visionary Paolo Soleri. Seeking to solve many of the world's problems in one architectural swoop, he is trying—with eager young helpers—to build an idyllic, energy-efficient, space-saving and environmentally correct community. However, its geometric precast concrete shapes have begun to weather in the three decades since the project was started. It looks more like a scruffy space station that crash-landed in the desert.

Wickenburg

If you take U.S. 89 southwest from Prescott, you'll discover a community of quite a different stripe. Wickenburg works to preserve its cowboy past instead of fretting about an Orwellian future. It calls itself the "Dude ranch capital of the world," a title well earned, since five guest ranches function in the attractive surrounding desert.

Wickenburg was first a gold rush boomtown and then an important ranching center. Today, it still looks like yesterday, with false front stores and boardwalks. And it proudly hosts one of the finest small museums in Arizona.

For area information • Wickenburg Chamber of Commerce, 216 N. Frontier St., Wickenburg, AZ 85390; (520) 684-5479.

Desert Caballeros Western Museum • *20 N. Old Railroad St. (at Wickenburg Way), Wickenburg, AZ 85358; (520) 684-2272. Monday-Saturday 10 to 4, Sunday 1 to 4.* ◻ The focal point of this museum is a full scale turn-of-the-century Western street scene. Excellent dioramas and artifacts recall the area's development from the Paleozoic to the present. An adjoining gallery displays Western art by such notables as Russell, Remington and Catlin.

Hassayampa River Preserve • *West side of Highway 60/93, three miles southeast town (P.O. Box 1162), Wickenburg, AZ 85358; (520) 684-2772. Wednesday-Sunday 8 to 5 from mid-September to mid-May and 6 to noon the rest of the year. Suggested donation $5.* ◻ This is a fine example of a riparian woodland along the course of the Hassayampa River. Once a stage stop and guest ranch, it was opened as a preserve in 1987 by the Nature Conservancy.

Chapter thirteen
THE WEST & SOUTHWEST
THE COLORADO RIVER CORRIDOR

W̲e discussed the Colorado River's aquatic playground in Chapter eight. A series of dams has turned the stream into a chain of lakes, disrupting the great stream's efforts to flow from the Grand Canyon into Mexico's Gulf of California.

This chapter is rather short. Other than the river itself, there aren't a lot of attractions along the river corridor, or elsewhere in southwestern Arizona. Away from the river, the region is mostly unpopulated desert. The area does have a few lures, however.

If you live elsewhere and plan to visit this area, we'd suggest coming in the spring or fall. Summers sizzle, with average daytime temperatures above 105 degrees. It's not uncommon for the mercury to crawl into the 120s. Winter nights, while pleasantly balmy, can get a bit cool. During spring and fall, temperatures are close to idyllic day and night.

As you approach these corridor communities, bear in mind that they aren't bastions of culture or architectural gems. Many, like Bullhead City, look hastily assembled. Few have significant tourist attractions other than their bordering reservoirs. Notable exceptions are Hoover Dam, Lake Mead National Recreation Area, the historic parks of Yuma and—well—there's that British bridge at Lake Havasu. Inland, you will discover Organ Pipe Cactus National Monument and Kitt Peak, both definitely worth a detour.

HOOVER DAM AND LAKE MEAD

Our tour starts in the north and wanders south to Yuma and then inland to Organ Pipe Cactus and Kitt Peak. We begin at the Arizona-Nevada border with Hoover Dam and Lake Mead. Visitor facilities for both are on the Nevada side. Just beyond is the attractive community of **Boulder City**, built in the 1930s as a construction town for the dam. Its nicely preserved art deco downtown area, Boulder Dam Hotel and Hoover Dam Museum are definitely worth a look. Boulder City is the only town in Nevada that prohibits gambling, although there's a casino between the town and the dam. Don't spend all of your money before your tour along the Colorado River corridor begins.

Hoover Dam and Lake Mead National Recreation Area • *601 Nevada Highway, Boulder City, NV 89005-2426; (702) 293-8906. Hoover Dam Visitor Center open daily 8:30 to 6:30. Alan Bible Visitor Center open daily 8:30 to 4:30.* ☐ A sparkling new visitor center was opened at Hoover Dam a few years ago, with exhibits, videos and a dramatic viewing platform. From the center, tours take visitors through the innards of one of the grandest engineering marvels of the world. Hoover Dam holds back the world's largest reservoir, **Lake Mead,** which has become a major aquatic playground. Lake Mead and **Lake Mohave** below the dam comprise Lake Mead National Recreation Area. For details of its marinas, lodgings, campsites and water sports, stop at the Alan Bible Visitor Center, a few miles into Nevada.

SOUTH TO QUARTZSITE

For area information (in order of appearance) • Kingman Area Chamber of Commerce, P.O. Box 1150 (333 W. Andy Devine Ave.), Kingman, AZ 86402; (520) 753-6106.

Bullhead Area Chamber of Commerce, 1251 Highway 95, Bullhead City, AZ 86430; (520) 754-4121.

Lake Havasu Area Chamber of Commerce, 1930 Mesquite Ave., Suite 3, Lake Havasu City, AZ 86403; (800) 242-8278 or (520) 453-3444.

Laughlin Visitor Bureau, Box 29849, Laughlin, NV 89028; (702) 298-3321.

Parker Area Chamber of Commerce, P.O. Box 627 (1217 California Ave.), Parker, AZ 85344; (520) 669-2174.

From Hoover Dam, you can choose between Arizona or Nevada for your southbound trip. Both routes miss the river until you reach Bullhead City. The Nevada route is the fastest, although we prefer the Arizona side, since it takes you to the interesting towns of Kingman and Oatman, and through the dramatic ramparts of the Black Mountains on historic Route 66.

To begin, follow U.S. 93 east from Hoover Dam through the dry Detrital Valley to **Kingman.** You'll want to poke about its weathered old downtown, check out historic Highway 66 monuments in Railroad Park and visit its fine museum:

Mohave Museum of History and Arts ● *400 W. Beale St. (Grand-view), Kingman, AZ 86401; (520) 753-3195. Monday-Friday 9 to 5 and weekends 1 to 5.* ◻ A cut above the typical small-town archive, this museum tells the story of this valley's settlement, from Native Americans through the silver and copper rush to the present. A major exhibit traces the life of gravel-voiced character actor Andy Devine, who was born in Flagstaff and grew up here.

From Kingman, take historic Route 66 west over the rugged Black Mountains toward Bullhead City. Take time to poke around funky **Oatman**, a mining camp turned tourist trap. Merchants will sell you feed for feral burros that hang around town waiting for handouts; don't let one of them follow you home. From here, the highway tilts downward and hits State Route 95 at the Colorado River's **Lake Mohave**. Turn north for the short drive into **Bullhead City.**

Most visitors find Bullhead interesting only for its water recreation. For retirees and Snowbirds, however, the greatest draw is its balmy winters. If you feel like pulling a few slot machine handles, you can drive across a bridge to Laughlin, or leave your car in a parking lot on the north end of Bullhead and catch a shuttle boat.

Heading south from Bullhead City, you'll stay rather close to the river until you bump into I-40. Drive eastward briefly and then head south on Highway 95 to **Lake Havasu City.** As we discussed in Chapter eight, the attraction here is the **London Bridge**, brought stone-by-stone from England and reassembled over a peninsula of Lake Havasu. Promoters call it the second most visited attraction in Arizona, after the Grand Canyon. It is interesting, sitting in the desert, looking like a left-over Roman ruin in North Africa. Unfortunately, an "English village" built around its base has become quite tacky.

From Havasu, continue south on Highway 95 to **Parker Dam**, which offers brief self-guided tours. If you turn west at the "business route" sign just below **Buckskin Mountain State Park**, you'll drive along the **Parker Strip**. It's a water recreation area lined with resorts, marinas and RV parks. The route takes you into **Parker**, an unassuming little town surrounded by the Colorado River Reservation. There's a new Native American casino here, in case you didn't spend all of your quarters in Laughlin. The **Colorado River Indian Tribes Museum** on the south end of town is worth a pause.

Below Parker, the highway swings away from the river, cuts arrow-straight through boring desert and hits I-10 at **Quartzsite**, which we have unkindly branded as the ugliest town in Arizona. You can stop by the little **Quartzsite Museum** on the north side frontage road if it's open; the hours are rather irregular. Before leaving town, go to the local cemetery and visit a curious pyramidal monument to Haiji Ali. He was a Syrian who came over as part of a late 19th century experiment to use camels for Southwestern desert transport. The program flopped so "Hi Jolly" hung around Quartzsite and became something of a local character.

YUMA TO ORGAN PIPE AND KITT PEAK

Below Quartzsite, highway 95 stays away from *Rio Colorado* until it hits **Yuma**, the only town of substance along the river. With a population topping 55,000, it offers a fine historic park, the "notorious" territorial prison and a museum fashioned from an elegant early day residence. From Yuma, you might want to swing west and follow I-8 into California, where you'll see sand dunes right out of a Lawrence of Arabia film.

For area information • Yuma Convention & Visitors Bureau, P.O. Box 10831 (377 S. Main at Giss Parkway), Yuma, AZ 85366-8831; (520) 783-0071.

THE ATTRACTIONS

Century House Museum • *240 Madison Ave., Yuma, AZ 85364; (520) 782-1841. Tuesday-Saturday 10 to 4.* ☐ Italian pioneer E.F. Sanguinetti made his fortune as a Yuma merchant and developer, and he spent a lot of it on this spacious 19th century house and garden. Today, the 1870s adobe is a fine museum with exhibits concerning early Colorado River sternwheelers, mining, railroading, settlers and Indian cultures.

Yuma Crossing Quartermaster Depot Historic Site • *100 N. Fourth Avenue at the Colorado River, (P.O. Box 2768), Yuma AZ 85366-5735; (520) 329-0404. Daily 10 to 5; visitor center and gift shop open 9:30 to 5:30.* ☐ This site preserves two important elements in Western history—a ford across the Colorado River that opened California to overland travelers from the east, and a major Army supply center. Several buildings survive from the original depot, which operated from 1864 until 1883. The original storehouse, office, commanding officers quarters and other structures have been refurbished and furnished to the period. A riverside trail links the Yuma Territorial Prison and the depot.

Yuma Territorial Prison State Historic Park • *Prison Hill Road (P.O. Box 10792), Yuma, AZ 85366-8792; (520) 783-4771. Daily 8 to 5.* ☐ Hollywood made this old prison more notorious than it really was. Actually, it was designed to be a model lockup with a library, schooling and even crafts classes. However, it had no air conditioning and summers were beastly, even if the guards weren't. It was closed in 1909 and what remains are a few cell blocks and the main guard tower built over a water tank. A museum constructed on the mess hall foundation displays prison artifacts, scowling photos of inmates and graphics concerning prisoners and the men who guarded them.

There's not much south of Yuma, other than the pleasantly dusty Mexican border town of **San Luis**, which offers a few handicraft and curio shops. If you head east on I-8 to **Gila Bend** and then swing south onto State Route 85, you'll hit the interesting old company mining town of **Ajo**. Check out its Spanish style colonnaded shopping plaza. Also worth a pause are the small **Ajo Historical Museum** in a former Indian mission, and an overlook to the **New Cornelia** open pit copper mine. From Ajo, continue south to one of our favorite patches of desert.

Organ Pipe Cactus National Monument ● *Route 1, Box 100, Ajo, AZ 85321; (520) 387-6849. Park open 24 hours; visitor center open daily 8 to 5.* ◻ Arizona's largest and most remote national monument preserves some of the world's most striking desert wilderness. It is named for a large cactus with multiple arms that reach upward from a common base, supposedly resembling organ pipes. This is but one botanical resident of this mountainous rock garden. It's busy with giant saguaro and hundreds of other desert plants, including 29 species of cactus.

Head briefly north from Organ Pipe and turn east at the oddly named town of **Why** onto State Route 86. You'll travel through the barren desert of the huge **Tohono O'odham Indian Reservation**. As you leave southwestern Arizona and approach Tucson, follow a winding road up to the world's largest astronomical facility.

Kitt Peak National Observatory ● *P.O. Box 26732, Tucson, AZ 85726-6732; (520) 620-5350. Daily 9 to 3:45; film and guided tours at 11, 1 and 2:30.* ◻ This busy complex offers extensive visitor facilities, including a new reception center, astronomical museum and theater. Among its exhibits are artifacts and crafts of the Tohono O'odham Indians, whose land the observatory occupies. Self-guiding tours take you into structures that house three of the observatory's 13 telescopes. A highlight attraction is the monster McMath solar telescope, built into an angular shaft thrusting 300 feet into the earth.

Chapter fourteen

PHOENIX & SURROUNDS

VALLEY OF THE SUN ATTRACTIONS

It will come as no surprise that the greater Phoenix area is a major destination for tourists as well as for job-seekers, retirees and Snowbirds. Although Phoenix boasts several mountain and desert parks, most of the lures here are man-made—fine museums, huge air conditioned malls and elegant resorts. Phoenix has been rated second in the nation for visitor services, accommodations and dining by the New York-based Zagat Guide. Phoenix and Scottsdale have more Mobile Travel Guide five-star resorts and four and five-diamond AAA resorts than any other area in the country.

With all of this, it is still a remarkably economical city in which to play tourist. A recent survey revealed that it was the third least expensive major city in the country for lodging and meals. Los Angeles costs nearly twice as much and New York is nearly three times as pricey.

For area information ● Phoenix and Valley of the Sun Convention and Visitors Bureau, 400 E. Van Buren St., Suite 600, Phoenix, AZ 85004-2290; (602) 254-6500. Also, there's a downtown visitor center at the northwest corner of the Hyatt Regency Hotel block, Adams and Second Street.

THE ATTRACTIONS

Arizona Hall of Fame Museum ● *1101 W. Washington St. (near 11th Street, in the former Carnegie Public Library), Phoenix, AZ 85007; (602) 255-4675. Weekdays 8 to 5.* ☐ The museum features photos and memorabilia of Arizona's "famous, not yet famous and perhaps infamous." A special exhibit honors the Navajo Code-Talkers, who used their little-known native language as the basis for a communications code in the Pacific during World War II.

Arizona Military Museum • *5636 E. McDowell Rd.; (602) 267-2676. Tuesday and Thursday 9 to 2, weekends 1 to 4.* ☐ This unprofessional but nicely done museum is housed in the Depression era Arizona National Guard arsenal. Exhibits trace the history of the military as it relates to Arizona, starting with Francisco Vásquez de Coronado's 1540 quest for the fictitious golden cities of Cibola, and continuing through Arizona's involvement in the Korean Conflict and Vietnam War.

Arizona Mining and Mineral Museum • *1502 W. Washington St. (Fifteenth Avenue), (602) 255-3791. Weekdays 8 to 5, Saturday 1 to 5; free.* ☐ Appropriate to Arizona, this museum focuses on the mining end of minerals, with core samples, tools and mine models, plus an extensive collection of rocks and gems. No ordinary rock house, it features unusual exhibits such as "pseudo fossils"—minerals that have fooled even experts into thinking they were of fossil origin.

Arizona Science Center • *Washington and Fifth in the new Heritage and Science Park; (602) 256-9388. Monday-Saturday 9 to 5, Sunday noon to 5.* ☐ The former Arizona Science and Technology Museum has moved to a new science and history complex as part of the $1.1 billion downtown renovation project. It's one of the most advanced science centers in America, with a heavy focus on medical advances, space age technology and computers.

Arizona State Capitol Museum • *1700 W. Washington (17th Avenue), Phoenix, AZ 85007; (602) 255-4675. Weekdays 8 to 5; tours at 10 a.m. and 2 p.m.; free.* ☐ Arizona outgrew its copper domed state capitol in 1972 and moved to an adjacent highrise. Sitting in the shadow of its replacement, the old Grecian style tufa and granite relic has become a museum of the state's early government. Senate and house chambers are furnished as they appeared when Arizona gained statehood in 1912, with wooden desks, tulip chandeliers and spittoons. Other rooms serve as muséums to the state's political past.

Desert Botanical Garden • *1201 N. Galvin Parkway (in Papago Park), Phoenix, AZ 85008; (602) 941-1225. September-May 9 a.m. to sunset, June-August 8 a.m. to sunset; gift shop open 9 to 5.* ☐ In Arizona's finest botanical garden, you'll see desert plants from around the globe, including more than half of the world's cactus varieties. March to May is the desert garden's peak blooming season. A special exhibit shows how the Hohokam and other Indians used plants to survive and thrive in this dry environment.

Hall of Flame Museum of Firefighting • *6101 E. Van Buren St. (in Papago Park), Phoenix, AZ 85008; (602) 275-3473. Monday-Saturday 9 to 5 and Sunday noon to 5; guided tours daily at 2.* ☐ Every kid of every age whose pulse is quickened by the shriek of a siren and the red flash of a fire engine will love this place. It's the world's largest museum of firefighting equipment, exhibiting glittering ranks of hand-drawn pumpers, early hook-and-ladder rigs and other smoke-chasing classics. More than 100 restored fire engines are on display.

The Heard Museum • *22 E. Monte Vista (Central Avenue), Phoenix, AZ 85004; (602) 252-8840 or 252-8848 (taped information). Monday-Saturday 9:30 to 5 (until 9 Wednesday) and Sunday noon to 5.* ◻ Quite simply, the Heard is the finest museum in Arizona and probably the world's greatest monument to Native Americans. Although it dates back to 1929, this treasury of American Indian cultures is a state-of-the-art facility. With more than 30,000 objects to draw from, its staff exercises artistic discipline in keeping displays both simple and topical. Major exhibits provide an enlightening study of Arizona's ancient and modern Indian cultures, with artifacts, graphics and mock-ups.

Heritage Square • *Sixth Street and Monroe (a block east of Civic Plaza); (602) 262-5071.* ◻ This is a scene from Phoenix yesterday—eight structures dating from the late 19th and early 20th centuries. They're gathered around an attractive patio garden, shaded by a curved-wood lath house. Surprisingly, all but one are in their original locations.

Phoenix Art Museum • *1625 N. Central Ave. (McDowell Road), Phoenix, AZ 85004; (602) 257-1222. Tuesday-Saturday 10 to 5 (Wednesday to 9), Sunday 1 to 5. Tours Tuesday-Sunday at 1 p.m., plus 6 p.m.* ◻ The American West, contemporary art and old world classics are featured in this large, versatile art museum. A major renovation and expansion program was completed in mid-1996, nearly doubling its exhibit space. Permanent collections include a gallery of Western Art, galleries of early European and American art, an Asian gallery, costume displays and decorative arts.

Phoenix Museum of History • *105 N. Fifth Street at Washington; (602) 253-2734. Monday-Saturday 10 to 5 and Sunday noon to 5.* ◻ Originally called the Arizona Museum and located elsewhere, the newly-named Phoenix Museum of History joined the recent move to the Heritage and Science Park. The gallery focuses on the region's history from the territorial era to the "Romantic Movement" of the 1920s. Exhibits include Hohokam artifacts, battleship Arizona mementos, an egg from a former Phoenix ostrich farm, a rifle collection and modern Kachina dolls.

Phoenix Zoo • *455 N. Galvin Parkway (in Papago Park), Phoenix, AZ 85072; (602) 273-1341. Daily 9 to 5 (7 to 4 in summer).* ◻ This would be a pleasant place to stroll even if it weren't stocked with 1,300 animals. Occupying 125 acres of Papago Park, the zoo encloses a fine slice of desert terrain. It's landscaped with giant eucalyptus trees, pools, trickling streams and shady patios. Among recent additions are the Baboon Kingdom and Tropical Flights rainforest.

Pioneer Arizona Living History Museum • *c/o Black Canyon Stage, Phoenix, AZ 85027; (602) 993-0212. Wednesday-Friday 9 to 3, weekends 9 to 4, shorter hours during the summer.* ☐ Since 1956, a non-profit group has been assembling an historic Arizona community on a chunk of desert 30 miles north of Phoenix. About 20 buildings—either originals or reconstructions—occupy the site. It's a sampler town of Arizona from its earliest Spanish days to statehood. Although the site seems a bit disconnected and exhibits need sprucing up, it's worth the drive. To reach it, follow I-17 north and take exit 225 (Pioneer Road) west.

Pueblo Grande Museum • *4619 E. Washington St. (44th Street), Phoenix, AZ 85034; (602) 945-0901. Monday-Saturday 9 to 4:45, Sunday 1 to 4:45.* ☐ Surrounded by the expanding city, this site preserves a large Hohokam settlement. There's little left of the village, which can be viewed from an overlook. Ridges and depressions suggest the shapes of an ancient ball court and canal banks. The museum does a fine job of presenting slices of life from the early days. Exhibits include a scale-model Hohokam home and artifacts taken from the site.

SCOTTSDALE, CAREFREE, CAVE CREEK AND FOUNTAIN HILLS

Once a cowboy village way out in the lonely desert, Scottsdale has become an upscale residential and commercial center, merging its expanding borders into Phoenix. Carefree and Cave Creek are two hamlets on the Valley of the Sun's fringe. Carefree is an attractive planned community while Cave Creek is a funky old mining town that draws folks to several "saloon restaurants" for cowboy steaks. Among Carefree's lures are the world's largest sundial, and El Pedrigal Marketplace, a shopping center that resembles a cross between Frank Lloyd Wright architecture and Tune Town.

Fountain Hills is a newly developing community in scenic desert slopes northeast of Scottsdale and southeast of Carefree. Its claims to fame are the world's tallest fountain, gushing from a downtown park, and a close-contact animal center called Out of Africa.

For area information • Carefree/Cave Creek Chamber of Commerce, P.O. Box 734 (748 Easy St.), Carefree, AZ 85377; (602) 488-3381.

Fountain Hills Chamber of Commerce, P.O. Box 17598, Fountain Hills, AZ 85269; (602) 837-1654.

Scottsdale Chamber of Commerce, 7343 Scottsdale Mall, Scottsdale, AZ 85251-4498; (602) 945-8481.

THE ATTRACTIONS

Cave Creek Museum • *Basin and Skyline, Cave Creek, AZ 85331; (602) 488-2764 or 488-3183. Wednesday-Sunday 1 to 4:30; closed in summer. Free; donations appreciated.* ☐ This typically small-town historical museum displays relics of Cave Creek's past as a mining and ranching center. A model pit house and Indian artifacts trace early Native American cultures in the area.

Cosanti • *6433 Doubletree Ranch Road (Invergorden), Scottsdale, AZ 85253; (602) 948-6145. Daily 9 to 5; $1 donation. Tours Monday 9 to 3.* ☐ Paolo Soleri is a visionary working on an environmentally correct city called Arcosanti, 68 miles north of Phoenix (see Chapter 12). Cosanti is his home, workshop and art studio in Paradise Valley, north of Scottsdale. Here, he and his students create bronze and ceramic bells and wind chimes and other decorator items. Like Arcosanti, his Cosanti studio has an extra-terrestrial look with pre-cast concrete freeform shapes. It suggests melted geometry, with a kind of doughy primitive look. Yoda would feel right at home here.

Fleischer Museum • *17207 N. Perimeter Dr., Scottsdale; (602) 585-3108. Daily 10 to 4; tours by appointment. Free; contributions accepted.* ☐ The grand atrium lobby and second floor of the Perimeter Center office building have been given over to a fine museum of American impressionistic art. Exhibits focus primarily on California and the west, although special shows are sometimes featured. Several bronze sculptures occupy a glass domed rotunda courtyard beyond the foyer.

Out of Africa • *Two S. Fort McDowell Rd. (near Beeline Highway), Fountain Hills, AZ 85269; (602) 837-7779 or 837-7677. Tuesday-Sunday 9:30 to 5.* ☐ Two animal enthusiasts intrigued with people-big cat relationships have turned their research project into a public attraction. Lions, tigers, panthers and assorted other critters are on display, and folks can watch animal handlers work with the big felines. These aren't training sessions, they say, but animal-human encounters. Visitors also can swim with tigers every day at 1:15 p.m. at the Tiger Splash.

Rawhide • *23023 N. Scottsdale Rd. (Pinnacle Peak Rd.), Scottsdale, AZ 85261; (602) 563-5600. Monday-Thursday 5 to 10 and Friday-Sunday 11 to 10 from October through May; daily 5 to 10 the rest of the year.* ☐ "How the West was fun," says the sign out front. Rawhide is the largest and best of several wanna-be cowboy towns in the area, with a couple of dozen false-front stores housing boutiques, curio shops, saloons and restaurants. Visitors can catch a stagecoach, witness a shoot-out, feed goats in a petting zoo and watch a "meller-drammer" in the Moonshine Theatre. An Old West museum boasts 5,000 items—from high-button shoes to antiques.

Scottsdale Historical Museum • *7333 Scottsdale Mall; (602) 945-4499. Wednesday-Saturday 10 to 5, Sunday noon to 4. Free; donations appreciated.* ☐ Small and nicely done, this museum exhibits original furniture of town founders Winfield and Helen Scott, along with artifacts and photos of the early days. Featured displays include an early American kitchen and a mock-up of a turn-of-the-century school room.

Taliesin West • *114th Street at Cactus, Scottsdale, AZ 85261; (602) 860-2700. Tours daily, on the hour 9 to 4 (at 8 and 11 in summer); desert walks Monday-Saturday at 9 and 11 a.m.; modest fees charged for tours. Bookstore open daily 8:30 to 5.* ◻ The former winter home and studio of legendary architect Frank Lloyd Wright, Taliesin West is an intriguing mix of concrete and stone that seems fused into the desert instead of rising from it. The complex sits on a 600-acre alluvial fan, sweeping down from the McDowell Mountains. Wright's designs involved the repeated play of geometric forms, using natural materials to embody nature, man and architecture. Taliesin West is mostly triangular, with red sandstone and concrete wedges and desert stone sculpted into the sloping hill. Docents give comprehensive tours of the facility while discussing Wright's architectural and personal philosophies.

TEMPE-MESA

These are essentially bedroom communities southeast of Phoenix. While not tourist centers, they offer a few worthy attractions.

For area information • Mesa Convention and Visitors Bureau, 120 N. Center St., Mesa, AZ 85201; (602) 969-1307.

Tempe Chamber of Commerce, P.O. Box 28500 (909 E. Apache Blvd.), Tempe, AZ 85285; (602) 967-7891.

THE ATTRACTIONS

Arizona Historical Society Museum • *1300 N. College Ave., Tempe, AZ 85281; (602) 929-0292. Weekdays 9 to 4, Saturday 10 to 4 and Sunday noon to 4; free.* ◻ Opened in 1996, this elegant facility captures Arizona's yesterdays, from the coming of the Spanish, the Mexican era, cowboys and bad guys to the 20th century irrigation projects that blossomed the desert. Particularly interesting is a "Futures Lab" which focuses on Arizona's planning for tomorrow. One of the state's finest museums, the structure is built around a sunny courtyard and gurgling stream.

Arizona State University Campus • *Visitor Center at the southeast corner of the campus, Apache and Rural Road. open weekdays 8 to 4:45; (602) 965-0100. Campus tours weekdays at 10:30 and 2; (602) 965-2604.* ◻ Green lawns and palms create a park-like setting for ASU's imposing gathering of brick buildings. The centerpiece is Frank Lloyd Wright's Gammage Center for the Performing Arts, a dramatic sandstone pink structure of circles within circles. The campus contains several art museums, a planetarium, geology museum and gallery of design.

Champlin Fighter Museum • *4636 Fighter Aces Dr. (Falcon Field, off McKellips Road), Mesa, AZ 85205; (602) 830-4540. Daily 10 to 5.* ◻ Snoopy would love this place. You can fantasize dogfights with the Red Baron and other aces at this impressive gathering of fighter planes from the two world wars, Korea, Vietnam and Desert Storm. Thirty-three planes, either restored originals or airworthy replicas, seem ready to take off into the wild blue yonder.

Confederate Air Force Museum ● *2017 McKellips Road; (602) 924-1940 or (602) 981-1945. Daily 10 to 4.* ◻ Arizona's Confederate Air Force, made up of World War II pilots and younger men with an interest in flying, is devoted to collecting, restoring and flying military aircraft of that war. Their collection, while not large, is impressive, including an airworthy Flying Fortress, a couple of C-47 Skymaster transports, a Grumman AF-2S submarine killer and a pair of training planes.

Mesa Southwest Museum ● *53 N. MacDonald St. (First Street), Mesa, AZ 85201 (602) 644-2230 or 644-2169. Tuesday-Saturday 10 to 5, Sunday 1 to 5.* ◻ This fine City of Mesa museum effectively captures the area's history, from the mysteries of the vanished Hohokam Indians to the legend of the Lost Dutchman Mine. It's housed in an attractive Spanish style structure surrounded by landscaped gardens. Among the professionally done exhibits are "Dinosaurs of the Southwest" with an animated *triceratops*; and Native American artifacts and reconstructions of their dwellings using native materials.

Mesa Historical Museum ● *2345 N. Horne St. (Lehi Road), Mesa, AZ 85201; (602) 835-7358. Thursday-Saturday 10 to 4; closed in summer.* ◻ Housed in a large 1913 schoolhouse, this busy museum exhibits antique farm machinery, a country store, grist mill, turn-of-the-century wedding gowns and other Mesa memorabilia. Murals in the old school auditorium trace the valley's settlement.

Tempe Historical Museum ● *Tempe Community Center (3500 S. Rural Road at Southern Avenue), Tempe, AZ 85282; (602) 731-8842. Tuesday-Saturday 10 to 4:30; free.* ◻ Tempe's early days are preserved in this collection of farm implements, historical photos, utensils, toys, furniture and clothing. Exhibits include a Model-T fire truck, post office and a prairie schooner.

PHOENIX-TUCSON CORRIDOR

Interstate 10 that runs diagonally between Phoenix and Tucson is Arizona's busiest freeway. Highway 79, just to the northeast, is a much more genteel route. Several tourist lures can be encountered along each.

For area information ● Apache Junction Chamber of Commerce, P.O. Box 1747, Apache Junction, AZ 85217; (602) 982-3141.

Greater Casa Grande Chamber of Commerce, 575 N. Marshall, Casa Grande, AZ 85222; (520) 836-2125.

The U.S. 60 freeway running southeast from Phoenix will take you to Apache Junction. It's a growing community in an attractive desert setting, below the grimly fascinating ramparts of the **Superstition**

Tonto National Monument preserves a small cliff dwelling surrounded by an attractive cactus garden.

Mountains. You've probably heard the tale of the Lost Dutchman Mine. A German prospector named Jacob Waltz supposedly found a rich gold cache in the Superstitions in the 1860s, although he died without revealing its whereabouts.

You can explore the foothills of these rough-hewn mountains and indulge in a bit of water sports by following State Route 88 northeast from Apache Junction. Known locally as the Apache Trail, it takes you to **Lost Dutchman State Park** with camping, picnicking and hiking and to the old mining town of **Goldfield**, which now functions as a rustic tourist attraction. Continuing east you'll pass the tiny and touristy hamlet of **Tortilla Flat** and then enter rugged **Salt River Canyon**, where dams of the Salt River project have created several reservoirs. An unpaved but passable road continues through the canyon's scenic and rocky ramparts to **Theodore Roosevelt Dam** and **Tonto National Monument** which preserves a small native cliff dwelling. It's open daily 8 to 5, with a nicely done interpretive center and a short trail leading to the ruin.

Florence

If you drive south from Apache Junction on Highway 79, you'll encounter the attractive Western style town of Florence. Check out the **Florence Townsite National Historic District** and the gingerbread trimmed **Pinal County Courthouse.** Save an hour or so for an interesting historical museum:

McFarland State Historic Park • *Main and Ruggles streets (P.O. Box 109), Florence, AZ 85232; (520) 868-5216. Thursday-Monday 8 to 5.* ☐ Pinal County got its start here; this adobe functioned as the courthouse, sheriff's office and jail from 1878 to 1891. Among its exhibits are the old courtroom with its jury box, wooden pews and judge's bench. A special display focuses on local boy-makes-good Ernest W. McFarland. He authored the G.I. Bill of Rights as a U.S. senator and served as chief justice of the Arizona Supreme Court.

As you continue south toward Tucson, Highway 79 becomes the **Pinal Pioneer Parkway,** passing through attractive desert gardens. Signs identify the roadside flora, so think of it as a 55-mile-an-hour nature trail. The highway eventually skirts the Santa Catalina Mountains and enters the northern portal of Tucson.

Interstate 10 is a much faster route between Arizona's two metropolitan centers, although it's considerably less interesting. However, it does offer three visitor lures:

Gila River Arts and Crafts Center • *Casa Blanca Road, P.O. Box 457, Sacaton, AZ 85247; (520) 315-3411. Daily 8 to 5; free.* ☐ More than 30 different tribes and 2,000 years of Native American history are represented in this modern cultural center on the Gila River Indian Reservation. It's actually a blend of four facilities—the Gila River Museum, with historical exhibits; the Arts and Crafts Center; Heritage Park, with reconstructions of Indian dwellings; and a restaurant serving fry bread and other typical Native American fare.

Casa Grande Ruins National Monument • *1100 Ruins Dr., Coolidge, AZ 85228; (520) 723-3172. Daily 7 to 6* ☐ Covered by a metal roof to keep it from melting back into the earth, this is the tallest and perhaps most mysterious of Arizona's many pueblos. It's four stories high with four-foot thick walls at the base to support its 2,800-ton mass. The structure was the centerpiece of a Hohokam village, occupied for about a century, until 1450 A.D. Archaeologists don't know why Casa Grande was built, nor why it was abandoned.

Picacho Peak State Park • *P.O. Box 275, Picacho, AZ 85241; (520) 466-3183.* ☐ This park at the base of a thumb-like peak has picnic areas and hiking trails, including a path to the 1,400-foot summit of the stone upcropping. Confederate and Union forces clashed near here in 1862 in the westernmost battle of the Civil War. These weren't regular troops, but members of the Texas Volunteers and California Volunteers. Although the Texans won the first skirmish, killing four Californians, they realized that reinforcements would soon arrive in this pro-Union territory, so they hightailed it back to Texas.

Chapter fifteen

TUCSON & BEYOND

TOURING "THE OLD ADOBE"

Arizona's second largest city rivals its big sister in both the quality and quantity of its tourist attractions. It offers a fine mix of indoor culture and outdoor recreation. Five mountain ranges rim Tucson's high desert basin and a 17,000-acre slice of this terrain has been preserved in Tucson Mountain Park. This vast swatch of desert shelters several major attractions.

One of Arizona's oldest cities, Tucson is a tempting blend of cosmopolitan, old pueblo and the great outdoors. All of this—and it claims to have more days of sunshine than any other major American city.

For area information ● Metropolitan Tucson Convention and Visitors Bureau, 130 S. Scott Ave., Tucson, AZ 85701; (800) 638-8350 or (520) 624-1817.

THE ATTRACTIONS

Arizona Historical Society Museum ● *949 E. Second St. (Park Avenue), Tucson, AZ 85719; (520) 628-5774. Monday-Saturday 10 to 4, Sunday noon to 4; free.* ☐ Located just outside the University of Arizona campus, it covers the area's settlement from the arrival of the Spanish to the development of modern Arizona. Uncluttered, informative exhibits tell the state's story with cattle brands, Bull Durham pouches, high-wheeled bicycles and period costumes.

Arizona-Sonora Desert Museum • *2021 N. Kinney Rd. (in Tucson Mountain Park), Tucson, AZ 85743; (520) 883-2702. Daily 8:30 to 5 October through February and 7:30 to 6 the rest of the year.* ◻ Planners re-invented the museum when they created this indoor-outdoor complex. It is the finest such center in Arizona, and Tucson's most-visited attraction. The museum takes its name from the states of Arizona, U.S.A., and Sonora, Mexico. Its primary focus is ecological, telling the story of the plants, animals and geology of the Sonoran Desert that covers much of these two states.

Arizona State Museum • *University Avenue at Park Avenue (c/o University of Arizona, Tucson, AZ 85721); (520) 621-6302. Monday-Saturday 10 to 4 and Sunday noon to 5; free.* ◻ Occupying two buildings just inside the University of Arizona's main gate, this museum focuses on prehistoric and modern Indian cultures of the Southwest. A display in the main exhibit building offers an excellent view of the lifestyle of the Apache, past and present. A mezzanine is stuffed with stuffed animals indigenous to Arizona, along with a gemstone and Hohokam exhibit.

De Grazia Gallery in the Sun • *6300 N. Swan Rd. (Skyline Drive), Tucson, AZ 85718; (520) 299-9191. Daily 10 to 4; free.* ◻ The late Ted De Grazia developed a large following for his impressionistic, whimsical style of painting. Simple, quick brush strokes created color-splashed Indians, Mexicans, roadrunners and other Southwestern subjects. After his death, a foundation was created to continue operating his rustic gallery and gift shop. Exhibits are changed periodically, drawn from his extensive collection, and replicas of his art is on sale.

El Presidio Historic District • *Bounded by Pennington, Church, Washington and Main.* ◻ Although its adobe walls have long since melted back into the sand, Tucson's original walled fortress retains some of its yesterday flavor. Many of its 19th century adobes house galleries and restaurants. Sign posts and plaques relate the history of homes dating back more than a century.

Flandrau Science Center and Planetarium • *Northwest corner of University and Cherry; (520) 621-4515 or (520) 621-STAR for recorded information. Museum and astronomy store open weekdays 10 to 5 and weekends noon to 5. Evening hours with public telescope viewing Wednesday-Thursday 7 to 9 and Friday-Saturday 7 to midnight. Museum admission and telescope viewing free; fees for star and laser shows in the planetarium theater.* ◻ This is a science museum as well as a planetarium. Push assorted buttons and levers to learn about holography, radio waves and Light Amplification by Stimulated Emission Radiation—and now you know that LASER is an acronym.

Fort Lowell Museum • *Craycroft and Fort Lowell (mailing address: 949 E. Second St., Tucson, AZ 85719); (520) 885-3832. Wednesday-Saturday 10 to 4; free.* ◻ Part of a large city park and recreation center, Fort Lowell Museum is a reconstruction of a military camp established in 1873. Structures include the commanding officers quarters with period furnishings and historical displays, and the "kitchen building," with exhibits of the fort's development and excavations of early Indian sites.

International Wildlife Museum • *4800 W. Gates Pass Rd. (Camino de Oeste), Tucson, AZ 85745; (520) 629-0100 or (520) 624-4024 (recording). Daily 9 to 5.* ⧠ The museum is enclosed in a curious architectural blend of feudal castle and French Foreign Legion fort. Exhibits, including more than 300 varieties of stuffed animals, are intended to "promote wildlife appreciation," says the brochure. Videos focus on conservation; graphics tell of the threat to the world's rain forests. However, one large room is filled with more than a hundred hunting trophies. Bodyless Cape buffalo, rhinos, elephants and assorted antelopes stare morosely from the walls in this room, which suggests massive hunting lodge.

Mission San Xavier del Bac • *San Xavier Road (9 miles south, off I-19); (520) 294-2624. Church, museum and gift shop open daily 9 to 6; Mass Saturday at 5:30 and Sunday at 8, 9:30, 11 and noon. Free; contributions appreciated.* ⧠ The "White Dove of the Desert," with its Spanish-colonial architecture, gleaming white walls and brown façade, is perhaps Arizona's most beautiful structure. Its roots reach back to the earliest days, when Spanish mission-builder Father Eusebio Kino ministered to the people of the village of Bac. Located on the San Xavier Reservation, it still serves Native Americans. Its handsomely restored sanctuary, chapel and other rooms are open to visitors.

Mount Lemmon Recreation Area • *Reached via the Catalina Highway from northeast Tucson. For information: Coronado National Forest, (520) 576-1542.* ⧠ The Catalina Highway spirals quickly from the saguaro-thick foothills of the Catalina Mountains to the piney forests of Mount Lemmon. Along the way, you'll see fantastic roadside rock formations that look like misplaced Easter Island statues. In winter, you can hit the slopes at Mount Lemmon Ski Valley. One of its lifts operates the year around for the benefit of sightseers; weekdays 11 to 5 and weekends 10 to 5 in summer and daily 9 to 4 in winter.

Old Tucson Studios • *201 S. Kinney Rd. (Tucson Mountain Park), Tucson, AZ 85746; (520) 883-6457 or 883-0100. Daily 9 to 9.* ⧠ Old Tucson is Universal Studios with hay bales—a working memorial to all those shoot-outs that have blazed across the Arizona landscape. It began in 1939 when Columbia Pictures built a set to produce one of the first big movie epics, *Arizona.* Twenty years later, an entrepreneur bought the old ruin, added more weather-worn buildings and created a permanent Western movie set. Since then, more than 150 oat-baggers have been filmed here. Visitors can watch shoot-outs on Main Street, tour a giant sound stage and sip suds in the Royal Oak Saloon.

Pima Air and Space Museum • *6000 E. Valencia Rd. (Wilmot), Tucson, AZ 85706; (520) 574-0462 or (520) 574-9658 (recorded mes-*

sage). Daily 9 to 5 (doors close at 4). ☐ If you've ever wanted to soar on fanciful wings of eagles, you'll love this place. More than 200 aircraft are on display, from a realistic full-scale model of the Wright brothers craft to a mach-3 Lockheed SR-71 Blackbird. Exhibits trace the development of aviation from pre-Wright brothers attempts to recent space flight.

Reid Park Zoo • *1100 S. Randolph Way (enter Lakeshore Drive off 22nd Street), Tucson, AZ 85716; (520) 791-4022. Daily 9:30 a.m. to 5 p.m.* ☐ This fine little zoo, landscaped with green lawns shaded by eucalyptus and palm trees, has a busy collection of giraffes, lions, tigers, hippos, primates and more. Some of its critters are housed in modern open-air enclosures; birds flit around a large aviary. About 400 creatures occupy the zoo, which conducts ongoing conservation, educational and scientific research programs.

Sabino Canyon • *Sabino Canyon Road; (520) 749-2327. Reached by tram only. From December through May, they run every half hour, daily 9 to 4:30; the rest of the year, hourly 9 to 4 on weekdays and 9 to 4:30 weekends. Sabino Canyon Visitor Center open 8 to 4:30 weekdays and 8:30 to 4:30 weekends.* ☐ Just minutes from downtown, this steep-walled chasm cuts deeply into the flanks of the Santa Catalina Mountains. Forests of saguaro cactus march from the banks of Sabino Creek up rugged canyon walls. Ultimately, they give way to forests of pine. Hiking trails lead into the more remote heights.

Saguaro National Park • *Tucson Mountain section off Sandario Road in Tucson Mountain Park; (520) 883-6366; open 24 hours; Red Hills visitor center open daily 8 to 5; free. Rincon Mountain section off Old Spanish Trail east of Tucson; (520) 296-8576; 7 a.m. to 6 p.m., visitor center open 8 to 5.* ☐ The two sections of Saguaro National Park serve the same function—to preserve and exhibit their giant cactus namesake, plus other desert flora. Saguaro West, the Tucson Mountain section, has more bountiful cactus gardens than its eastern counterpart, although it doesn't have the elevation range. Saguaro East, off Old Spanish Trail, climbs through five climate zones from the desert to conifer ramparts of the Rincon Mountains, offering a rich cross section of desert topography.

Tohono Chul Park • *7366 N. Paseo del Norte (northwest corner of Ina and Oracle), Tucson, AZ 85704; (520) 742-6455. Daily 7 a.m. to sunset; exhibit hall, gift gallery and Tea Room open Monday-Saturday 8 a.m. to 5 p.m. and Sunday 11 to 5. Free; contributions accepted.* ☐ Privately endowed Tohono Chul preserves a patch of desert landscape in the middle of Tucson. Nature trails, patios, shade ramadas, two gift shops, an exhibit center and a Southwest style tea room provide refuge from the growing city.

Tucson Botanical Gardens • *2150 N. Alvernon Way (Grant), Tucson, AZ 85712; (520) 326-9255. Daily 8:30 to 4:30 daily; gift shop open Monday-Saturday 9 to 4 and Sunday noon to 4.* ☐ Once the estate of a local nurseryman, the garden rambles over five and a half acres, with pleasant paths leading through lush plant life. Among its displays are an Australian garden, herb garden, historical garden with English ivy and such, and a Tohono O'odham garden with crops typical of early Native Americans.

Tucson Mountain Park • *Eight miles west of downtown; (520) 883-4200. Daily 7 a.m. to 10 p.m.* ☐ This huge Pima County park sprawls over 17,000 acres of rough-hewn Tucson Mountain foothills. It provides instant desert wilderness to residents of the nearby city. Within the park's boundaries are three other attractions—the Tucson Mountain section of Saguaro National Park, Arizona-Sonora Desert Museum and Old Tucson Studios (listed here separately). Park facilities include picnic areas, hiking and riding trails and a campground.

Tucson Museum of Art • *140 N. Main Ave. (Alameda, next to El Presidio Historic District), Tucson, AZ 85701; (520) 624-2333. Monday-Saturday 10 to 4 and Sunday noon to 4, Tuesday-Saturday 10 to 4.* ☐ Galleries are arranged along downward spiraling ramps in this contemporary museum on the edge of El Presidio Historic District. The complex also includes a sculpture garden and five houses built between 1850 and 1907. Galleries display large collections of Western art and pre-Colombian artifacts.

University of Arizona campus • *Community Service Center at Cherry and University open Monday-Friday 8 to 5 and Saturday 9 to 2; (520) 621-5130.* ☐ Located in the heart of Tucson, the university's expansive campus is a major cultural resource as well as an important learning center. Eight museums and galleries occupy its sturdy red brick buildings. Three major public attractions—Flandrau Science Center, Arizona State Museum and Arizona Historical Society Museum—appear above on this list.

SOUTH TO NOGALES

Interstate 19 provides a fast link between Tucson and the twin border towns of Nogales, Arizona and Mexico. The first substantial habitat you'll encounter, other than dusty little Sahuarita, is the planned community of **Green Valley**. Nearby is the Titan Missile Museum, a grimly fascinating reminder of the cold war.

Twenty miles south of Green Valley is dusty little **Tubac**. Arizona's oldest Spanish community, it's now a haven for artists, individualists and a few retirees. Slices of Arizona's history are preserved in a state park here, and in a national historic park a few miles south.

Continuing below Tubac, you'll soon hit Mexico at **Nogales**, which offers the best *Latino* shopping of any Arizona border town. On the Arizona side, Nogales offers a historical museum that's worth a pause.

For area information • Green Valley Chamber of Commerce, P.O. Box 566 (108 W. Continental, Room 187), Green Valley, AZ 85622; (520) 625-7575.

Tubac Chamber of Commerce, P.O. Box 1866, Tubac, AZ 85646; (520) 398-2704.

Nogales-Santa Cruz County Chamber of Commerce, 123 W. Kino Park Place, Nogales, AZ 85621; (520) 287-3685.

ATTRACTIONS, IN ORDER OF APPEARANCE

Titan Missile Museum • *Green Valley Road (Exit 69, then west), Green Valley, AZ 85614; (520) 625-7736. Open 9 to 5 Wednesday-Sunday from May through October and daily from November through April. One-hour tours; last tour at 4 p.m.* □ This is one of the most fascinating tours in Arizona, through a decommissioned Titan missile silo. The tour begins with a video about the history of the Titan and its deadly nuclear delivery capability. Then visitors are taken deep into the "hardened" command center and to the silo itself, where a 110-foot-tall Titan is aimed skyward. Of course, it has been rendered harmless.

Tubac Presidio State Historic Park • *P.O. Box 1296, Tubac, AZ 85646; (520) 398-2252. Daily 8 to 5.* □ Little remains of the presidio that was built here in 1752, but an exhibit center effectively traces its history. Nicely done displays take you from Tubac's days as a 17th century Pima Indian village through its Spanish, Mexican and American periods. Exhibits include a set of wrist irons tied to a post that served as the town's jail, plus period weapons, religious art and friars' frocks.

Tumacacori National Historic Park • *P.O. Box 67, Tumacacori, AZ 85640; (520) 398-2341. Daily 8 to 5.* □ Father Kino erected a small adobe here in 1691 and began preaching to local Indians. Half a century later, construction began on a more elaborate structure. Today, Tumacacori Mission is a noble ruin, standing forlornly on a grassy field. An adjacent interpretive center features a diorama of the mission in its heyday, relics from the old church and an artistically-produced video of missionaries ministering to the Indians.

Pimeria Alta Historical Society Museum • *136 N. Grand Avenue and Crawford Street (P.O. Box 2281), Nogales, AZ 85621; (520) 287-4621. Tuesday-Friday 10 to 5, Saturday 10 to 4. Free; donations encouraged.* □ This museum personifies the close ties between the twin towns of Nogales. Photos, documents and pioneer artifacts trace the history of both communities. Although not professionally done, it's quite interesting, with exhibits such as a hand-drawn fire pumper, a pictorial history of the twin towns and archeological artifacts.

Chapter sixteen
EASTERN ARIZONA
THE LAND OVERLOOKED

Most visitors to Arizona, preoccupied with the Grand Canyon, the Red Rock country and the desert resorts of Phoenix and Tucson, overlook the eastern third of the state. This is a pity, since this remote, thinly populated area contains some of Arizona's most interesting attractions and some of its most varied terrain.

We begin with the state's southeastern wedge, where the traveler will discover Arizona's earliest roots.

THE COWBOY CORNER

What we've chosen to call the Cowboy Corner is Cochise County, a history-laden 90-mile by 70-mile rectangle on Arizona's southeastern edge. It could as well be called the Cochise Corner in honor of the Chiricahua Apache warrior, or the Copper Corner, for the great copper mines around Bisbee.

Some of America's most dramatic historical pageants were played out here. Francisco Vásquez de Coronado passed through in 1540 on his quest for the Seven Cities of Cibola. Cochise made a futile stand against intruding whites from 1858 until 1869, and then Geronimo took up the lance of resistance until his final surrender in 1886. On October 26, 1881, in a dusty alley in Tombstone, three men died in the most celebrated gun battle in Western history.

These events are recorded in a variety of historic sites and monuments scattered about this intriguing corner of Arizona. In our *Ari-*

zona Discovery Guide, we outline a drive that hits the high spots. We offer an abbreviated version here.

Tombstone

To approach the Cowboy Corner, drive east from Tucson on I-10, then turn south on U.S. 80 and follow it to Tombstone, the "town too tough to die." The town itself is the main attraction, with a mix of museums, boutiques, restaurants and saloons in old Western style buildings. They stand alongside boardwalks where the boots of Wyatt Earp, Doc Holliday, Johnny Ringo and Bat Masterson once clunked. The town has several museums and gift shops thinly disguised as museums. Only a few are serious attractions, which we list below.

For information • Tombstone Chamber of Commerce, P.O. Box 339 (Allan and Fourth streets), Tombstone, AZ 85638; (520) 457-9317 or (520) 457-3929.

THE ATTRACTIONS

Boothill Cemetery and Gift Shop • *Highway 80; (520) 457-3348. Daily 7:30 to 6; free.* ◻ You don't often find a cemetery that accepts Visa and MasterCard. Of course, that's only in the gift shop, through which you must pass to view the graves of Tombstone's fallen. Frank and Tom McLaury and Billy Clanton—victims of the O.K. Corral shootout—lie side by side on this sloping hill. More than 250 other citizens are buried here. Grave markers remind you that life was often short and death was quick in the Wild West, for many were victims of gunshots and other violence. One poor soul was "hanged by mistake," according to his grave marker.

Tombstone Courthouse State Historic Park • *219 E. Toughnut St. (Third Street), Tombstone, AZ 85638; (520) 457-3311. Daily 8 to 5.* ◻ This imposing brick structure served as the Cochise County Courthouse from 1882 until neighboring Bisbee snatched away the county seat in 1931. It's now a museum of Cochise County yesterdays, with a restored sheriff's office, courtroom and various exhibits. Assorted versions of the O.K. Corral shootout hang on the courthouse walls.

The O.K. Corral and Camillus Fly Photo Studio • *Allen Street (between Third and Fourth); (520) 457-3456. Daily 8:30 to 5; shootout re-enactments several times daily in summer, less frequently in the off season.* ◻ The O.K. Corral has been corralled into a major tourist attraction. Among its exhibits are Camillus S. Fly's photo studio, and several 19th century rigs, including a hearse that once toted unfortunate cowboys to Boothill. Near the scene of the shootout, beside Fly's studio, mannequins mark the position of the combatants when their guns started blazing.

Bird Cage Theater • *Sixth and Allen streets; (520) 457-3421. Daily 8 to 7 (shorter hours in the off-season).* ◻ This should be one of Tombstone's better attractions, for it's the town's only original and intact gambling hall-theater-saloon. However, the museum is cluttered with many items unrelated to the theater's lively history. Among authentic relics are dusty four-by-six foot bird cage "cribs" suspended from upper walls, where fallen angels entertained their gents.

Sierra Vista and Fort Huachuca

The most direct route from Tombstone to Sierra Vista is a number-less road across the desert. To find it, head south on Tombstone's Sumner Street and just keep going. It becomes Charleston Road as it approaches Sierra Vista.

This burgeoning community offers no specific tourist lures, al-though next-door **Huachuca City** is home to the West's oldest still-active Army fort. And there, you'll discover a fine military museum. To get there, head west through Sierra Vista on Fry Boulevard. It leads right to the Fort Huachuca gate, where you'll need a pass to get in. It comes with a map of directions to the museum.

From Fort Huachuca, take Fry Boulevard back to the Highway 90-92 junction in Sierra Vista and turn right, following 92 south toward Bisbee. If you'd like to check out a sheltered canyon woodland, turn right onto Ramsey Canyon Road and follow it into **Ramsey Canyon Preserve**. It's a sanctuary operated by the Nature Conservancy. As you continue along Highway 92, watch for a sign to the right that will steer you into mountainous woodlands and the **Coronado National Memorial**.

For area information ● Sierra Vista Chamber of Commerce, 77 Calle Portal, Suite A-140, Sierra Vista, AZ 85635; (800) 288-3861 or (520) 458-6940.

THE ATTRACTIONS

Fort Huachuca Museum ● *U.S. Army Garrison, Fort Huachuca, AZ 85613-6000; (520) 533-5736. Weekdays 9 to 4, weekends 1 to 4; free.* ☐ This is one of Arizona's great surprises, an outstanding museum sit-ting among the barracks of an old Army fort. It has a dual focus—the history of the Southwest and the history of the fort, which are fre-quently linked. The museum's best feature is a large open exhibit por-traying a patrol at evening's rest, somewhere on the desert. Tents are pitched, a campfire crackles, a distant coyote howls and a mannequin soldier strums a guitar.

Coronado National Memorial ● *4101 E. Montezuma Canyon Rd., Hereford, AZ 85615; (520) 366-5515. Visitor center open daily 8 to 5; free.* ☐ This small preserve in the wooded flanks of the Huachuca Mountains honors Francisco Vásquez de Coronado's entry into present-day Arizona in 1540. However, he missed this spot; his trek took him about ten miles to the east. But this land was available so, what the heck, the National Park Service took it. The interpretive center offers fine exhibits on Coronado's wanderings and the settling of this part of the American West. After checking out Coronado, visitors can follow hiking trails into the wooded slopes of Montezuma Canyon.

Bisbee

From Coronado Memorial, follow Highway 92 east and then Route 80 briefly north to Bisbee. It's a yesteryear mining town whose outskirts are marked with headframes and tailing dumps. The sturdy downtown area is busy with 19th century brick buildings, and Victorians grace steeply sloped neighborhoods.

For area information • Bisbee Chamber of Commerce, P.O. Box BA, Bisbee, AZ 85603; (520) 432-5421.

THE ATTRACTIONS

Bisbee Mining & Historical Museum • *Five Copper Queen Plaza, P.O. Box 14, Bisbee, AZ 85603; (520) 432-7071. Daily 10 to 4.* ☐ This imposing brick building originally housed the Phelps Dodge mining company headquarters. Exhibits weave the story of the people and mines that transformed a frontier town into a sophisticated mini-city. Displays include photos of early mining activity, equipment and a make-believe shaft with cutaways of mining methods as they evolved through the years.

Bisbee Restoration Association Museum • *37 Main Street (Subway Street), Bisbee. Daily 10 to 3; free.* ☐ Located in the old Fair Mercantile Building, this museum looks more like an overstocked antique shop. If you like historic clutter, you'll love this collection of old magazines and photos, spinning wheels, typewriters, period costumes, china, lace and the list goes on.

Lavender Pit • *Adjacent to Highway 80, immediately south of town.* ☐ Tours aren't necessary to visit this gigantic brown, yellow and pale green hole in the ground. You can simply park and walk to the fenced-off edge. A sign advises you that the great terraced pit is more than a mile long, three-fourths of a mile wide and 950 feet deep. More than 380 million *tons* of material came out of this hole.

Queen Mine Tour • *118 Arizona St., Bisbee, AZ 85603; (520) 432-2071. Mine tours daily at 9, 10:30, 2 and 3:30.* ☐ Hour and a half tours of this now-closed mine, usually led by former miners, lead deep into the side of a mountain. There, participants learn about old and new mining techniques and the history of this particular operation.

Bisbee to Willcox

Continue east from Bisbee toward **Douglas,** which sits on the Mexican border. It was a smeltering center for the Bisbee mines, and offers none of Bisbee's hilly charm. If you like old buildings, head downtown to the impeccably restored **Gadsden Hotel** at 106 G Avenue. If you don't, head north from Douglas on U.S. 191 (shown on some older maps as U.S. 666). Follow it about 25 miles through a high prairie to its junction with State Route 181. This takes you to **Chiricahua National Monument,** which preserves a slice of Arizona history and some of its most impressive geological formations.

As you depart the monument, turn north from the access road onto State Route 186. If you don't mind dust and bumps, turn left about nine miles above the Chiricahua junction and follow a dirt road to **Fort Bowie National Historic Site.** Otherwise, stay on 186 and follow it to **Willcox,** sitting astride Interstate 10. It's home to the **Rex Allen Cowboy Hall of Fame** and **Museum of the Southwest.**

For area information • Willcox Chamber of Commerce and Agriculture, 1500 N. Circle I Rd., Willcox, AZ 85643; (800) 200-2272 or (520) 384-2272.

THE ATTRACTIONS

Chiricahua National Monument • *Dos Cabezas Route, Box 6500, Willcox, AZ 85643; (520) 824-3560. Visitor center open daily 8 to 5.* ☐ This pocket-sized preserve, covering only 12,000 acres, shelters some incredibly complex rock formations and five of the seven North American life zones. Wind and rain have eroded a 27-million-year-old volcanic rhyolite deposit into fantastic shapes, and several hiking trails wind among them. These rocky ramparts were the refuge of the Chiricahua Apaches during their 25-year war with the U.S. Army.

Fort Bowie National Historic Site • *P.O. Box 158, Bowie, AZ 85605; (520) 847-2500. Visitor center open 8 to 5; free.* ☐ Reaching this remote site requires an eight-mile drive on a dirt road and then a 1.5-mile hike. Fort Bowie was built in 1862 to protect the vital Apache Pass during the army's war with the Chiricahuas. All that remains now are weathered ridges of adobe and stone walls—and a lot of history. Signs mark the sites of the former buildings and describe their uses.

Museum of the Southwest • *1500 N. Circle I Rd., Willcox, AZ 85643; (520) 384-2272. Monday-Saturday 9 to 5, Sunday 1 to 5; free.* ☐ This small and nicely done museum, in the Willcox Chamber of Commerce building, focuses on early Indian and cowboy life in this corner of Cochise County. It offers a fine display of Indian artifacts, graphics on Apache life patterns and details of the Chiricahua War.

Rex Allen Arizona Cowboy Museum • *Railroad Avenue near Malley Street (P.O. Box 995), Willcox, AZ 85644; (520) 384-4583. Daily 10 to 4.* ☐ They call him the "Arizona Cowboy," and he was that before he became a movie, TV and rodeo star. Rex Allen grew up on a homestead ranch near Willcox. After achieving fame and certainly fortune, he returned home to finance this small museum. Exhibits trace his rise to stardom, with movie posters, some of his gaudy boots and cowboy clothes, sheet music and even a badly-done oil painted by Rex.

THE EASTERN MOUNTAINS

We now leave the Cowboy corner and travel to the far reaches of eastern Arizona. If you head east from Willcox on I-10 and turn north on U.S. 191, you'll shed the high prairie and climb into the foothills and forests of the White Mountains. You then enter an agricultural valley where—surprisingly—cotton is the main crop. Two towns serve as its commercial center.

Safford-Thatcher

Although not tourist towns, Safford and next-door Thatcher offer a couple of tourist surprises. Still a-building, Safford's **Discovery Park** is shaping up as a fine science and history center. The campus of Eastern Arizona College in Thatcher contains the fine little **Museum of Anthropology.** Outdoor lovers may want to follow State Route 366 (the Swift Trail) south of Safford into the ramparts of **Mount Graham**, one of Arizona's highest peaks, at 10,713 feet.

For area information • Safford-Graham County Chamber of Commerce, 1111 Thatcher Blvd., Safford, AZ 85546; (520) 428-2511.

THE ATTRACTIONS

Discovery Park • *C/o Mt. Graham International Science and Culture Foundation, 1651 32nd St., Safford, AZ 85546; (520) 428-6260. Daily 10 a.m. to 10 p.m.* ☐ A focal point of this new museum is a planetarium operated in conjunction with the nearby Mount Graham International Observatory. Other exhibits include "The Story of Cotton" in Gila Valley, "The World of Mining" with a model underground drift mine, "Wonders of the Land" featuring exhibits on Graham County's five climate zones and "Lives of People," regarding the area's pre-Colombian and various contemporary cultures.

Museum of Anthropology • *On the campus of Eastern Arizona College, Church at College Avenue (P.O. Box 1186), Thatcher, AZ 85546; (520) 428-8310. Weekdays 9 to noon and 1 to 4 during the school year. Free; donations accepted.* ☐ Missed by most visitors, this is an impressive little museum featuring the early peoples of central Arizona. Its focal points are two remarkably detailed dioramas—one showing life here 11,000 years ago when giant bisons and ground sloths roamed about, and another depicting a typical pueblo of 300 A.D.

North to Clifton/Morenci and Springerville

From Safford, head east about 12 miles on Highways 70/191 and then branch northeast, following 191 through rocky desert foothills to the twin mining towns of Clifton and Morenci. This is a booming copper area and your drive will take you through a moonscape of tailing dumps and other unearthly gouges. You'll first travel through tired old **Clifton**, a blue collar town with a sagging Main Street that forks to the left off the highway. Its tattered old buildings are worth a browse.

From there, Highway 191 makes a wide sweeping turn up through terraced mining pits and tailing dumps to the neatly arrayed company town of **Morenci**. It's neatly arrayed because the original Morenci was dismantled and moved to this spot after rich copper or was found beneath it. If your timing is right, take the **Phelps Dodge mine tour** through its massive open pit operation.

The author sits like a bump on a petrified log on the Giant Logs Trail, at Petrified Forest National Park.

North of here, U.S. 191 becomes the **Coronado Trail,** winding steeply through more tailing dumps and then through the alpine beauty of Apache-Sitgreaves National Forest. Several turnouts along the way will help you appreciate the scenery.

You'll eventually wind up in another pair of towns, **Eagar** and **Springerville.** Quite different than Clifton-Morenci, these are commercial centers in a farming and ranching valley surrounded by wooded mountains. Although remote, this area offers a surprising array of lures, including two major archaeological sites. One is near Springerville; the other between Springerville and St. Johns. Springerville also has a couple of small museums; you can learn about these from the Round Valley Chamber of Commerce.

For area information ● Greenlee County Chamber of Commerce, P.O. Box 1237, Clifton, AZ 85533; (520) 865-3313.

Round Valley Chamber of Commerce, P.O. Box 31 (148 E. Main St.), Springerville, AZ 85938-0031; (520) 333-2123.

THE ATTRACTIONS

Phelps Dodge mine tour ● *Free tours weekdays at 8:30 and 1:15. Call (520) 865-4521, extension 1435 for reservations, or stop at the Phelps Dodge employment office just above Morenci on Highway 191, opposite the fire station. Tour groups meet at the Morenci Motel 15 minutes prior to departure.* ☐ These three-hour tours of the Morenci Mine operation include the world's second largest open pit mine and various ore processing facilities.

Casa Malpais Pueblo ● *Museum at 318 Main Street in Springerville; open Wednesday-Sunday 9 to 5. Casa Malpais Pueblo is nearby and tours depart the museum at 9, 11 and 2:30.* ☐ A downtown storefront visitor center contains a few relics from Casa Malpais Pueblo. From here, visitors are taken to the pueblo site, which was occupied for about 200 years and abandoned around 1400 A.D. Although not large, it's one of the most intriguing in the Southwest, with a huge ceremonial kiva and a remarkably intact complex of pueblos.

Raven Site Ruin • *White Mountain Archaeological Center, HC 30, Box 30, St. Johns, AZ 85936; (520) 333-5857. Museum and gift shop open daily May through mid-October 10 to 5. Modest fee for 40-minute tours.* ☐ A private foundation was established in the early 1990s to protect and excavate this 800-room Anasazi-Mogollon ruin on a low hill above the Little Colorado River. It's one of the largest in the Southwest, although only a few rooms have been unearthed. Visitors are taken on 40-minute tours of the site, where excavation is continuing.

North to the Petrified Forest

Drive three miles northwest of Springerville and take the Highway 180/191 fork north toward Holbrook and Petrified Forest National Park. You'll pass **Lyman Lake State Park** with swimming, boating and camping, and then the small prairie town of **St. Johns**. Go west and then northwest on U.S. 180 and you'll encounter the southern entrance to **Petrified Forest National Park**. Drive through the park, loop over I-40 through the **Painted Desert** and then take the freeway west to Holbrook.

For area information • Holbrook-Petrified Forest Chamber of Commerce, 100 E. Arizona St., Holbrook, AZ 86025; (520) 524-6558.

Petrified Forest National Park • *P.O. Box 2217, Petrified Forest, AZ 86028; (520) 524-6228. Park gates and visitor centers open daily 8 to 5; longer in summer.* ☐ This park in a high, windy prairie is full of trees, although they've all turned to stone. Petrified logs are scattered like broken columns of fallen temples over the preserve's 93,533 acres. Driving northwest on Highway 180, enter the park's southern gate, follow a 27-mile scenic drive and exit the northern gate, at Interstate 40 about 25 miles east of Holbrook. You actually get two attractions for the price of one. The drive takes you through a section of the **Painted Desert** north of the park. This multi-chromatic desert stretches for 200 miles across Arizona, along the northern edge of the Little Colorado River.

Holbrook to Globe-Miami

The town of Holbrook is comprised mostly of motels and restaurants that serve visitors to nearby Petrified Forest National Park. It does offer one lure, the **Courthouse Museum** in the town's still-active courthouse at Arizona and Navajo Streets. It has the usual pioneer relics, and the Chamber of Commerce office is located here. Both are open weekdays 8 to 5, plus evenings 7 to 9 in the summer.

From Holbrook, a long drive through mixed terrain will take you nearly half the length of the state to the mining towns of Globe and Miami. To begin, follow signs from Holbrook's Main Street to Highways 180 and 77 south, and then continue straight ahead on State Route 77. It cuts a direct line through bunchgrass prairie, and then begins climbing into the White Mountains as it passes through hamlets of **Snowflake** and **Taylor.**

As pine trees replace bunchgrass, you'll hit **Show Low.** It's a mountain vacation retreat, although it offers no specific visitor lures. Pick up U.S. 60 here and take it south into the huge **White Mountain Apache Reservation.** After winding through pretty pine forests, it drops downhill through the adjacent **San Carlos Indian Reservation,** where the trees begin to thin out. Leaving the reservation, you follow a dramatic spiral through spectacular **Salt River Canyon**, which is rimmed by jagged peaks, buttes and fluted ridges.

After ten miles of twisting canyon and another 20 miles of rocky mountainous terrain, you hit **Globe** in the arid Cobre Valley. Copper marks its past, present and future. The great open pits were abandoned a few years ago, then mining resumed recently, bringing a bit of prosperity to this old brick-front town. It offers a few items of visitor interest, including impressive vistas of multi-colored tailing dumps.

For area information • Greater Globe-Miami Chamber of Commerce, P.O. Box 2539 (1360 N. Broad), Globe, AZ 85502; (800) 448-8983 or (520) 425-4495.

THE ATTRACTIONS

Gila County Historical Museum • *1330 N. Broad St. (Highway 60, north of town), Globe, AZ 85502; (520) 425-7385. Monday-Saturday 10 to 4. Free; donations appreciated.* ☐ The museum occupies a 1914 Spanish style bungalow that served as the Dominion Mine rescue station. Exhibits include a furnished turn-of-the-century miner's cabin, a tack room with saddles and other cowboy stuff, an early bedroom setting, a wet plate camera and other relics.

Besh-Ba-Gowah Archaeological Park • *Near Globe Community center, a mile southwest of town, off Jesse Hayes Road; (520) 425-0320. Daily 9 to 5.* ☐ Archaeologists and craftsmen have re-created Arizona's most realistic ancient Indian dwellings at Besh-Ba-Gowah. Climb a rough wooden ladder and peer into a second-floor room where pottery, gourds, ears of corn and a plant fiber whisk broom are arranged as they might have been 600 years ago. The adjacent museum has fine graphics and implements of the Salado people who occupied this pueblo.

Historic downtown Miami • *Town Hall information desk is on Keystone Avenue, open 8:30 to 12 and 1 to 5; (520) 473-4403.* ☐ Next-door Miami, considerably more sleepy than Globe, is a virtual museum of weathered 19th century structures. A walking map available at the Town Hall will direct you past its more interesting buildings.

From Globe, you can follow State Route 77 south to Tucson, thus completing an ambitious loop of southeastern and far eastern Arizona.

Chapter seventeen
FOUR CORNERS COUNTRY
NAVAJO-HOPI LAND

The large Navajo and Hopi reservations in northeastern Arizona encompass some of the state's most interesting terrain, from starkly beautiful canyons to netherworld sandstone spires. They also provide an opportunity to witness two proud nations in transition—working to preserve their old ways while embracing many of our new ones.

The combined reservations cover about 29,000 square miles, encompassing all of northeastern Arizona and spilling over into Colorado, Utah and New Mexico. That's nearly as big as New Hampshire, Vermont, Massachusetts and Connecticut combined.

The Navajo reservation, largest in America, covers 25,000 square miles. The Hopi Nation is much smaller, about 4,000 square miles. By an unfortunate whim of the federal government, Hopi turf is entirely surrounded by the Navajo Nation. The Hopi reservation does, however, encompass some of the tribe's ancestral lands. One pueblo, Old Oraibi, has existed for more than 800 years. Dating from 1150 A.D., it may be the oldest continually occupied settlement in America.

Navajos are America's largest Indian tribe, numbering about 150,000 on the reservation, with several thousand more living elsewhere. Hopi population on the reservation is around 10,000. Navajos tend to live on their ranches and farms, while the Hopi prefer village life in the pueblos—commuting to the their agricultural lands.

245

SOME VISITOR TIPS

Sovereign nations • When you enter reservation lands, you technically leave Arizona and enter sovereign nations. You don't need a passport, of course, and both tribes welcome visitors. However, they are self governing and some of their laws differ from those outside. Alcohol is prohibited in Hopi-Navajo land; you cannot buy a drink at any reservation establishment or a can of beer in a market.

Permits • As on other reservations, permits are required for hunting or fishing, and you don't need Arizona licenses. These permits are readily available through tribal offices and at some trading posts and stores; fees are modest.

Driving laws • Safety belt use is required on the dual reservations, as it is in the rest of the state. Navajo police use radar to enforce the speed limit, although they aren't fanatics about it.

What time is it? • Here's a point of minor confusion: Arizona does not switch to daylight saving time, and neither does the Hopi Nation, but the Navajo Nation does.

Photography • The Hopi forbid kind of photography—still, movie or video camera. Photography is permitted in Navajo lands.

Dining • The Hopi, more traditionalist than the Navajo, have several distinctive dishes. The best place to find traditional Hopi fare—in fact, one of the *only* places—is the Tunosvongya Restaurant at the Hopi Cultural Center. Try the *chil-il ou gya va*, a spicy blend of pinto beans, beef and chilies, or *nok qui*, a stew with lamb, baked green chilies and Indian fry bread.

Shopping • Navajos have long been noted for their artistry with hand-woven wool blankets and turquoise and silver jewelry—particularly the squash blossom necklace. The Hopi produce fine basketry, pottery, silver jewelry and detailed, brightly-colored *kachina* (or *katsina*) dolls, carefully whittled out of cottonwood. Traditional *kachinas* are regarded as spiritual messengers. Navajo and Hopi artistry, like all native crafts, has been altered by the tourist market. The Navajo turquoise and silver jewelry trade actually was created in the late 1800s by the Fred Harvey Company. Don't be surprised to see a Levi-clad Hopi *kachina* in a craft shop, or one toting a camera.

Scores of roadside stands offer a bewildering variety of Navajo crafts, particularly in the western part of the reservation on routes to the Grand Canyon. Prices generally are better than those in the shops, although quality control may be better in some of the established trading posts. Both Navajo and Hopi officials work to ensure that anything sold on the reservation is authentic.

For area information • Navajoland Tourism, P.O. Box 663, Window Rock, AZ 86515; (520) 871-6659, 871-6436 or 6659.

Office of Public Relations, The Hopi Tribe, P.O. Box 123, Kykotsmovi, AZ 86039; (520) 734-2331, ext. 360.

NAVAJO-HOPI DRIVE

The Hopi-Navajo terrain may surprise you. Much of it is barren grassland, punctuated by startling scenery. Canyon de Chelly is one of the most interesting chasms we've ever seen; Monument Valley looks even more dramatic than it appears in photos, although it's smaller than one might think. After you've driven for hours across the reservation, seeing nothing but an occasional farmhouse, a great redwall butte may appear on the horizon or a cathedral-like spire may crop up in a pasture. Although the Hopi are famous for their distinctive pueblos, don't expect to see quaint Indian villages on the Navajo reservation. You'll see occasional log and mud hogans and some modern ones made of lumber. However, most Navajo towns differ little from ours.

Natural and historic lures of Navajo-Hopi land are widespread so we've again devised a driving route. Our starting point is **Page**, which is notched into the far northwestern tip of the Navajo Nation.

Drive south on U.S. 89, and then turn east onto U.S. 160. Look for a small sign indicating **dinosaur tracks**, which are imprinted into hardpan on a side road just north of the highway. Several locals usually are there to point out the tracks and tell you a bit about them. They'll splash them with water to accent them for photos. A small gratuity will be appreciated.

You soon enter **Tuba City**, the largest town on the Navajo reservation. Mormons settled here in 1877, and then sold out to the government when they realized that they were on Indian land. It was the reservation's administrative center until offices were moved to Window Rock on the far eastern side in 1930. The town offers an interesting architectural mix—old cut sandstone government buildings, ordinary bungalows, mobile homes and typical octagonal hogans.

THE HOPI NATION

Follow Highway 264 south from Tuba City into the Hopi Nation. Most of their celebrated pueblos occupy three mesas, simply called First, Second and Third. Some are true cliff dwellings, perched on shelves and niches high above the valley floor.

These pueblos, while intriguing, are not models of neatness. The earthy style of these ancient dwellings does not blend well with non-biodegradable objects such as car parts and tin cans. The gentle Hopi are more into spiritual things than landscaping. Look beyond the litter and realize that you are seeing people and dwellings that were here before Columbus set sail, before the Spanish began their intrusions into this peaceful land. The Hopi may have occupied this area for as long as man has wandered in the Southwest. Most anthropologists agree that they're descendants of the Anasazi.

Among the more interesting pueblos you'll encounter on this drive are **Old Oraibi** (*oh-RYE-bee*), **Kykotsmovi** (*Kee-KOTS-mo-vee*), **Shungopovi** (*Shung-O-PO-vee*), **Shipaulovi** (*Shih-PAW-lo-vee*) and

Mishongnovi (*Mih-SHONG-no-vee*). Did you get those pronunciations? Note that the accent is on a middle syllable.

To learn more about the people and their ancient pueblos, visit the fine cultural complex on Second Mesa in the heart of the Hopi Nation. Coming from the west, it's to the left on the main highway:

Hopi Cultural Center and Museum • *P.O. Box 7, Second Mesa, AZ 86043; (520) 734-6650. Museum and cultural center open Monday-Friday 8 to noon and 1 to 5 the year around, plus weekends 9 to 3 from May to mid-October. Gift shops generally open daily 9 to 5.* ☐ This handsome sandstone colored pueblo style complex includes a museum, gift shops, the Tunosvongya Restaurant and a motel. The nicely done museum has collections of modern and ancient pottery, murals portraying traditional villages, a hand-woven bridal robe and other things Hopi. A diorama of Keet Seel, a ruin in Navajo National Monument, shows how it appeared in 1200 A.D.

Hopi dances • The Hopi still perform centuries-old ceremonial dances in traditional dress. Some are private while others may be witnessed by visitors, and these are usually held on weekends. Although schedules aren't usually posted in advance, you can check with the cultural center to see if a dance is planned in the area. Photography, video taping and recording are forbidden at the dances.

BACK TO THE NAVAJO NATION

Leaving Hopi land, follow Highway 264 east until you approach the Navajo village of **Ganado**. Watch for signs on the right to an interesting historic complex:

Hubbell Trading Post National Historic Site • *P.O. Box 150, Ganado, AZ 86505; (520) 755-3475. Daily 8 to 6 in summer and 8 to 5 the rest of the year. Free.* ☐ The oldest active trading post on the reservation, Hubbell was established in 1876. It's both an historic landmark and an active trading post. You can buy canned goods, bolts of cloth or harnesses, or curios, souvenirs and books. A large barn next to the venerable stone store once housed the post's livestock. Several old wagons are on display out back. At the visitor center museum, you'll learn about the vital role of the Western trading post, which provided a commercial and cultural link between Indians and whites.

Window Rock

Pressing eastward on Highway 264, you'll next hit Window Rock, right next to the New Mexico border. It looks like a typical American community, although the culture is definitely Navajo, as you'll learn at the museum and crafts center, on the main highway near the border.

Navajo Tribal Museum • *In the Arts and Crafts Center (P.O. Box 308, Window Rock), AZ 86515; (520) 871-4090. Weekdays 9 to 4:45. Free; donations appreciated.* ☐ This well-planned museum exhibits the skeleton of a 180-million-year-old *dilophosaurus*, plus displays tracing native occupation of the region from the basketmakers of 50 A.D. to the present. Artifacts include pottery, projectile points, metates and such. (A new structure just beyond the craft center may house the museum by the time you arrive, or the facility may be used for a visitor center and tribal offices.)

From the tribal museum, go back to the town's only traffic signal and turn north onto Highway 12. After half a mile, watch on the right for a sign pointing toward the community's namesake. A few blocks off the highway, **Window Rock** is a natural arch sculpted through Kayenta sandstone. It occupies a small, nicely landscaped park. As you approach the park, you'll pass the 1930s style masonry buildings of tribal headquarters.

North to Canyon de Chelly

From Window Rock Tribal Park, press northward on Route 12, which takes you through imposing beige and red rock formations. When you reach the town of **Fort Defiance,** stay alert for a right hand turn at a service station to stay with the highway. Otherwise, you'll continue straight ahead into the town.

Pressing northward, you'll dip into New Mexico (marked by a sign) and then back into Arizona (not marked). This is an appealing drive into the pines of the Chuska Mountain foothills, offering picnic sites, campgrounds and a couple of fishing lakes. As further enhancement, the area is marked with occasional sandstone cliffs, buttes and spires. Particularly dominant to the east is a thick, towering butte with a wide alluvial skirt, called Black Pinnacle. Beyond small **Tsaile Lake,** you'll see the campus of Navajo Community College on your left. It has a fine little museum worthy of pause:

Hatathli Museum • *Navajo Community College, just inside the east entrance of campus; (520) 724-3311. Weekdays 8:30 to 4:30; donations appreciated.* ❑ This all-Navajo museum is housed in the octagonal Hatathli Center. Exhibits trace Navajo and other Native American cultures. Handicrafts and artwork are available at a sales gallery.

Just beyond the college, you'll reach the hamlet of **Tsaile.** From here, Highway 64 leads westward into the side door of Canyon de Chelly National Monument, about 25 miles west. However, before heading in that direction, we suggest that you continue another ten miles north on Route 12 to see a spectacular proscenium of red rock cliffs above the town of **Lukachukai.** Having done so, return to Tsaile Junction and head west toward the national monument.

Canyon de Chelly National Monument • *P.O. Box 588, Chinle, AZ 86503; (520) 674-5436. Visitor center open 8 to 6 from May to September and 8 to 5 the rest of the year; free. The center has a small museum with graphics tracing canyon occupation from basketmakers to Anasazi cliff dwellers of the 12th and 13th centuries. Ranger programs,*

The impossibly slender spire of Spider Rock rises from the bottom of Canyon de Chelley, one of several attractions on the huge Navajo and Hopi reservations.

from late May through early September. ◻ Canyon de Chelly and its adjoining Canyon del Muerto are unexpectedly beautiful steep-walled ravines, dropping a thousand feet to neat patchwork farms on the valley floor. Lining the banks of a meandering stream, these lands are still being tilled, as they have been since the 1300s. Coming from Tsaile, you'll first encounter Canyon del Muerto, following the North Rim Drive. Continue to the visitor center and then take the South Rim Drive along Canyon de Chelly. Both scenic drives have turnouts with graphics describing the splendid canyon vistas.

Four Corners, Monument Valley & Navajo Nat'l Monument

From Canyon de Chelly, drop down into the small town of **Chinle** and head north, following Highway 191 past several imposing freestanding red rock mesas. At U.S. 160, head east through **Mexican Water,** following signs to **Four Corners** where the borders of Arizona, New Mexico, Colorado and Utah merge. It's interesting mostly for its geographic oddity; a flat concrete monument with the four state seals marks the spot. It's in a Navajo tribal park and the monument is rimmed with dozens of souvenir stalls and small cafés.

Retrace your route on U.S. 160 through more imposing red rock formations and stay with the highway until you reach the town of **Kayenta**. Turn north for a visit to the Navajo Nation's most famous attraction:

Monument Valley Tribal Park ● *P.O. Box 360289, Monument Valley, UT 84536; (801) 727-3287. Daily 8 to 7 mid-March through September and 8 to 5 the rest of the year; last admission 30 minutes before closing.* ◻ Just inside the park, a small visitor center perched on a ridge offers great views of the valley below. From here, an extremely rough road leads down to the famous buttes, spires, pinnacles and fins of Monument Valley. Should you not want to abuse your vehicle, a dozen or more tour operators are parked nearby, waiting to take you down by jeeps, flatbed trucks with seats affixed to the bed, or other rigs. These are some of the most imposing formations on earth, although you may be surprised that the legendary valley is actually rather small.

From Monument Valley, return to Kayenta and continue west on U.S. 160 for the last major attraction of Navajo-Hopi land:

Navajo National Monument ● *HC 71, Box 3, Tonalea, AZ 86044; (520) 672-2366 or 672-2367. Interpretive center open 8 a.m. to 4:30 p.m. Lookout trail open during daylight hours.* ◻ This preserve shelters three of the most complete Anasazi ruins and one of the finest small museums in the state. Betatakin Ruin can be seen from an overlook near the visitor center museum, and you can visit it on ranger walks. Keet Seel, the "star" of Southwest's Indian ruins, is eight miles away and can be seen only with an advance permit. Inscription House is so fragile that it's closed to visitors. Back at the interpretive center, the excellent museum features stone tools, pottery and other artifacts found at the three ruins. You can crawl inside a reconstructed living unit that's so realistic the occupants appear to have just stepped out.

THE OTHER INDIAN NATIONS

If you'd like to learn more about Native Americans, Arizona is the ideal place to do so. The Navajo and Hopi nations offer good previews of contemporary Indian life. However, these are only two of 20 reservations in the state, and each tribal homeland has its own characteristics, arts and crafts.

Native American lands occupy 27 percent of Arizona—more than any other state. Further, Arizona has America's largest native population—around 200,000. It's one of the few places where Native Americans have the land and resources to maintain their own identity as members of viable communities. They are a major force in the state, both culturally and politically. Most reservations welcome visitors and many have fine natural attractions, and hunting and fishing areas.

Some reservations encompass lands that have been with the same tribes for centuries. Several Hopi villages, for instance, are among the oldest continually occupied settlements in America.

About three-fourths of Arizona's native people live on reservation land. It is communally owned and those who occupy it do not pay property taxes. As American citizens, they pay other state and federal tariffs, except some sales taxes.

Indian gaming

Because reservations are sovereign nations independent of most state laws, many tribes have gone into the gaming business. Indian casinos are scattered throughout Arizona and much of the rest of the country. Interestingly, there's also a tribal-owned casino in Nevada, where gambling is legal statewide; it's near Laughlin on the Colorado River. Tribes also have taken advantage of sales tax exemptions to operate smoke shops, where they can sell discounted cigarettes. You won't find many liquor sales, however, despite a potential savings on this heavily taxed product. Most reservations in Arizona prohibit the sale of alcohol—to their own people or anyone else.

More than a century has passed since the last Native American tribe yielded to white settlement and moved to reservations. Yet, they weren't granted citizenship until 1924, and they weren't given the right to vote until 1948. This must have been particularly galling, since many of them fought in World War II, including famed Iwo Jima flag-raiser Ira Hayes, a member of Arizona's Pima tribe.

For more information ● Native American Tourism Center, 4130 N. Goldwater Blvd., Suite 114, Scottsdale, AZ 85281, (602) 945-0771.

Arizona Commission of Indian Affairs, 1645 W. Jefferson St., Phoenix, AZ 85007, (602) 542-3123.

Chapter eighteen

DOWN MEXICO WAY

EXPLORING SOUTH OF THE BORDER

Arizona shares a long border and many ethnic ties with Mexico. Indeed, Southwestern cooking, architecture and even cowboying are heavily influenced by our neighbors to the south. One out of six Arizonans trace their roots to Mexico.

Visiting the Mexican state of Sonora through any of the six border crossings is a simple matter. At most points, you can merely walk across the international boundary to nearby shopping areas, restaurants and cantinas. Bear in mind that these aren't typical Mexican cities, any more than Arizona border towns are typically American. Each is influenced by the presence of the other. With the exception of Sasabe, these towns cater heavily to tourists, with an inordinate number of curio shops and restaurants. While you won't experience a typical slice of Mexico, you'll enjoy browsing through these bordertown shops. They offer bewildering selections of leather goods, ceramics, costume jewelry, turquoise and silver, onyx and wood carvings, embroidered clothing and glassware. Also, some of the simpler and more traditional Mexican Indian handicrafts are quite nice.

Most Mexican border towns are many times larger than their Arizona counterparts. A major reason for this is the "twin plant" program in which American-owned plants take advantage of inexpensive Mexican labor. Hundreds of thousands have flocked to the border towns, since—by Mexico's standards—wages paid at these plants are high.

Since most towns have shopping areas right next to the border, we recommend parking and walking across. U.S. Customs officials are

254 — CHAPTER EIGHTEEN

more picky than their Mexican counterparts, and you might get stuck in a long line of cars, trying to get back into Arizona. Also, American car insurance policies aren't recognized in Mexico. Incidentally, it's best to avoid weekend visits, when most border crossings are extremely busy.

Health matters ● We've traveled extensively in Mexico without getting anything worse that diarrhea. However, that's awfully unpleasant, so take precautions. Follow a few simple rules and your trip across the border should be both happy and healthy:

1. Although no specific shots are required for entry into Mexico, we'd recommend getting hepatitis inoculations, particularly if you plan to spend some time there. New vaccines now offer long-term protection against both hepatitis A and B, so you no longer have to cope with that uncomfortable and short-term gamma globulin shot. Check with your physician for details.

2. Drink the beer, not the water. Most Mexican cities don't have inadequately treated public water supplies. Tap water is safe for bathing and cooking (if it's boiled), but not for drinking or brushing your teeth. Most hotels will furnish you with bottled water and it's readily available in stores and street stalls.

3. In restaurants, particularly out-of-the-way ones that don't cater to tourists, avoid rare meat, poultry and fish. Also avoid salad vegetables that may have been rinsed with untreated water or handled by unwashed hand. And steer clear of iced drinks, since freezing doesn't kill the bacteria that can bring havoc to visiting intestines. The best rule is to eat only cooked food that's served while it's still hot. If it has been allowed to cool, it can be re-contaminated by careless handling.

4. Never eat food offered by street vendors; you don't know where it's been. If you buy fruit from a public market or street vendor, eat only what you can peeled yourself, such as oranges or bananas.

5. Since freezing doesn't kill most infectious bacteria, ice cream may not be safe unless you can confirm that the milk used has been pasteurized. The same is true for milk you drink or pour on breakfast cereal. (Cereal? We always have tortillas for breakfast in Mexico.)

Entry formalities ● If you're an American or Canadian citizen, you need only to declare your citizenship for visits of 72 hours or less, if you aren't going beyond a border town. If you plan to stay longer and/or go deeper, you'll need a Mexican Tourist Card and an automobile permit. These can be obtained quickly at the border, or from the Mexican Consulate, 553 S. Stone Ave., Tucson, AZ 85701; (520) 882-5595. The office is open weekdays from 8 to 2. You'll need proof of citizenship such as a birth certificate, passport, voter's registration certificate or military ID. A driver's license won't work. For a vehicle permit, you *must* carry proof of ownership, such as the registration slip.

Auto insurance ● Don't drive anywhere in Mexico without Mexican auto insurance. Although insurance isn't mandated by law, your vehicle might be impounded if you're involved in an accident. Few American insurance policies extend coverage to Mexico and even if they do, Mexican officials won't recognize them. If you have a rental car, make sure your rental agreement permits driving into Mexico, and get proper insurance coverage. Mexican auto insurance is available on both sides of the border. Rates are similar to American premiums.

Shopping ● American money is widely accepted in border towns, so don't bother with currency exchanges unless you're going into the interior. Expect to haggle over prices in curio shops. The rule of thumb is to counter with a third of what they ask, then meet somewhere in the middle. Don't embarrass the poor shopkeeper and take all the fun out of haggling by paying full price. Because of lower labor costs and a favorable exchange rate, you'll find many good buys. Booze is cheap because of the lack of tax, and Mexican-made liquor such as tequila and brandy are less than half the U.S. price. However, there are limits on what you can bring back; see below.

"Se habla Ingles?" ● You won't have to resort to your high school Spanish in the border towns; English is spoken at virtually every shop, motel and restaurant.

Driving the interior ● It's generally as safe as driving across Arizona, although there's a major difference. Once you get away from the border, service facilities are scarce and car parts even scarcer. For an extended trip into Mexico, take spare parts such as fan belts, water pumps and hoses—things that might fail. And don't forget the tools needed to install them. Also, take plenty of bottled water in case you're stranded for a while. Paved Mexican roads are often narrower than ours. Watch out for potholes, tractors and cows who seem oblivious to the risk of colliding with a car. Because of open ranges in the state of Sonora and elsewhere, we make it a rule never to drive after dark. Unleaded gasoline is plentiful in border towns, less so as you travel south. You may want to filter your gasoline through a fine sieve or cloth, particularly if you have a fuel-injected vehicle.

Returning to Arizona ● You can bring back $400 worth of duty-free goods per family member, plus one quart of liquor per adult. Mexico enjoys favored nation status with the U.S., and certain handicrafts can be imported in excess of the $400 limit. Check with a U.S. Customs office to see what's currently on the list.

THE BORDER TOWNS

While none of the border towns are cool in summer, Nogales and Agua Prieta—at nearly 4,000 feet elevation—are a bit more livable. San Luis, below Yuma, is near sea level; expect to sizzle if you plan a summertime visit.

Agua Prieta ● This is Mexico's twin to Douglas. The two towns rub shoulders at the border, and Mexican shops are less than a block from the boundary. With about 70,000 inhabitants—ten times as many as

Douglas—Agua Prieta offers fair shopping variety. It's not as abundant as Nogales or San Luis, however. Downtown here is more of a conventional mix of businesses, with gift shops tucked among department stores, *farmacias* and professional offices. Paved highways lead from here into the interior; it's the most direct driving route to Mexico City.

Naco ● A hamlet south of Bisbee, Naco is one of our favorite border towns. If there's such a thing as scruffily cute, this is it. Naco is more like an interior village—uncrowded, with little Mexican shops behind dusty pastel store fronts. You won't find much of a shopping selection here, but there's one good-sized liquor store. The wide (although pot-holed) streets with center dividers give the place a nice colonial charm.

Nogales ● Opposite Nogales, Arizona, it's the largest of the border towns, with a population exceeding 200,000. Predictably, it's also the best place to shop. Scores of curio and liquor stores are crowded into the Calle Obregon, a shopping area that starts just a block from the border. Narrow arcades are stuffed with stalls. Some carry a variety of crafts, curios and general junk, while others specialize in leather goods, fabric, glassware and such. You'll find an abundance of shops within a few blocks of the border, so it's best to park and walk in. Several lots on the Arizona side offer all-day parking for a few dollars. One, adjacent to a McDonald's restaurant, has spaces large enough for rec vehicles. Since this is the largest of Arizona's border towns, the vehicle crossing can be quite congested at times.

San Luis ● South of Yuma, San Luis is an agricultural community of 50,000 or so. Its weathered old business district offers several shops within two blocks of the border. Selections are fairly good, although it's a distant second to Nogales for shopping variety. You can park free in Friendship Park on the American side; the lot closes at 9 p.m.

Sasabe ● At the bottom of Highway 286 southwest of Tucson, this is the smallest, least crowded and most typically Mexican of all the border towns. A handful of residents occupy its weathered buildings. There are no tourist shops or other facilities here, or in its Arizona twin. Only dirt roads lead south from here, so Sasabe obviously gets very little through traffic. Incidentally, the border station is closed between 8 p.m. and 8 a.m.

Sonoita ● Opposite Lukeville below Organ Pipe Cactus National Monument, Sonoita is about three miles from the border. A few shops are within walking distance of Lukeville although there isn't much of a selection. You might like to drive 63 miles south to **Rocky Point** (Puerto Peñasco), where you can swim, snorkel and fish in the clear waters of the Gulf of California. It has several tourist hotels and restaurants. Remember that you need a Mexican Tourist Card and vehicle permit to go south of Sonoita. The Sonoita-Lukeville border station is closed between midnight and 8 a.m.

Chapter nineteen

AFTERTHOUGHTS

OUR ARIZONA FAVORITES

We said at the beginning that this book is free of outside bias, for it has no paid listings or advertising. However, it certainly isn't free of *our* bias. Just for the fun of it, we've compiled "Ten Best" lists of our favorite things in Arizona. The first selection on each list is our top pick, followed by the next nine in alphabetical order. In this manner, we have no losers among the Ten Best, only winners and runners-up.

Arizona's ten best towns and cities

1. Tucson • It has it all—urban conveniences, varied cultural offerings, a world class university, interesting attractions and excellent climate (except for peak summer heat). Surrounding mountains and desert offer lures for outdoor enthusiasts.

2. Bisbee • This venerable copper mining town has found new life as a tourist and art center. We love the sturdy old downtown and steeply tiered residential areas. The mining scars aren't pretty although they add drama to the setting.

3. Carefree/Cave Creek • Take your pick of modern (Carefree) or Old West (Cave Creek). They're beyond the Valley of the Sun's congestion, in an attractive desert setting, yet within half an hour's drive of the urban action of Pboenix and Scottsdale.

4. Flagstaff • Think of it as a mini Tucson, with colder winters but milder summers. Northern Arizona University and several fine museums give it cultural depth. It's surrounded by natural attractions, and within a short drive of the Grand Canyon and several Indian ruins.

5. Fountain Hills ● The best of Arizona's new planned communities, Fountain Hills offers modern conveniences and beautiful homes in a rugged desert setting.

6. Mesa ● This is where we'd live if we lived in the Valley of the Sun. It's on the outer edge of congestion, yet within a short drive of Arizona State University, Phoenix and other lures. We like its nicely preserved old fashioned downtown area.

7. Prescott ● It's an appealing, self-contained little community tucked against forested mountains. Several colleges, galleries, a handsome old downtown area and a friendly Western attitude make this one of Arizona's most desirable communities.

8. Safford ● Tucked off by itself in southeastern Arizona, Safford is a prim little farm town in an agricultural valley. An exceptional new science and history center and an adjacent college give it some cultural depth, and nearby Mount Graham offers outdoor pursuits.

9. Sedona ● We'd retire here in a minute if we could afford it, and spend every evening watching the sundown light and shadow show against those fantastic red rock formations.

10. Wickenburg ● If you like to play cowboy, this is the place, dude. A pretty desert setting, an excellent museum, and old style downtown and surrounding dude ranches make this the best little cowtown in Arizona.

Arizona's ten best retirement towns

1. Tucson ● With extensive retirement facilities, affordable housing and the attractions we've already mentioned, the Old Pueblo again tops our list.

2. Apache Junction ● The rugged backdrop of the Superstition Mountains, water play lures of the nearby Salt River Canyon and affordable housing make this a fine place to retire.

3. Catalina ● The town itself isn't much more than a widening of Highway 77 asphalt. What we're really recommending is the two nearby retirement villages of Sun City Vistoso and Saddlebrooke with their extensive amenities. We like the nearness of Tucson and the adjacent Santa Catalina Mountains.

4. Green Valley ● The surrounding desert is rather bland, although careful planning has created an ideal site for the good life. Green Valley offers ample shopping, reasonable prices and the nearby lures of Tucson.

5. Fountain Hills ● Home prices are on the high side; otherwise, Fountain Hills provides a great retirement environment with its nicely planned housing developments and robust desert setting.

6. Florence ● Mix a historic downtown area with some modern housing in the suburbs and a convenient location between Phoenix and Tucson, and you have an excellent retirement community.

7. Pine/Strawberry ● Folks who need pine trees with their retirement will like these two woodsy communities tucked under the

Mogollon Rim north of Phoenix. Winters are nippy but certainly warmer than in North Dakota.

8. Prescott • In addition to its cultural lures, ample shopping, collegiate atmosphere and nice setting, Prescott offers extensive senior programs and good medical facilities. One of four residents is retired.

9. Sedona • We again select Sedona for its stunning red rock backdrop. With warm summers and rather mild winters, it's a great place to be at leisure—if you can afford it.

10. Yuma • No, it's not a pretty place. However, a good selection of inexpensive homes and mobile home parks, ample shopping and interesting historic sites make Yuma quite attractive. It gets hotter than the hinges of Hades in summer but what the heck. You're retired; be a Sunbird and fly north!

Arizona's ten best snowbird roosts

1. Apache Junction • Both alphabetically and preferentially, it tops our list of Snowbird retreats. Although it isn't on the popular Colorado River corridor, it offers water sports in the nearby Salt River Canyon; the lures of Phoenix are a short drive away.

2. Bullhead City • It ain't pretty, but it can be fun. Bullhead has an abundance of RV and mobile home parks, and the gaming centers of Laughlin, Nevada, are just across the Colorado River.

3. Lake Havasu City • The best planned of the Colorado River corridor communities, Lake Havasu offers lots of water sports, good shopping and—oh, yes—that misplaced bridge.

4. Lake Mead National Recreation Area • This isn't a community, although it's certainly a Snowbird roost. RV parks at Lake Mead marinas offer water play, and the casino action of Las Vegas is less than an hour away.

5. Parker • This friendly little town is ideal for Snowbirds on a budget and those who love water sports. The adjacent Parker Strip is lined with RV and mobile home parks.

6. Phoenix-Scottsdale • This is your roost if you want to be in the middle of the action, with cultural pursuits and plenty of shopping. And if you're a Cactus League baseball fan, look no further. Five teams play here and Phoenix now has its own major league club, the Arizona Diamondbacks.

7. Mesa-Tempe • These two bedroom communities in the southeastern part of the Valley of the Sun offer some of the same advantages as Phoenix and Scottsdale, with a greater selection of mobile home parks and cheaper space rent.

8. Quartzsite • So all right, it's ugly. But if you want inexpensive RV parking, you may want to join the legions that descend on this sun-baked patch of desert. The gem shows and swap meets are a blast.

9. Tucson • For all of the reasons we listed above, this is a great place to spend a winter or a lifetime. Tucson has a good assortment of RV parks and resorts, apartments and condos.

10. Yuma • Snowbirds double Yuma's population in winter, so why not join them? Ample shopping, interesting historic sites and the Colorado River playground make this a good choice.

Arizona's ten best places to find jobs

1. Phoenix • Hands down, Phoenix is the job center of Arizona. With a low unemployment rate and a broad employment base, this is where we'd start knocking on doors.

2. Buckeye • This small town on the fringes of the Valley of the Sun is actively promoting light industry and it's away from the congestion of Phoenix-Mesa-Tempe.

3. Chandler • Fast growing Chandler offers a good mix of space-age firms, high tech, general manufacturing, construction and retail.

4. Flagstaff • This dynamic western Arizona city's job count increased by more than 30 percent in the past decade. Lumbering, tourism, high tech manufacturing and education are leading job sources.

5. Gilbert • Little Gilbert just keeps expanding, and the job market expands with it. The fastest growing Arizona city of the Eighties, it continues to move right along. Gilbert and its neighboring communities offer a diversified job base.

6. Glendale • Like its booming neighbors, Glendale has a constantly expanding job base. Its varied employment picture includes manufacturing, high tech, construction, retailing and services.

7. Goodyear • The first of several West Valley towns started by the Goodyear Tire and Rubber Company, it is host to such firms as McKesson, Rubbermaid and Lockheed Martin.

8. Litchfield Park • Another of the Goodyear towns, this attractive planned community offers a growing job base; employment has increased 45 percent in the past ten years.

9. Sierra Vista • This prairie town offers the best job market in Arizona's southeast, which admittedly isn't as good as the Valley of the Sun. However, Sierra Vista is working to attract more light industry.

10. Tucson • The Old Pueblo isn't growing as fast as Phoenix, and most folks here like that. However, as Arizona's second biggest city, it offers a large and varied employment base.

Arizona's ten best tourist attractions

1. Grand Canyon National Park • We might even call this incredible gorge *America's* best attraction. The pity is that most people see it only from the rim. To really love the canyon, you should hike down into it or run the wild rapids of the Colorado River.

2. Arizona-Sonora Desert Museum • If we had time to visit only one museum in Arizona, it would be this one on the outskirts of Tucson. You'll receive a quick education about the flora, fauna and history of the state's great desert reaches.

3. Canyon de Chelly National Monument • Located on the Navajo reservation, this steep-walled gorge with ancient pueblos tucked into its sheer flanks is often overlooked by visitors. Of Arizona's natural attractions, only the Grand Canyon surpasses its grandeur.

4. The Heard Museum • If we had time to visit only two museums in Arizona, this would be the other one. Devoted exclusively to the study of Native Americans, this outstanding Phoenix archive contains the world's best treasury of Indian culture.

5. Hoover Dam/Lake Mead National Recreation Area • When Hoover Dam was completed in 1935, it was the world's highest, holding back the world's largest reservoir. It's still an awesome thing, and Lake Mead is a grand place to play on the water.

6. Mission San Xavier del Bac • The "White Dove of the Desert" near Tucson is one of America's most beautiful early day missions. And it's one of the few still serving Native Americans.

7. Monument Valley Tribal Park • This is where they film those great car commercials. Although smaller than most people think, this park on the Arizona-Utah border has some of America's most dramatic sandstone buttes, spires and fins.

8. Oak Creek Canyon • Awesome red rock shapes, a sparkling stream and thick forest combine to create one of Arizona's most beautiful settings—and one of its favorite playgrounds.

9. Organ Pipe Cactus National Monument • Arizona's largest national monument contains striking examples of the great Sonoran Desert that covers much of southern Arizona and northern Mexico.

10. Wupatki National Monument • This large national monument north of Flagstaff preserves scores of pre-Columbian Indian ruins. It's the best of several ancient pueblos in the area.

USEFUL ARIZONA BOOKS
(In addition to the one you're holding)

Now that you've purchased this book and we've gotten your money—assuming you aren't still thumbing through it in the bookstore—we will recommend further reading.

General travel information

Arizona Discovery Guide by Don and Betty Martin; Pine Cone Press, Inc., 631 Stephanie St., #138, Henderson, NV 89014. "A remarkably useful travel companion for motorists, RVers and other explorers," this statewide travel guidebook tells readers where to go, what to see and where to eat and sleep.

Arizona Milepost Guide by William Hafford; Arizona Highways Books. A milepost-pegged guide to fifteen tours.

Arizona Scenic Drives by Stewart Greene; Falcon Press, P.O. Box 279, Billings, MT 59103. This book features a series of descriptive drives through the state.

Arizona Travel Planner distributed free by the Arizona Office of Tourism, 1100 W. Washington St., Phoenix, AZ 85007, call (800) 842-8257 or (602) 542-TOUR. A concise guide to the state, section by section, listing attractions, mileages, campgrounds, chambers of commerce, tour operators and other essentials.

Roadside Geology of Arizona by Halka Chronic; Mountain Press Publishing Company, P.O. Box 2399, Missoula, MT 59806. Scholarly yet highly readable guide to geological formations that visitors see as they travel Arizona's highways.

RVing America's Backroads: Arizona by Kitty Pearson and Jim Vincent; Trailer Life Books, Agoura, Calif. Full-color, attractively-illustrated guide to Arizona, oriented to the RV set, with suggested driving tours in various areas of the state.

Travel Arizona: The Back Roads by Joseph Stocker; Arizona Highways, 2039 W. Lewis Ave., Phoenix, AZ 85009. Sixteen tours, with illustrations, maps and color photos.

What Is Arizona Really Like: A Guide to Arizona's Marvels by Reg Manning; Reganson Cartoon Books, P.O. Box 5242, Phoenix, AZ 85010. Humorously written insider's look at Arizona with cartoon illustrations, by the former cartoonist for the *Arizona Republic.*

Relocation and retirement

The Book of Lists, published annually by the *The Business Journal*, 2910 N. Central, Phoenix, AZ 85012; (602) 230-8400. Although it doesn't provide specific job listings, it publishes names, phone numbers and addresses of the area's largest firms.

The Phoenix Job Bank, published by Bob Adams., Inc., 260 Center St., Holbrook, MA 02343. A "how-to" book for job-seekers, with lists of major Phoenix and Tucson employers, job descriptions and techniques for successful job-hunting.

Retirement Living by Sally Ravel and Lee Ann Wolfe; Conari Press, 713 Euclid Ave., Berkeley, CA 94708. Although it's oriented to northern California, it contains useful information in planning for retirement and selecting a retirement community.

History, ghost towns and reference

Arizona Place Names, re-print of a 1935 edition by Will C. Barnes, University of Arizona Press, Tucson. Thorough, comprehensive guide to the origin of Arizona's geographic names.

Arizona's Best Ghost Towns by Byrd Howell Granger; Northland Press, P.O. Box N, Flagstaff, AZ 86002. A helpful guide with maps and nice sketches.

Desert Wildflowers; Arizona Highways, 2039 W. Lewis Ave., Phoenix, AZ 85009. Gorgeous photos of desert blossoms, with descriptions and times to catch peak blooming periods.

History of Arizona by Robert Woznicki, PH.D.; Messenger Graphics, 110 S. 41st Ave., Phoenix, AZ 85009. A highly-readable treatment of the state's history; not comprehensive, but filled with interesting vignettes and personality sketches.

The Story of Superstition Mountain and the Lost Dutchman Mine by Robert Joseph Allen; Pocket Books, New York. A readable narrative of the Dutchman mine mystery, with some very questionable suppositions.

Hiking, camping, wildlife viewing

Arizona Day Hikes by Dave Ganci; Sierra Club Books. It describes a hundred day hike trails throughout the state.

Arizona Wildlife Viewing by John N. Carr; Falcon Press, P.O. Box 279, Billings, MT 59103. This small full-color book advises hikers and strollers where to see what kind of wildlife in the state's parks and recreation areas; compiled in cooperation with park and recreation departments.

A Hiker's Guide to Arizona by Steward Aitchison and Bruce Grubbs; Falcon Press, P.O. Box 279, Billings, MT 59103. A well-written guide with maps and black and white photos.

Hiker's Guide to the Superstition Wilderness by Jack Carlson and Elizabeth Stewart; Clear Creek Publishing, P.O. Box 24666, Tempe, AZ 85285. A fine little guide to trails in the Superstitions, brightened by the history and legends of the Lost Dutchman mine.

Outdoors in Arizona: A Guide to Camping by Bob Hirsch; Arizona Highways, 2039 W. Lewis Ave., Phoenix, AZ 85009. A good mix of campsite listings, color photos and history and vignettes about the state's out-of-doors.

Outdoors in Arizona: A Guide to Hiking and Backpacking by John Annerino; Arizona Highways, 2039 W. Lewis Ave., Phoenix, AZ 85009. Suggested hikes from desert to mountain to prairie, with maps and photos.

Native Americans

A Clash of Cultures: Fort Bowie and the Chiricahua Apaches by Robert M. Utley; for sale by the Superintendent of Documents, U.S. Government Printing Office, Washington, DC 20402. Also at national monuments and historic sites.

American Indians of the Southwest by Bertha P. Dutton; University of New Mexico Press. A good general guide to present and past Southwestern Indians.

The Complete Family Guide to Navajo-Hopi Land by Bonnie Brown and Carol D. Bracken; Bonnie Brown and Carol Bracken, P.O. Box 2914, Page, AZ 86040. It's a bit unprofessionally done, but helpful, with lists of attractions, places to dine and sleep; several children's pages to amuse the youngsters.

Geronimo: A Man, His Time, His Place by Angie Debo; University of Oklahoma Press, Norman, OK 73019. An award-winning biography of the famous Apache warrior; probably the most comprehensive Geronimo study ever written.

Hohokam Indians of the Tucson Basin by Linda M. Gregonis and Karl J. Reinhard; University of Arizona Press, Tucson. Scholarly, readable account of Tucson's early peoples.

Southwestern Indian Tribes by Tom Bahti; KC Publications, Inc., Box 14883-A, Las Vegas, NV 89114. Attractive guide to Arizona and New Mexico tribes with maps and color and black and white illustrations; nicely detailed photos of artifacts.

Visitor's Guide to Arizona's Indian Reservations by Boye De Mente; Phoenix Books/Publishers, P.O. Box 32008, Phoenix, AZ 85064. A thorough, well-written guide with lots of detail and maps.

HOW TO TALK LIKE AN ARIZONAN

Well, of course Arizonans speak English, although there's a generous sprinkling of Spanish and Indian words in there. Many Arizona place names have Spanish and Indian roots. This pronunciation guide—prepared with the aid of Brian C. Catts of the University of Arizona's Office of Public Service—will help you talk like a native.

Ajo *(AH-hoe)* — Town in southern Arizona; the word means "garlic" in Spanish.

Anasazi *(Ana-SAH-zee)* — Early Arizona Indian tribe; the name means "the ancient ones."

Apache *(Ah-PAH-chee)* — Central and southeastern Arizona tribe.

Athabaskan *(A-tha-BAS-kan; "a's" pronounced as in apple)* — Canadian Indian tribe; ancestors of the Navajo and Apache.

Bowie *(BOO-ee)* — Fort in southeastern Arizona, now a national historic site; also a tiny town on Interstate 10.

Canyon de Chelly *(du SHAY)* — Arizona national monument, whose name is often mispronounced.

Canyon del Muerto *(MWAIR-toh)* "Canyon of Death," a ravine adjacent to Canyon de Chelly.

Carne *(CAR-nay)* — Meat.

"Cerveza fria, por favor" *(Sehr-VE-sa FREE-ah, por fah-VOR)* — "Bring me a cold one, please."

Chemehuevi *(Tchem-e-H'WAY-vee)* — Southern Colorado River tribe of Yuman origin. Meaning of tribal name is unknown.

Chinle *(Chin-LEE)* Navajo town, the gateway to Canyon de Chelly.

Chiricahua *(Cheer-i-COW-wa)* — Southeastern Arizona Apache tribe made famous by Cochise and Geronimo's rebellions.

Cholla *(CHOY-ya)* — Large family of Arizona cactus.

Coconino *(Co-co-NEE-no)* — Arizona place name, given to a national forest, county and plateau south of the Grand Canyon.

Colorado *(Coh-lo-RAH-doh)* — Red.

El Tovar *(El To-VAR)* — Historic hotel at the Grand Canyon's South Rim.

Gila *(HEE-la)* — A river in southern Arizona.

Guadalupe Hidalgo *(Wa-da-LU-pay Hee-DAL-go)* The treaty ending the Mexican War, signed in 1848.

Havasupai *(Hah-vah-SOO-pie)* — "Blue-green water people" who occupy beautiful Havasu Canyon; also called Supai.

Hohokam *(Hoe-hoe-KAHM)* — Prehistoric tribe occupying deserts of Southern Arizona about AD 200 to 500; means "those who have gone."

Huachuca *(Hwa-CHOO-ka)* — Army fort in southern Arizona with an historic museum; also the name of a mountain range.

Hopi *(HOE-pee)* — Indian tribe, most likely Anasazi descendants.

Hotevilla *(HOAT-vih-la)* — Hopi village on Third Mesa. The name means "skinned back" or cleared off.

Hualapai *(HWAL-a-pie or WAH-lah-pie)* — Western Arizona Indian tribe; the name means "pine tree people."

Huevos Rancheros *(WHEY-vose ran-CHER-ohs)* — Popular Spanish style breakfast with eggs and picante sauce.

Kykotsmovi *(Kee-KOTS-mo-vee)* — Hopi administrative center, on Third Mesa below Oraibi, also called New Oraibi. It means "the place of the mound of ruins."

Maricopa *(Ma-ri-KOH-pah)* — A name given to the Pipa tribe, which shares a reservation with the Pima.

Mescalero *(Mess-kah-LAIR-o)* — Arizona-New Mexico Apache tribe. The name is Spanish, referring to mescal cactus, a traditional food source.

Moenkopi *(Mu-en-KO-pee)* —Third Mesa Hopi village; "place of running water."

Mogollon *(MUGGY-yon)* — Ancient Indian tribe occupying eastern Arizona about AD 200 to 500; also Mogollon Rim, the abrupt southern edge of the Colorado Plateau.

Mohave *(Mo-HA-vay)* — Very common Arizona place name, referring to Indian tribe and a county in western Arizona. It's spelled "Mojave" in California.

Navajo *(NAH-VAH-hoe)* — America's largest Indian tribe, descended from the Athabascan band of Canada.

Nogales *(No-GAH-less)* Twin Arizona-Mexico border towns; the word is Spanish for "walnuts."

Ocotillo *(O-co-TEE-yo)* — Spiny-limbed desert bush with red blossoms.

Oraibi *(Oh-RYE-bee)* — Hopi settlement on Third Mesa; the name means "place of the Orai stone."

Paloverde *(PAW-lo-VAIR-day)* — Desert tree distinctive for the green bark of its limbs.

Papago *(PAH-pa-go)* — Spanish word for "bean eaters," referring to a Southern Arizona Indian tribe, which has since re-adopted its traditional name of "Tohono O'odham."

Pima (PEE-mah) — Central and southern Arizona tribe. The name was a Spanish mistake. When questioned by early explorers, they responded *"Pi-nyi-match,"* which means "I don't understand." The Spanish thought they were identifying themselves.

Prescott *(PRESS-kit)* — The proper way to pronounce the name of that town in central Arizona.

Quechan *(KEE-chan or KAY-chan)* — Indian tribe near Yuma area; also known as Yuma Indians.

Saguaro *(Sa-WHA-ro)* — Large cactus; its blossom is Arizona's state flower.

San Xavier *(Sahn Ha-vee-YAY)* — Spanish mission south of Tucson; some locals pronounce it *Ha-VEER.*

Sichomovi *(si-CHO-MO-vee)* — Hopi settlement on First Mesa; means "a hill where the wild currants grow."

Sinagua *(Si-NAU-wa)* — Ancient north central Arizona tribe; lived in the area about 900-1000 A.D. It comes from the Spanish words *sin agua*—"without water."

Shungopovi *(Shung-O-PO-vee)* — Hopi settlement on Second Mesa; means "a place by the spring where tall reeds grow."

Tempe *(Tem-PEE)* — City east of Phoenix.

Tohono O'odham *(To-HO-no Ah-toon)* — Traditional Papago tribal name; it means "people of the desert who have emerged from the earth."

Tubac *(TU-bahk)* — Arizona's first settlement; below Tucson.

Tumacacori *(Too-mawk-ka-COR-ee)* — Spanish mission below Tucson.

Tusayan *(TU-sigh-yan or TUSSY-yan)* — Sinagua Indian ruin near Desert View in Grand Canyon National Park; also a town outside the south entrance station.

Ute *(Yoot)* — Large Great Basin Indian tribe; few members are in Arizona. It means "the tribe" in the Shoshoni and Comanche language.

Verde *(VAIR-day)* — Spanish for "green."

Wahweap *(WAH-weep)* — Ute Indian for "bitter water"; the name of a large marina at Glen Canyon National Recreation Area.

Wupatki *(Wu-PAT-key)* — National monument northeast of Flagstaff. The word is Hopi for "tall house."

Yaqui *(Ya-KEE)* — Small Indian tribe southwest of Tucson, near Tohono O'odham Reservation. Origin of name unknown; it might simply mean "the people," a self-reference used by many early tribes.

Yavapai *(YA-va-pie)* — Central Arizona tribe. The name might mean "crooked mouth people" or "people of the sun."

Yuma *(YOO-mah)* — Large tribal group near the city of Yuma; the name is derived from *lum,* which means tribe. The original name is Quechan (see above), which the tribe is again using.

INDEX: main listings indicated by *bold face italics*

REMARKABLY USEFUL GUIDEBOOKS
from *PINE CONE PRESS*

Critics praise the "jaunty prose" and "beautiful editing" of Pine Cone Press guidebooks by Don and Betty Martin. In addition to being comprehensive and "remarkably useful," their books are frank, witty and opinionated.

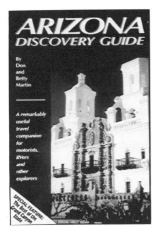  

ADVENTURE CRUISING
This book focuses on small ship cruises, listing over a hundred cruise lines and hundreds of worldwide itineraries. "Cruise closeups" provide an intimate look at more than a dozen different voyages.   — *352 pages; $15.95*

ARIZONA DISCOVERY GUIDE
This detailed guide covers attractions, scenic drives, hikes and walks, dining, lodgings, RV parks and campgrounds. A "Snowbird" section helps retirees plan their winters under the Arizona sun.   — *408 pages; $15.95*

ARIZONA IN YOUR FUTURE
This is an all-purpose relocation guide for job-seekers, retirees and winter "Snowbirds" planning a move to Arizona. It provides essential data on dozens of cities, from recreation to medical facilities. — *272 pages; $15.95*

THE BEST OF THE WINE COUNTRY
Where to taste wine in California? Nearly 300 wineries are featured, along with nearby restaurants, lodging and attractions. Special sections offer tips on selecting, tasting, serving and storing wine.   — *336 pages; $13.95*

LAS VEGAS: THE BEST OF GLITTER CITY
This is a delightfully impertinent insiders' guide to the world's greatest party town, with detailed descriptions of the Ten Best casinos, restaurants, shows, attractions, bars, bargains, buffets and more! — *256 pages; $14.95*

NEVADA DISCOVERY GUIDE
This guide covers all of Nevada, with a special focus on gaming centers of Las Vegas, Reno-Tahoe and Laughlin. A special section advises readers how to "Beat the odds," with casino gambling tips.   — *416 pages; $15.95*

More books and ordering information on the next page

NORTHERN CALIFORNIA DISCOVERY GUIDE

This detailed guide to the Golden State's upper half takes you from San Francisco Bay and the scenic north coast to the Wine Country, Gold Country, the "Big Valley" and the lofty Sierra Nevada. **—356 pages; $12.95**

OREGON DISCOVERY GUIDE

From the wilderness coast to the Cascades to urban Portland, this book takes motorists and RVers over Oregon's byways and through its cities. It's another in the Martins' new Discovery Guide series. **— 352 pages; $12.95**

THE TOLL-FREE TRAVELER

This handy pocket or purse sized companion lists hundreds of toll-free phone numbers for airlines, hotel and motel chains, rental car agencies and more. It's also packed with useful travelers' tips. **—162 pages; $8.95**

THE ULTIMATE WINE BOOK

It's the complete wine guide, covering the subject in three major areas: wine and health, wine appreciation and wine with food. It's loaded with useful information for both casual and serious wine lovers. **— 176 pages; $8.95**

UTAH DISCOVERY GUIDE

This remarkably useful driving guide covers every area of interest in the Beehive State, from its splendid canyonlands to Salt Lake City to the "Jurassic Parkway" of dinosaur country. **— 360 pages; $13.95**

WASHINGTON DISCOVERY GUIDE

This handy book takes motorists and RVers from one corner of the Evergreen State to the other, from the Olympic Peninsula and Seattle to Eastern Washington's wine country and great rivers. **— 372 pages; $13.95**

MARTIN GUIDES ARE AVAILABLE AT MOST BOOK STORES, OR YOU CAN ORDER DIRECTLY FROM THE PUBLISHER

Order from us and we'll charge you only a nickel shipping! Add five cents to the prices listed above and send us your check or money order.

Send your order to: *Pine Cone Press, Inc.*
631 N. Stephanie St., #138, Henderson, NV 89014
Got a question? Call (702) 558-8242